Kobe University Monograph Series in Social Science Research

Series editor

Takashi Yanagawa, Graduate School of Economics, Kobe University, Kobe, Hyogo, Japan

The Kobe University Monograph Series in Social Science Research is an exciting interdisciplinary collection of monographs, both authored and edited, that encompass scholarly research not only in the economics but also in law, political science, business and management, accounting, international relations, and other sub-disciplines within the social sciences. As a national university with a special strength in the social sciences, Kobe University actively promotes interdisciplinary research. This series is not limited only to research emerging from Kobe University's faculties of social sciences but also welcomes cross-disciplinary research that integrates studies in the arts and sciences. Kobe University, founded in 1902, is the second oldest national higher education institution for commerce in Japan and is now a preeminent institution for social science research and education in the country. Currently, the social sciences section includes four faculties—Law, Economics, Business Administration, and International Cooperation Studies—and the Research Institute for Economics and Business Administration (RIEB). There are some 230-plus researchers who belong to these faculties and conduct joint research through the Center for Social Systems Innovation and the Organization for Advanced and Integrated Research, Kobe University.

This book series comprises academic works by researchers in the social sciences at Kobe University as well as their collaborators at affiliated institutions, Kobe University alumni and their colleagues, and renowned scholars from around the world who have worked with academic staff at Kobe University. Although traditionally the research of Japanese scholars has been publicized mainly in the Japanese language, Kobe University strives to promote publication and dissemination of works in English in order to further contribute to the global academic community.

More information about this series at http://www.springer.com/series/16115

Yuka Kaneko
Editor

Civil Law Reforms in Post-Colonial Asia

Beyond Western Capitalism

KOBE UNIVERSITY

Springer

Editor
Yuka Kaneko
Graduate School of International
Cooperation Studies
Kobe University
Kobe, Hyogo, Japan

ISSN 2524-504X ISSN 2524-5058 (electronic)
Kobe University Monograph Series in Social Science Research
ISBN 978-981-13-6202-6 ISBN 978-981-13-6203-3 (eBook)
https://doi.org/10.1007/978-981-13-6203-3

Library of Congress Control Number: 2019931525

This Springer imprint is published by the registered company Springer Nature Singapore Pte Ltd.
The registered company address is: 152 Beach Road, #21-01/04 Gateway East, Singapore 189721, Singapore

Contents

Contributors

Yoshifumi Akanishi Kinki University Law School, Higashi Osaka, Japan

Beatrice Jaluzot Lyon Institute of East Asian Studies (CNRS, ENS de Lyon), Sciences-po Lyon, Lyon, France

Yuka Kaneko Graduate School of International Cooperation Studies, Kobe University, Kobe, Japan

Shiro Kawashima Department of Law, Doshisha University, Kyoto, Japan

Hong Hai Nguyen Department of Civil-Economic Laws, SRV Ministry of Justice, Hanoi, Vietnam

Rudy Faculty of Law, University of Lampung, Lampung, Indonesia

Shiori Tamura Faculty of Law, Thammasat University, Bangkok, Thailand

List of Tables

Introduction

Purpose: Review of Legal Reforms in Asian Emerging Economies

This book is an attempt to analyze the outcomes of "legal reforms" in Asian late-developing countries, under multiple foreign pressures such as the negotiation for entry to the World Trade Organization (WTO) and the legal technical assistance led by international development agencies such as the World Bank and the Asian Development Bank (ADB) as well as bilateral official development aid including Japan since after the end of the Cold War. While numbers of preceding researches have attempted at the evaluation of the "progress" of legal reforms in response to the prescription given by international donors based on the "Washington Consensus" or the policy orientation in pursuit of economic growth through the promotion of foreign investments, less academic works have been directed to the evaluation of the "outcomes" of such legal reforms. A series of practical arguments were led by the World Bank in the mid-1990s to initiate the legal reforms in emerging economies (Shihata 1991; World Bank 2001, 2003), which was succeeded by the attempts of numerical evaluation of the progress of legal reforms, such as the Governance Indicators (Kaufman 1996–2017), and the Report on the Observance of Codes and Standards (ROSC) by the World Bank and the International Monetary Fund (IMF). Various attempts have also been made by the academics to provide theoretical justifications for such legal reforms toward the "Washington Consensus," including the contingency theory (Pistor and Wellons 1999; Hansmann and Kraakman 2000, etc.), the legal origin theory (La Porta et al. 1996, 2008, etc.), and the legal transplants (Reimann 1998; Pistor et al. 2000, etc.). Although critical arguments were raised by the school of critical legal studies questioning the outcomes of legal reforms led by the international development agencies as another mistake repeating the failure of "Free Law Movement" in the 1960s (Trubek & Gualanter 1974; Trubek 2006; Ginsburg 2009), the leading international agencies only responded by incorporating some additional projects meant for gender and socio-environmental considerations, without changing the mainstream policy orientation of "Washington Consensus" (Santos 2006).

Perhaps, there should be an alternative for a legal reform that goes beyond the given model of capitalist growth, to search out a harmonious design of law to balance both economic and social policy needs. The goal of such an alternative legal reform would be a redefined "development" toward the human development incorporating redistribution, rather than a utilitarian maximization of total wealth. A role of the donors in legal technical assistance could also be reconsidered reflecting the redefined "development." Efforts have not yet been made sufficiently enough to identify the mode of assistance to better balance the policy needs (Davis & Trebelicock 2008). Although an influential scholarly opinion suggests a laissez-faire approach so as to let each government choose its own way of legal reforms (Tamanaha 1995, 2009), the authors of this volume find it unrealistic that recipient countries of legal assistance can enjoy freedom in choosing their own legal designs, given the increasing pressures of international donors for the transplant of particular models. Asian legal reforms are in a need of an escort runner, instead of demanding donors, in an attempt of searching out better suitable legal designs for each socio-economy.

This book intends to take a stance of such an escort runner in the legal reforms. Targets are the Southeast Asian countries, particularly the late-developing countries, often referred to as the CLMV countries (Cambodia, Laos, Myanmar and Vietnam), who are under perpetual foreign pressures for socialist market economic reforms, the negotiation for WTO entry, and the conditionalities to the structural adjustment loans extended by international development agencies. The ultimate goal of this volume is to induce a hint for alternative legal designs through an attempt of evaluating the outcomes of legal reforms in these target countries.

A particular focus will be upon the basic sphere of private law, centering on the civil code, in the very intersection where the norms of civil, commercial, and consumer laws interact to enable a chance of alternative design of law. For Asian developing countries, where the unification of law system has been a desire since the colonial independence, the greatest meaning has been placed on having a civil code.

It is understandable that the lawmakers of market reformist economies have chosen to have the integrated code system that can be a basis of hierarchic application of basic principles to all spheres of legal reforms. Judges can apply the upper principles of the code to the single-row models brought by the donors in the commercial field, to maintain the unified norm beyond the conflicting border of civil and commercial spheres. Japan's legal technical assistance to the CLMV countries has been known for the focus on the drafting of civil code and civil procedure code, as in the cases of Vietnam Civil Code in 1995, 2005, and 2015, the 2008 Civil Code of Cambodia that came into force in 2011, the draft Civil Code of Laos which is on a debate at the parliament as of 2017, and the civil procedure code reform in Myanmar. Often, the benefit of supporting such basic codes has been interpreted as an attempt of exporting a legal regime from Japan to other Asian nations (Taylor 2005). However, the positive meaning of supporting the basic codes may be found differently. When influential donors bring in the investor-friendly models in the sphere of economic laws, a hierarchical order of norms under the basic code can function as the basis of systemic interpretation to balance the conflicting policy considerations in the intersection of norms. This basic code drafting by the Japanese legal assistance has often met with inter-donor conflicts as a natural result of normative intersection between civil and commercial spheres (Kagawa & Kaneko 2007; Hammergren 2014), leaving questions to be rediscovered.

Methodology: Historical and Spatial Perspectives in Comparative Asian Law

As for a methodological standpoint, this book is concerned with the dynamics of legal changes that occurs at the boundaries between different legal systems. "Legal transplant" or legal technical assistance by donor agencies is a typical external pressure that urges for change (Kaneko 2009, 2010a, b, 2011). Donors who introduce the Anglo-American legal model have overwhelming influence, such as the World Bank, Asian Development Bank (ADB), and the USA, but they are not the only participants; donor support based on continental law systems such as Japan, France, and the Netherlands continues to provide thoughtful involvement. Further, there are many instances where legal reform is imposed as a condition in the negotiation of trade agreements such as WTO accession negotiations, bilateral investment treaties (BITs), and free trade agreements (FTAs). Also, foreign laws are routinely designated as the governing law in marketplace economic contracts for trade and investment, and inevitably flow into the country.

On the other hand, the legal system of the recipient country in Asia is complicated by the crisscrossing of the remnants of previous eras, stemming from the inherent laws that have existed as sophisticatedly codified system since before colonization; the laws of the colonial powers that were introduced during the colonial era (French law in Cambodia, Laos and Vietnam; English law in Myanmar; Dutch law in Indonesia, etc.) mostly took over the heart of inherent contract law and property law that existed in the colonies while maintaining only narrow area of civil relation such as marriage and inheritance in the name of "custom" (*adat*); the endeavor of post-independence law to overcome such "pluralism" of narrow civil custom and greedy colonial law; influence of socialist law; and the contemporary legal transplants in the path of industrialization and development, such that one country's current legal system is the overall result of each historical path.

In order to understand the dynamics of these changing laws, this book will combine two methodological perspectives. The first is a historical perspective in which the trends in legal changes will be understood on the time axis. The second is to ascertain the spatial range as to how far the codified law extends across social phenomena.

Historical Axis: Colonial Law and Legal Pluralism

Historical axis is an indispensable viewpoint in understanding the present form of civil law in Asian countries. Many Asian laws today are still struggling to cover the influence of colonial law. In Indonesia from 1848 onward until today, the Netherlands Civil Code of 1838 is basically preserved with certain exceptions, without subsequent development to follow the case law development in the Netherlands nor to follow the new Civil Code of 1992. In Myanmar, "Indian Code" which is the codification of the English case law introduced in British colonial era is still literally applied as "Burma Code" today, in contrast to Singapore and Malaysia where the case laws and legislations continuously catch up with trends in Britain though maintaining the similar basis of law derived from "Indian Code" to Myanmar. Vietnam, Laos and Cambodia where the Indochina Civil Code was applied under French rule, despite the overwhelming influence of the inflowing English-U.S. law, chose to rebuild their civil codes in the midst of the socialist market economy transition, despite the overwhelming influence of the inflowing Anglo-American law in contemporary legal transplants.

It is not that these Asian jurisdictions have never attempted a graduation from the colonial influence. Rather, they have straggled hard for the establishment of sui generis law, and yet the task involved unimaginable difficulties. The goals of the post-independence lawmaking were not only to overcome the capitalist exploitation structure engraved in the colonial law, but also to reintegrate the pluralistic normative order formed by the colonial reign. The "unity within diversity" of the current law is, however, not an easy task to be reached (Benda-Beckmann 2006). Particularly in the Asian emerging economies that have long been in civil war under the Cold War structure, the integration of the legal norm is only a movement of a few decades. The normative axis in the integration has been swaying with the fluctuation of "development" definition. We cannot grasp the breadth and depth of the problems of present Asian law unless we start with putting ourselves in such historical flow of legal changes.

Spatial Axis: Interaction in the Boundary of Norms

The spatial range that the law covers is an essential aspect in discussing the significance of donor involvement in the drafting of codes. To what extent do formal laws cover socioeconomic events? Within the internal structure of formal laws, to what extent do the general principles of the civil code apply, and from what point do the contract freedom prevails? What is the point that mandatory provisions of the commercial law, consumer protection law, and labor law start to intervene, and what is the demarcation between them? Is it the role of the court to elaborate such a demarcation by a flexible interpretation of general principles? Furthermore, where does the realm of customary law begin? In such an intersection of formal and customary laws, how can we reconcile the individualist value of modern civil codes with the collective modes of legal capacity (such as the "household" and the "community") and the collective property rights of such intermediate groups (such as common rights, water usage rights, and fishery rights of village communities).

Moreover, how can we differentiate the treatments of civil customary laws and customary commercial laws or *lex mercatoria* that embodies an ultimate capitalist liberalism of contract autonomy? It is sometimes hard to decide which form of customary norm is more consistent with the individualist ideology of modern codes, when in the dimension of commercial activities individuals are buried within the corporate personality as the labor force, while civil customary law allows individuals to actively cooperate in pursuit of postmodern values such as equity and ecology through their connection with common properties, contrary to the prejudice commonly held that civil customary law suppresses individual freedom by pre-modern value.

In the social reality of the Asian emerging countries that are struggling to catch up economically, customary civil law and customary commercial law often directly conflict and an aspect occurs where the codified formal law cannot provide clear rules for resolution. For example, regarding disputes over land, one of the main themes dealt with in each chapter of this book, property rights that have survived in the rural customs of each country are not recognized by the authoritative registration systems that are introduced by codified formal law, or even if recognized, they are easily lost to the freedom of commercial contract, making much of the bona fide purchaser with considerations, administrative decisions favoring such contractual freedom to encourage land transferability, and the judicial decisions lacking the independence to reverse administrative decisions. As another example, contract law amendments for the consideration of consumer protection are often stacked in these economies, while the gradual formation of judicial case law through the interpretation of general principles such as the good faith is unrealistic, particularly in countries with socialist legal tradition such as Vietnam and Laos where the judiciary's authority to interpret the law is constitutionally restricted, while in Myanmar and Cambodia the judges have insufficient interpretive ability.

A complicacy is added by the contemporary context of "regional integration" that crosses national borders; countries that inherited different legal systems from Britain, France, and the Netherlands during the colonial era are now struggling to form unified law across the differences in their systemic bases. The difficulty that the former colonial powers suffered in the formation of unified laws in the modern European Union is also reflected in the geopolitical confrontation of the legal systems in the former colonies in Asia and Africa. The attempt of regional integration at the level of the ASEAN Economic Community (AEC) will face the similar difficulties, having wide varieties of countries in terms of the paths from the independence from the colonial law. For example, there are countries like Myanmar, which was among the countries that inherited the British Indian Code (such as the Contract Act of 1872 and the Sale of Goods Act of 1930) but has not subsequently adopted any modern amendments to the British law (such as the development in consumer protection law) and maintains the frozen colonial law. The AEC is an inherently difficult project as a coalition of countries that have different degrees of influence from the colonial laws.

Two Axes Combined: Multiple Spheres of Law

When we combine two axes of historical and spatial perspectives, we may better recognize and describe the complicacy of the conflicts between legal norms inevitably occurring in multiple spheres of legal regime: in the phase where pre-colonial inherent law encountered colonial law, the phase of post-independent lawmaking in sought of *sui generis* law to overcome the colonial law, and the phase of contemporary "legal transplant" in which global models introduced by the international donors seek to wash away the *sui generis* law that has been built up.

The colonial powers mainly adopted "pluralism" in Asian colonies, whereas the "assimilation" policy was adopted in African colonies. In the pluralist approach, the colonial legal system was only applied to colonists and their contractual counterparts, while the inherent local laws were maintained to the social relations between local people. This "pluralism" brought about the binary separation of civil and commercial legal spheres. If the inherent law that existed prior to colonization was a unitary system which did not differentiate civil and commercial laws for the securitization of the basis of livelihoods of people, in the colonial era the spatial limit of the application of such inherent law was narrowed to the scope of civil law in narrow sense such as family law and inheritance law, while a capitalist commercial law system was introduced to broadly cover the regular areas of contract mechanisms of law and property law; as a result of this binary system, the inherent unitary legal system for contract and property laws was negated or expressed merely as "custom" not amounting to the law.

Of course there is the irreplaceable intellectual assets of the pioneers who researched civil customary law in the colonial era from the viewpoint of legal sociology or anthropology, such as Van Vollenhoven who garnered respect for the customary law (Adatrechtbundels) of the Dutch East Indies, Izutaro Suehiro who is known for his "Kankou Chousa" (survey of customary laws) of Japan's colonies, the English translation of the law code "Manugye Dhammathat" by D. L. Richardson in British Burma, and the codification of customary law in the Annam Code and Tonkin Code by A. Bonhomme in French Indochina. Yet while their work was academically diligent, it isolated the narrow civil customary law from the core of the inherent system of contract and property laws, and in the sense they permitted the promotion of the exploitative commercial law of nineteenth-century capitalism to establish the "colonial law."

The colonial reign aggressively constructed a legal system that aimed at the profit maximization in the context of the nineteenth-century capitalism, while having legal designs far from the law of the country of origin. The land title registration system, for example, that featured an absolute constructive effect for the promotion of transactions in Asian colonies has never been introduced back in suzerain countries up to the twenty-first centuries.

The greatest factor that prescribed the legislation of Asian countries after the colonial independence could be the impact of development assistance initiated under the Cold War structure. Modernization theory based on development economics urged the lawmaking as the instrument of the economic growth.

Dual-economy model was criticized, making the conflict between the agriculture protective policy orientation and the economic development route through foreign capital invitation overwhelming. As the result, the path of post-colonial lawmaking for *sui generis* law in each country strays. Under the land law, the law reform aiming at the facilitation of transfer of farmland and agricultural population to commercial and industrial sectors undermined the philosophy of farmland reform after independence. Under the transaction law, foreign law was selected by contract autonomy of the applicable law, resulting in virtually the same private and commercial dualism as the colonial era.

The binary structure of colonial law still defines the legal systems of the Asian emerging economies today. While the *sui generis* law of each country has progressed toward an establishment of integrated legal system, the intervention of Western donors is once again reviving the binary structure of colonial law, as if fighting again a geopolitical battle between different legal families (Davis and Trebelicock ibid.). While the first boom in legal technical assistance occurred in the post-colonial independence period, led by the "Free Law Movement" of the USA underneath the Cold War structure, the second boom was revived in the 1990s after the collapse of the Soviet Union, applying legal designs modeling after colonial law in the sense that its targets are largely concentrated on the sphere of commercial law, restoring the dualistic separation of civil and commercial spheres.

The Japanese ODA took a unique position in this historical phenomenon of legal technical assistance, began in the mid-1990s, maintained its attitude centering on the drafting and implementation of civil laws through its 20-year history. Perhaps, the nature of the contribution of civil-oriented legal assistance should be better evaluated in the context of overcoming the binary structure of civil and commercial legal spheres in Asian economies, historically doomed by colonial law, and revitalized by the contemporary donor assistance in pursuit of economic growth via investment promotion.

The battle of legal norms has been fought throughout the history. A work of spatial mapping of such historical changes of law may be required, by combining two axes of historical and spatial perspectives, to understand the significance of legal reforms of Asian economies, in the forefront of the struggle for a new legal system that can lead us beyond the vestiges of 19th century Western capitalism.

Structure of This Book

Part I: Historical Review of Civil Law Changes

In the following chapters of this book, the authors will delve into the meaning of legal changes led by the drafting of basic codes in civil sphere through a combination of two axes of historical perspective dating back to colonial law and a spatial retrospective on the confrontation of civil and commercial norms.

The first part of this book will explore the historical path stemming back to the Asian colonial law demonstrating the nature of capitalist legislation that emphasized the promotion of economic transactions, threatening the local laws of daily living. The attempt of post-independence law got to the wall, as we are pursuing the time axis incorporated into the global model again centering on promotion of commercial transactions brought by the contemporary donor assistance.

Beatrice Jaluzot (Chap. 1) analyzes the history of the formation of civil law regime in the French Indochinese colonies, where the "pluralism" was applied. It was an experimental process in which the French Civil Code was applied to French citizens, while the local law was considered to be applicable to the local people. The author contends that the colonial law was something formed independently by the colonies, rather than a simple transplantation from the home, and had started its own change through the interface with local laws at the colonial courts. Especially in Vietnam under the strong influence of Chinese law in the public law sphere because of the Chinese-oriented strong syntactic law (Saaron Code) that did not reflect the local civil norms according to her view, French colonists embarked on the civil customary law codification (1932 Tonkin Civil Code, 1936 Annam Civil Code). Jalzot argues a case law of legal interpretation appeared in the colonial court, suggesting that there was the possibility that the colonial civil law would have made its own development without Japan occupation. On this point, the readers may be reminded that the Japanese academic contribution on Vietnamese law studies pointed out that the Saaron Code contained some aspects different from either Chinese law or the French Civil Code, such as an equal couple property and the customary common properties, and suggested the restoration of the Vietnamese inherent norms which were denied by French colonists (Makino 1994; Takeda 2003). Here is an issue of historical exploration that has not been fully tried yet over the role of colonial law: whether it was negative to the intrinsic law or a developmental amendment to it.

Yuka Kaneko's article (Chap. 2) raises a similar question of the impact of colonial law in the context of British colonies. In the British colony, the "Indian Code," which is generally regarded as the codification of the English case law, was introduced, but its essence was quite different from the English origin, leaving rooms for reexamination. Indian 1872 Contract Act applied a mere facade of "consideration" and lacked thwart, the judgment enforcement by a third party known as the British case law of privity doctrine. By denying the doctrine, it embodied the promotion policy of commercial transactions as envisaged by the New York Civil Code of fashion at the time.

Though Myanmar has maintained the status quo of colonial law, it will not suffice in this era of change in global contract law in realizing the contractual justice. The path of contract law reform will not be a mere process of catching up, but rather be a repositioning of the pre-colonial Burmese norms to guide the contract interpretation in the local context of justice.

Meanwhile, in Thailand, which had escaped colonization, a codification movement took place by the hands of local drafters. Shiori Tamura (Chap. 3) provides a thorough review of the drafting process of the Book I and II in 1925 of the Civil and Commercial Code of Kingdom of Siam, going into the influence of German law mediated by Japan's legal development support at the time and brings in a historical perspective overlapping with the way of legal development assistance by contemporary donors. It was not a case of "legal transplant" with international support from a donor country in contemporary sense, but rather an independent "reception" of foreign model laws, which was rather comparable to the case of the Japanese civil code. While the Siamese drafters are said to pursue "reception" of the German Civil Code, the Japanese Code was for them a guideline and navigator toward this goal. This feature could be recognized especially in the provisions on the remedies for non-performance of obligation, whose construction could be quite controversial due to the essential heterogeneity between the German and Japanese concepts, making us reconsider the policy reason behind.

The goal of law-making after the colonial independence was to overcome the exploitative nature of colonial law. Its implication was also a return to the agrarian and sustainable intrinsic law order that existed before colonization. Rudy article (Chap. 4) summarizes the historical path of the land law reform in Indonesia in its attempt to overcome the colonial law. Indonesia's 1960 Basic Agrarian Law was established in abolition of the property provisions under the Netherlands Civil Code adopted in Indonesia since 1848. While introducing the new concept of land right *Hak Milik* emphasizing the difference from the Western concept of ownership, the goal of the 1960 Basic Agrarian Law was similar to that of the 1952 Agricultural Land Act of Japan, in the principle of restriction on farmland to the cultivators. At the same time, the binary order of registered formal rights and unregistered customary rights created by colonial law was also a search for unification.

Part II: Outcomes of Contemporary Legal Reform Assistance

The second part of this book will, from the viewpoint of understanding the range of civil norms in target countries, collect a series of articles contributed by the scholars who have been involved in the code drafting projects in Asian market reform countries.

Hong Hai Nguyen (Chap. 5), the drafter of the 2015 Civil Code in Vietnam, introduces the drafting policy in Vietnam held by the drafting team reflecting the national political goal striving for the economic growth. The civil code has been given the position and role as a legal fundamental basis, or the "constitution of the private law" and therefore its provisions were expected to be general and stable in order to not only meet the present practical requirements but also give proper forecasts to catch the continuous changes of socio-economy, creating a foundation for building and improving the private law system in the future.

Shiro Kawashima's article (Chap. 6) approaches the practical reality of the Civil Procedural Code of Vietnam at the trial site. In the area of this basic procedural law, since the start of this century Southeast Asian country has seen major reforms, including the new civil procedure laws adopted in Vietnam in 2004 and Cambodia in 2006. In both cases, the new laws were promulgated as a result of the support by foreign countries including Japan. The goal of both projects was the legislation of the "adversary system," which is a basic form in a modern code of civil procedure. However, in the outcomes, the nature of "adversary system" shows remarkable differences between these two civil procedure codes. The enactment process for the codes itself appears to be having an effect upon the realistic utilization and operation of civil procedure in the society, as well as its future development.

Yoshifumi Akanishi (Chap. 7) explores the issues of compulsory execution system in Myanmar, which maintains the British colonial law codified as "Burma Code" in the nineteenth century. While the civil execution law is an area of diversity reflecting the difference of social system and policy orientations, the author contends that still there is technical commonness which should be a target of international convergence for the facilitation of civil execution as the change of the nature of capitalist economy from 19th to 21st centuries. A comparative approach to Japan and Myanmar laws is deepened particularly through a practical viewpoint focusing on the real property execution based on monetary claims.

The last article by Yuka Kaneko (Chap. 8) is the review of contract law reforms in the Asian market reform countries to which Japanese projects of civil code drafting support have been extended since the 1990s. The author questions the destination of normative pluralism of code systems, maintaining the binary structure of civil code as modernist ideal and commercial code as merchandize practice. The integration of civil and economic contracts chosen by the 1995 Russian Civil Code was not always followed by the Asian reforms, as in the case of the Vietnamese Civil Code (1995/2005/2015) which outsources the commercial code, land code, and consumer law as if following the structure of Japanese code system. This pluralist approach may cast a question on the policy outcomes of the drafting support for civil code which is not self-sufficient as a basic law of capitalist market regime, particularly when plentiful individual laws are introduced in the commercial area in response to the foreign models brought by international donors.

Throughout these chapters, this book is a look at the dimensions of the formation of basic civil law and the drafting support thereof in the Asian emerging economies that are facing with the complicacy of policy choices in each historic struggle for the reestablishment of the regime of *sui generis* law. Each attempt of creating a unitary order of normative interpretation, amid the pressure of contemporary legal transplants by international powers, is a promising summary of long-term projects toward a new legal regime beyond greedy capitalist model, that will continue to deserve for keen observation.

This book is a result of the 2014–2016 research grant from the Ministry of Education, Culture, Sports, Science and Technology in the category of basic research program (B) titled "Comparative Law Research regarding the Deepening of Basic Civil Law in the 20 Years of Asian Legal Technical Assistance," led by Yuka Kaneko.

References

Benda-Beckmann, F. (2006). The multiple edges of law: Dealing with legal pluralism in development practice. *World Bank Legal Review, 2.*

Davis, K. & Trebelicock, M. (2008). The relationship between law and development: Optimists versus skeptics. *American Journal of Comparative Law, 56*, 895.

Ginsburg, T. (2009). Symposium: The future of law and development. 104 *Northwestern University Law Review 186*, http://www.law.northwestern.edu/lawreview/colloquy/2009/39/

Hammergren, L. (2014). *Justice reform and development*. Routledge.

Hansmann, H. & Kraakman, R. (2000). The end of history for corporate law. Yale Law School Working Paper No. 235; Harvard Law School Discussion Paper No. 280.

Honduce, E. (1994). Protection of weak parties in contract law. *Civil and Commercial Law Journal, 109*(4–5), 661–691.

Kagawa, K. & Kaneko, Y. (2007). *Hou Seibi Shien-Ron – Seido Kochiku no Kokusai Kyoryoku Nyumon* (Legal techical assistance theory—Introduction to international cooperation in system development) Minerva Shobo.

Kaneko, Y. (2009). An Asian perspective on law and development. 104 *Northwestern University Law Review 186*, http://www.law.northwestern.edu/lawreview/colloquy/2009/39/

Kaneko, Y. (2010a). A procedural approach to judicial reform in Asia: Implications from Japanese involvement in Vietnam. *Columbia Journal of Asian Law, 23*(2), 315–358.

Kaneko, Y. (2010b). An alternative way of harmonizing ownership with customary rights: Japanese approach to Cambodian land reform. *Journal of International Cooperation Studies, Kobe University, 18*(2), 1–21.

Kaneko, Y. (2011). Accompanying legal transformation: Japanese involvement in legal and judicial reform. In J. A. S. Cordero (Ed.), *Legal culture and legal transplants, Vols. I & II, International Academy of Comparative Law, 2012.*

Kaufmann, D., Kraay, A. & Mastruzzi, M. (1996–2017). Governance matters IV: Governance indicators. World Bank Policy Research Working Paper 3630.

La Porta, R., Lopez-De-Silanes, F. & Shleifer, A. (2008). The economic consequences of legal origins. NBER Working Papers No. 13608.

La Porta, R., Lopez-De-Silanes, F., Shleifer, A. & Vishny, R. W. (1996). Law and finance. NBER Working Papers No. 5661.

Makino, T. (1994). Annan no Reicho Keiritsu ni Arawareta Kazoku Seido. (Family System that Emerged from Annam's Lê Dynasty Criminal Law). *Shina Kazoku Kenkyu*, Seikatsusha.

Pistor, K., Raiser, M. & Gelfer, S. (2000). Law and finance in transition economies. 8 *Economics of Transition* 325.

Pistor, K. & Wellons, P. (1999). *The role of law and legal institutions in Asian economic development 1960–1995*, New York: Oxford University Press.

Reimann, M. (1998). Stepping out of the European shadow: Why comparative law in the United States must develop its own agenda. 46 *American Journal of Comparative Law*, 637.

Santos, A. (2006). The world bank's uses of the 'rule of law' promise in economic development. In D. Trubek & A. Santos (Eds.), *The New Law and Development: A Critical Appraisal.*

Shihata, I. (1991). World bank and 'governance' issues in borrowing members. *World Bank in a Changing World, 53.*

Takeda, Y. (2003). Hou to Shokuminchi Shugi – Betonamu ni okeru Furansu Kindai Houdounyu o Meguru Ichikosatsu" (Law and Colonialism—A Consideration of the Introduction of Modern French Law to Vietnam). *Keiai University International Research, 12*, 1–22.

Tamanaha, B. (1995). The lessons of law and development studies. *American Journal of International Law, 89*, 470.

Tamanaha, B. (2009). Distinguishing law & development from legal development. 104 *Northwestern University Law Review 186*, http://www.law.northwestern.edu/lawreview/colloquy/2009/39/

Taylor, V. (2005). New markets, new commodity: Japanese legal technical assistance. *Wisconsin International Law Journal*, *23*(2), 251–281.
Trubek, D. (2006). The rule of law in development assistance: Past, present and future. In D. Trubek & A. Santos (Eds.), *The new law and development: A critical appraisal*.
Trubek, D. & Gualanter, M. (1974). Scholars in self-estrangement: Some reflection on the crisis in law and development studies in the United States. *Wisconsin Law Review*, 162–1102.
World Bank. (2001). *Initiatives in legal and judicial reform*. World Bank.
World Bank. (2003). *Initiatives in legal and judicial reform*. World Bank.

Part I
Historical Review of Civil Law Changes

Chapter 1
Civil Law in the French Asian Colonies

Beatrice Jaluzot

1.1 Introduction

South-East Asian countries are going through a process of legal transformation. The end of dictatorships and the radical change of the socialist model make place for new societies where economic liberalism—which, to a large extent, includes civil liberties—has become mainstream. Viet Nam and Laos opted for a socialist market economy in 1986, Cambodia followed in 1995, and Indonesia adopted a democratic political system in May 1998, just as Myanmar did in 2012. This major turning point has proven to be a success, as economic growth in the region has clearly increased. However, this change of paradigm faces legal infrastructures inherited from the past, and among them from the colonial past.

Which legal legacy in the field of civil law comes from French colonization? The answer is not easy, but we may try to address the very first part of this question: which civil law was developed in the Asian colonies by lawmakers? Much recent research is concerned with French colonization and its legacy in the former empire, however, rare is that which deals with Southeast Asia. This is a real shortcoming, as legal construction has been extremely abundant in this region.

The French colonial empire spread over three present-day countries: Viet Nam, Laos, and Cambodia. At some point of the colonization, all three were imbedded in the Indochinese Union. The Union, well known as "Indochina", was the result of a

---

Beatrice Jaluzot—LL.B. University of Paris II; LL.M. Münster University; Ph.D. University of Lyon 3.

B. Jaluzot (✉)
Lyon Institute of East Asian Studies (CNRS, ENS de Lyon), Sciences-po Lyon, Lyon, France
e-mail: beatrice.jaluzot@ens-lyon.fr

Y. Kaneko (ed.), *Civil Law Reforms in Post-Colonial Asia*,
Kobe University Monograph Series in Social Science Research,
https://doi.org/10.1007/978-981-13-6203-3_1

national policy which aimed at converging several divided countries. Paul Doumer[1] mainly conducted this process between 1887 and 1900. Step by step the Union gathered six countries and territories with various legal status. Cochinchina was settled in the south of modern-day Viet Nam and had been annexed by the French government in 1862. Its status was that of a colony under direct French administration. Through the Oudong Treaty between the King of Cambodia and France, the country became a protectorate from 1863 and its status was comforted by the French-Siamese Treaty of July 15th, 1867. Annam, located in modern-day central Viet Nam, became a protectorate in 1883, just as the Tonkin, in the north of Viet Nam, did in 1884. Tonkin's main city, Hanoi, became Indochina's capital city in 1901. Laos became directly administrated as a result of a long lasting war between France and Siam (i.e. modern-day Thailand), which ended with the treaty of October 3rd, 1893.[2] It became part and parcel of the Union in 1899. The trading post of Kouang-Tchéou-Wan in the Guangzhou bay was the last territory to join the Union in 1900. It had been conceded under a 99 year lease by China, according to an agreement of November 16th, 1899. As the First World War arose in Europe in 1914, the French occupation started to decline; it recovered more intensity in the 1930s but ended with the Japanese occupation at the eve of the Second World War.

From the French point of view, the major characteristic of the Southeast Asian territories was its economic orientation. The main interest of the French government was to secure its local commercial interests than to build a new settlement for its population. As a result, when compared to other colonies such as Algeria, the French population was very low there. Local French administration strived to protect French commercial efficiency.

Positive civil law in Indochina reflects the situation that was very unstable and economic oriented. Parallel to the consolidation of the administrative structure of the French occupation, the French government developed a legal framework, which tightened gradually. All those rules were gathered in a collection of legislation, which accelerated from 1928 and reached more than 15,000 pages in 1939.[3]

Step by step the French occupation produced a local private law system, which was the result of a melting between local law and French law, but despite the geographical proximity, was never harmonized. The civil law construction was firstly concerned with judicial organization; therefore, civil law procedure is the domain most furnished with legal rules. The second step of the legal construction aimed at governing issues

[1]Paul Doumer, 1857–1932, Governor-General of Indochina between 1896 and 1902, after being a several-time finance minister, he became President of the French Republic in 1931. He was shot to death in 1932.

[2]M. P. E. Cressent, "Le Laos", in: Exposition coloniale, Indochine Française. Section d'administration générale. Direction de l'administration de la justice. La justice en Indochine. Organisation générale. La justice indigène, Hanoï, Imprimerie d'Extrême-Orient, 1931, p. 82, available on the portal Gallica, http://gallica.bnf.fr.

[3]Gouvernement général d'Indochine - Direction des archives et des bibliothèques, Recueil général de la législation et de la réglementation de l'Indochine, Hanoï, Imprimerie d'Extrême-Orient, 1939, spé. p. VIII, available on the portal Gallica, http://gallica.bnf.fr.

related to the personal status and the third step focused on property. To some extent, legal governance also expanded to commercial practices and credit securities.

This paper will first present the fundamental nature of civil colonial law as a hybrid legal construction; it will then focus on real property in order to give some light on the origins of its contemporary status.

1.2 French Civil Colonial Law as a Hybrid Legal Construction

French colonial law in East-Asia was built between 1862 and 1939. This short time wasn't enough to reach sufficient maturity. Even if its dynamics was turned toward a higher level of unity, the main characteristics of colonial French law remain as volatility and territorial division on one hand and hybridity as the result of the melting of French and local laws on the other hand.

1.2.1 A Volatile and Divided Legal Construction

Legal construction in Indochina was striving to improve its coherence, but still, it remained an empirical construction, suffering under its lack of consistency. Christian Bruschi wrote that colonial law was obviously shaped "under empiricism and territorial division, floating along historical and geographical circumstances."[4]

Colonial law grew up in an evolving and uncertain environment. It was the result of a changing ideology toward colonialism and concerns about its development varied according to the national French history. On a local level, colonial law was divided, as it was strictly based on a principle of territoriality of rules.

1.2.1.1 A Law Founded on Instable Ground

Colonization unfolded under a changing ideology and a disrupted historical context.

The colonial administration was confronted by the uncertainties of colonialism as a political project. At first it was moved by the ideology of the French Revolution and the ideal of human equality but later on the Republic gives up this ideal. At first colonialism was undertaken by military power, and then it was controlled by civil power.

The primary ideal of colonization was "assimilation", which meant that local people would be considered as French citizens.[5] This is the starting point of the

---

[4]Ch. Bruschi alnalyses this evolution from the point of view of state nationaly law in: "La nationalité dans le droit colonial", Procès, cahier d'analyse politique et juridique, 1987/88, n° 18, pp. 29 et s.
[5]Idem.

French legal settlement and for other territories under direct French administration.[6] At first, this was the guide followed by lawmakers to structure the legal status of local people. This ideology is given up at the end of the 19th century by the French Republic, which decided to make a clear difference between French people and local people.[7]

Colonization was a state program conducted by the military, mainly naval forces. In many cases, it was the result of French military intervention in local armed conflicts. This is the case of Laos and Cambodia, whose Kings were fighting against Thai or Chinese domination. As a result, the very first local organization was a military one and its governance passed through a transfer process to civil power. This civil power was held by the French administration that also possessed large legislative power.[8] The Indochinese Union (Indochina) was created by governmental decrees in 1887 in order to rationalize the regional administration.[9] Its government was based in Hanoi and the whole administrative organization was reframed, just as its economic and financial structures were.[10] The metropolitan government decided to support the project of railway construction, which lasted 35 years. It was financed by three state monopolies over alcohol, salt and opium. This imposed a heavy burden on local taxes that resulted in contentions being raised by opponents to the French occupation. Obviously, the French state needed to make efforts in return in order to be accepted by the local people.

Governmental policy towards colonies was also closely related to national history. Southeast Asian colonization started under the reign of Napoleon 3rd, who lost his position in the French-Prussian war of 1870. After five years of disturbance, the 3rd French Republic was formed in 1875 and lasted through WW1 until the beginning of WW2 in 1939. Every single event held back the French government from its empire, but as soon as each was over, the process of reinforcement of the French position in the colonies went further. As a result, colonial legal structures increased dramatically.

In the colonies, the legal order imposed by the French authorities was increasingly disputed and when the situation became threatening, they reacted by reinforcing the legal framework. In Southeast Asia, the Japanese occupation stopped the French occupation and after the end of the war, the French government was never able to return to its previous position. This was the path to independence for all of the

[6]A. F. Garrigues, "Du droit applicable aux indigènes et des Juridictions le prononçant. La Cochinchine", in: Exposition coloniale, Indochine Française, op. cit., pp. 43, 44, 80, available through Gallica.

[7]Ch. Bruschi, op. cit.

[8]E. Saada, "Citoyens et sujets de l'Empire français, Les usages du droit en situation coloniale", Genèse, 2003, 4 (n° 53), pp. 4–24.

[9]Décret du 17 octobre 1887, JO, 1887, 18 Oct. 1887, p. 4610, available though Gallica.

[10]J. Godard, Rapport de mission en Indochine du 1er janvier au 14 mars 1937, coll. Mémoires asiatiques, L'Harmattan, 1994, p. 16.

countries, which also involved judicial autonomy. For instance, Cambodia enacted a new Constitution in 1947 and three codes: civil, commercial and criminal by 1956.[11]

Colonial civil law was based on those very fluctuating conditions; moreover, it was extremely diverse from place to place.

1.2.1.2 A Territorially Fragmented Law

Enforcement of law in the French colonies was governed by the rule of territoriality: only local law applied to civil relations. But local laws were diverse as the Indochinese territory was split into many autonomous entities.

The territoriality principle governs the enforcement of law in the colonies. Lampue writes: "the validity of legal acts accomplished in Metropolitan France shall be checked through Metropolitan law, without any consideration to the place where the question is raised. But, the validity of legal acts occurring in an overseas territory shall only be checked through a law enforced in that territory."[12]

Metropolitan France controlled territories through two types of legal regime: colony and protectorate. According to the colony system, the overseas territory was controlled by "direct administration" under the responsibility of the French government, as was the case of Cochinchina. According to the protectorate system, the country officially kept its sovereignty and the local administration remained and was still empowered. The protectorate system was the result of a treaty signed by both countries; therefore, it differs from place to place and was quite often subjected to renegotiation.[13]

However, the status of civil legal rules was almost the same in every part of Indochina. In Cochinchina, which was under direct administration, French administration should have taken over the whole local organization. Due to practical issues, local courts were first recognized as competent for local people and for implementing local law.[14] After a while, Annamite laws remained in force for local people, but French courts became in charge of their implementation.[15] Cambodia became a protectorate in 1863 but its status changed to colonial status with the treaty of June 17th, 1884, which resulted in the general reform of local courts by Royal ordi-

---

[11] Khong Phirun, Crouzatier, Jean Marie, Les études sur le droit cambodgien, in: Bilan et perspectives des études Khmeres: langue et culture, P. Lamant (éd.), L'Harmattan, Paris, 1997, pp. 83–90, p. 86.

[12] «la validité des actes juridiques accomplis dans la métropole doit être examinée au regard de la loi métropolitaine en quelque lieu que la question puisse être posée devant le juge, mais les actes qui interviennent… dans un territoire d'outre-mer ne doivent être appréciés que suivant la loi ayant force obligatoire dans… ce territoire», A. Ortolland, André, Les institutions judiciaires à Madagascar, L'Harmattan, 1993, p. 294.

[13] Ch. Bruschi, op. cit., pp. 29 et s.

[14] Ainsi le traité du 25 juillet 1864 prévoit le maintien des juridictions indigènes, jusqu'à l'installation des juridictions françaises, par un arrêté du 21 décembre 1864: Garrigues, op. cit., p. 43.

[15] Id., p. 45.

nances.[16] In Annam, local courts were maintained, but they were placed under the Resident's control, who represented the French state in the country.[17] Tonkin came under French power with the Treaty of Hue on June 6th, 1884[18]; the sovereignty of the King remained but courts were reframed step by step under French instructions.[19] Laos was a colony with French administration and the Governor-General of Indochina reorganized the courts system through an instruction of September 30th, 1895. It maintained local courts for local matters.[20]

The main consequence of this situation was the jurisdiction of various court systems extending over the same area, governed by different status and containing competing authority over law enforcement. The courts were in charge of implementing French law on the one hand and local laws on the other. Law enforcement was extremely complex, expensive and suffered under a lack of legal security. Still, this mixed situation produced a mixing of French and native laws that ended up in the creation of a hybridization of local law.[21]

1.2.2 The Hybridization of Local Civil Laws

Enforcement of civil law rules was governed by the rule of personal status, which was not sustainable. According to this basic rule, settled from the beginning of the colonization process, French law applied to French people whereas local laws applied to local people. Colonial law was only there to fill in the gap between both laws in order to ensure colonial order. The main purpose of colonial law was to assert French power on the territories and to maintain control over French colonists settled abroad. French lawmakers refrained from ruling on local civil issues concerning indigenous people and French authorities wanted to preserve local institutions.

Colonial law was shaped by the French colonial administration and the support of the Metropolitan Government. French power struggled with local anti-colonialist movements, and as a result colonial law was to a wide extent made out of compulsory and criminal rules, its fundamental logic was that of a colonial public order. Those pragmatic and political concerns shaped the main features of French colonial law and contrary to some other types of colonization, it was not supported by any ideological philosophy.

[16] P. Nicolas, "Du droit applicable aux indigènes et des Juridictions le prononçant. Le Cambodge", in: Exposition coloniale, Indochine Française. op. cit., p. 118.

[17] A. Bonhomme, "Du droit applicable aux indigènes et des Juridictions le prononçant. L'Annam", in: Exposition coloniale, Indochine op. cit., pp. 155–174, disponible sur Gallica, spé. p. 172.

[18] L. A. Habert, "Du droit applicable aux indigènes et des Juridictions le prononçant. Le Tonkin", in: Exposition coloniale, Indochine Française. op. cit., pp. 175–212, disponible sur Gallica.

[19] Id., p. 182.

[20] Cressent, op. cit., p. 84.

[21] Cf. Bourgon, Jérôme, "Le droit coutumier comme phénomène d'acculturation au Japon et en Chine", Extrême Orient - Extrême occident, 2001, n° 23, pp. 125–143.

However, indigenous law was administered by colonial courts, which meant that French judges were entrusted with its jurisdiction and by this way with figuring out and shaping local laws. This resulted in a close connection between laws and provided a path to the emergence of new local laws, deeply influenced by French law but never harmonized with it.

1.2.2.1 The Recognition of Local Laws

Maintaining the implementation of indigenous law for local people came primarily from a practical constraint: the implementation of the French civil law in colonial territories was simply impossible. The language of the law—legal language expressed in French—differed deeply from the local languages; French rules were foreign rules and needed to be acknowledged by the local people in order to be enforced. The French Civil Code, made for a different civilization, ignored deep-rooted Asian traditions such as the cult of the dead.[22] Moreover, regarding protectorates, treaties stipulated the respect of existing political and legal structures. According to the scholar Henry Solus, "for colonial lawyers, it is unthinkable to impose French laws which do not cover all social situations of the colonies and are not adapted to them."[23]

The boundary between local and French law was designed through the criteria of nationality: French law applied to French and Europeans; local laws applied to indigenous people. For instance, in Cochinchina, an Imperial Decree of July 25th, 1864 which settled the judicial organization stipulated that commercial and civil matters involving "Europeans" were entrusted to French courts (Article 14), whereas Annamite law shall apply to "any convention and any civil or commercial dispute between Indigenous and Asian people" (Article 11). As a consequence, this ruling created a dual court system, namely a French court system charged with the implementation of French law and a local court system in charge of indigenous law.

Such an organization was unlikely to last a long time and in fact, in Indochina just as in the rest of the French colonial empire, colonial courts became more and more concerned with local laws. This can be explained by a few reasons. As a foreign power in a new society, French courts were in a position to arbitrate local conflicts. French colonial power was also interested in keeping the peace between local people in order to maintain control over the social situation.

Therefore, colonial law provided links between both court systems. In Cochinchina, but not in Cambodia or Annam,[24] non-European people could bring their conflicts to colonial courts if both parties agreed. More generally, the French government decided to establish special chambers in charge of indigenous law within

---

[22]Cf. for instance "Question de droit usuel", Pháp-Viên Báo, 1931, Mai 1931, Première année, n° 1, pp. 396–398, consultable sur Gallica.

[23]«Pour les juristes coloniaux, il est impensable de plaquer les lois françaises qui ne couvrent pas toutes les situations sociales des colonies et qui sont si peu» faites pour elles, H. Solus, traité de la condition des indigènes en droit privé, 1927, pp. 228–234.

[24]Garrigues, op. cit., p. 71.

the colonial appeal courts; this was the case in Cochinchina from 1881,[25] in Tonkin from 1905[26] and in Annam by par ordinances of the King of 1913 and 1925.[27]

As a result, French courts were empowered to pronounce indigenous law.[28] This was a difficult task as most judges were French-born jurists that were temporarily sent to the colonies, they did not have easy access to local legal resources. The courts' knowledge of local laws came through two ways: translation of ancient texts and testimonies from lettered people (local scholars) on unwritten usages. In order to improve the quality conflict resolution, judges endeavored to obtain legal writings on indigenous rules. The bias of the process was that French jurists formulated indigenous law. Impairment and substantial change of local laws derived from this process.

The first bias is that ancient texts were chosen and gathered by French authorities,[29] but it didn't seem to have big consequences in Southeast Asia, as Chinese tradition was extremely influential and it provided for uniform codification. Chinese code was translated and codified with minor changes by the Emperor Gia Long in 1812, and the Annamite code was enforced in Cochinchina,[30] Tonkin,[31] and Annam,[32] probably also with less influence in Cambodia.[33] The Annamite code was translated into French with the support of French authorities, its best achievement is due to Paul Philastre.[34] French courts based many of their judgments on this text. But this had many drawbacks. The Code was more of a penal code; most of its sanctions were punishments and very often corporal. Its substantial structure was completely different form the civil law code, which judges were used to.[35] Moreover, in many cases it didn't provide for a solution as new types of conflicts emerged with the colonization.

In Cambodia, Adhémar Leclère translated the Khmer codes. But in 1930, L. P. Nicolas, who was then judge there writes: "There are no witnesses of the past anymore

---

[25]"D. 25 mai 1881 portant réorganisation de la justice en Cochinchine", JO, 1881, 31 mai 1881, pp. 2994–2997, Article 10 al. 2.

[26]Habert, op. cit., p. 182.

[27]Bonhomme, op. cit., p. 172.

[28]Cf. also E. Saada, passim.

[29]Comp. For Islamic law F. Renucci, "Le juge et la connaissance du droit indigène. Eléments de comparaison entre l'Algérie et la Lybie", in: Durand, Bernard, Favre, Martine (éd.), Le juge et l'Outre-mer: Médée ou les impératifs du choix, t. 3.

[30]Garrigues, op. cit., pp. 41 et s.

[31]Habert, op. cit., p. 196.

[32]Bonhomme, op. cit., p. 173.

[33]Nicolas, op. cit., p. 113.

[34]P.-L.-F. Philastre, Etudes sur le droit annamite et chinois. Le Code annamite. Nouvelle traduction complète comprenant: Les commentaires officiels du Code, traduits pour la première fois; de nombreuses Annotations extrates des Commentaires du Code chinois: des Renseignements relatifs à l'histoire du droit, tirés de plusieurs Ouvrages chinois: des Explications et des Renvois. Seconde édition, tome premier, Paris, Ernest Leroux, 1909.

[35]Bonhomme, op. cit., p. 173.

who could testify of the traditional Khmer law before the French occupation... The only available sources are the works of Mg Cordier and Adhémar Leclère."[36]

Only at the end of the colonial era, in the 1930s, legal exchanges between local and French law become more effective and in 1931 a French-Annamite law review was created, under the supervision of a native lawyer and published in both languages, French and Vietnamese.[37]

In some parts of Indochina, those difficulties were increased with the diversity of the people living there and the need to respect their own traditions. French authorities introduced a special status for them. For instance, colonial law in Cochinchina acknowledged Asian people (Asiatiques), that is Chinese people,[38] and in Annam, special jurisdiction was dedicated to the implementation of the customs of Moï people.[39]

In official texts, indigenous law is called "law and local usages",[40] but they were soon called "customs" by French lawyers, and as such considered as insufficient. Colonial courts called for a new codification. It would create a hybrid law, melting indigenous and French law together.

1.2.2.2 The Creation of a Hybrid Law Under the Influence of French Law Makers

New legal rules were set in every country of the Indochinese Union. The designation is quite unclear as they were sometimes presented as the introduction of Civil law as such without mentioning any reference to local laws. As a matter of fact, those acts were deeply adapted to the local context and provisions were often drafted by following case law settled by the courts.

In Cochinchina, French civil law had been promulgated by a decree of July 25th, 1864 and its implementation aimed at European people. Regarding local people, a governmental decree of October 3rd, 1883[41] promulgated large parts of the Napoleon code related to legal status, besides marriage and inheritance law.[42] By this enactment, the content of French law was adapted to the local context; especially it took polygamy issues into account.

[36]«Il n'est plus aujourd'hui de témoins du passé qui pourraient évoquer la traditionnelle justice khmère avant l'occupation française»... «les seules sources accessibles sont les travaux de Mg Cordier et Adhémar Leclère», cited by Nicolas, op. cit., p. 113.

[37]Pháp-Viên Báo - Revue judiciaire franco-annamite. Hanoi, 1931–1932, Gallica

[38]Arrêté présidentiel du 23 août 1871 déterminant les individus de race asiatique soumis à la loi annamite, 1871.

[39]Bonhomme, op. cit., pp. 172 et s.

[40]Cf. par ex. D. 25 juill. 1864, Article 29: «lois et usages locaux».

[41]D. 3 Oct. 1883 portant organisation de l'état civil des indigènes, suivi par un "précis de législation annamite" comportant le livre 1er du code civil français titres IV, V, VI, VII, VIII, IX, X & XI, 1883, JO 11 Nov. 1883, pp. 5833–5840.

[42]Garrigues, op. cit., p. 76.

In Cambodia the King, under the treaty of June 17th, 1884, was forced to accept that the colonial power would be empowered to conduct "any administrative, judicial, financial and commercial reform the Republican government would consider as necessary."[43] As a directly administrated country, its legal status was framed following the Cochinchina model and French civil codes; especially civil and commercial codes were promulgated by an order of the governor of Cochinchina (under the French administration) of May 19th, 1883.[44] Those codes governed only westerners. Some years later the King promulgated criminal and criminal procedure codes by an ordinance of November 20th, 1911. Civil matters were enacted by a royal ordinance of February 25th, 1920, and enforced on July 1st.[45] This civil code was structured into four parts: persons, goods, obligations, and legal acts; it is based on the enactment of local rules translated by Leclère and Aymonier and drafted under the cooperation of the dignitaries of the Crown.[46]

In Annam, the French administration strived to respect local civil rules although it didn't undertake their enactment, but in 1931 Albert Bonhomme, then in charge of legal matters in Annam, considers it as a necessity.[47] Local rules, especially the Annamite code were enforced in Tonkin, but in 1931, the year of the Colonial Exposition, compilation of the civil laws was under way and criminal, criminal procedure, civil and commercial procedure codes were already promulgated.[48] This happened at a stage where legal transformation was largely advanced and Habert, general administrator of Justice for Indochina, mentioned the case law drawn up by the chamber for indigenous law in the Court of Appeal and claimed it to be "highly respected".[49]

Laos is a special case, as French administration decided to promulgate French laws as soon as possible. Those laws were hastily drafted, however with some support of the native people, and their enactment was a failure for lack of preparation. The governor of Indochina had to postpone their enforcement several times and finally decided to suspend it indefinitely in 1924.[50]

The result of legal development in Indochina is that the gap between local civil laws was never filled and that indigenous laws ended in a melting of traditional

[43] Cité par Boudillon, 1915, p. 99: «toutes les réformes administratives, judiciaires, financières et commerciales auxquelles le gouvernement de la République jugera... utile de procéder...».

[44] A. Boudillon, A., Le régime de la propriété foncière en Indochine. Ce qui a été fait - Ce qu'il faudrait faire. Rapport présenté à M. Le Ministre des colonies, Larose, Paris, 1915, disponible sur Gallica: http://gallica.bnf.fr/ark:/12148/bpt6k751226, p. 102.

[45] Ordonnance royale du 24 août 1924, entrée en vigueur le 25 novembre 1924: Nicolas, P., "Du droit applicable aux indigènes et des Juridictions le prononçant. Le Cambodge", in: Exposition coloniale, Indochine Française. Section d'administration générale. Direction de l'administration de la justice, Hanoï, 1931, 1931, Gallica, p. 118.

[46] S. E. Chuun, ministre de la justice, M. Penn suppléant, M Keth, Président de la plus haute instance, M. Chéa suppléant du ministre de l'intérieur, Cf. Nicolas, op. cit., pp. 113–154, disponible sur Gallica, p. 148.

[47] Bonhomme, op. cit., p. 174.

[48] Habert, op. cit., p. 199.

[49] Idem: «une jurisprudence qui fait autorité».

[50] Cressent, op. cit., pp. 89–91.

laws and French civil law into a new legal order, deeply renewed by the continental tradition and under the scrutiny of French judges.

These phenomena can be better observed through a tangible example and the case of land law stands as one of the most significant.

1.3 Land Law

French economic and commercial interests involved in the French Asian colonies put real property at the center of legal disputes and land law claims represented an important part of judicial work. This situation was common throughout the whole colonial empire.[51] As for Indochina, the French government ordered a special report by Auguste Boudillon, who was the general inspector of land and domain registry.[52] Boudillon spent more than one year between 1911 and 1913, traveling through the countries and analyzing all of the difficulties causing this situation. Boudillon's report was drafted in 1912 and published in 1915.[53] A complementary report was submitted after WW1, in 1924.[54] This exhaustive and well-documented survey ended in a general reform of land law in Indochina.

After an overview on the structural conflict which confronted the colonialists and local people, the answer imposed by the colonial power will be outlined.

1.3.1 The Conflict Between Legal Systems

In the field of land law, French law deeply conflicted with indigenous laws.

1.3.1.1 The Enforcement of French Land Law in the Indo-Chinese Union

French land law was enforced through two ways. In territories under direct administration, as a basic principle, French law, and therefore real property law, directly applied. Although the imposition of this rule on local people was disputed, its imposition on French and European residents was generally accepted.[55]

---

[51]Cf., par ex. Merle, Isabelle, "La construction d'un droit foncier colonial: de la propriété collective à la constitution des réserves en Nouvelle-Calédonie", Enquêtes, 1999, 7, pp. 97–126.

[52]That is "inspecteur de l'enregistrement et des domaines".

[53]A. Boudillon, op. cit.

[54]Boudillon, A., La réforme du régime de la propriété foncière en Indochine. Rapport présenté à M. le Gouverneur général de l'Indochine, août 1924, Imprimerie d'Extrême Orient, Hanoï, 1927, disponible sur Gallica.

[55]Boudillon, 1915, p. 31.

In protectorates, the conflict between legal systems regarding land law claims found its answer in general principles of French international private law. But the conflict rule for this matter, and contrary to the contemporary rule which provides for the law of the land, was the personal law of the parties.[56] This was the source of many difficulties and brought some inefficient solutions for disputes. For instance, the property of alluvia produced by a watercourse depended on the nationality of its owner and varied according to whether the owner was French or a native.[57] We can suppose that these rules were mainly shaped in order to preserve colonial commercial interests and that it violated the rights of the local people.

Regarding the forced imposition of French law, local land laws were weak, suffering from lack of unity and lack of enforcement. Even if most countries recognized the Annamite rules as land law, its enforcement varied from place to place and was very loose in some regions. Consequently, indigenous laws could not resist the imposition of French law.

1.3.1.2 Differences Between Local Laws

In 1915, Auguste Boudillon explained very precisely the state of the law in each country: Cochinchina,[58] Cambodia,[59] Annam,[60] Tonkin,[61] Laos[62] and Kouang-Chéou-Wan.[63] In each country, the local law consisted of various rules, quite often coming from the Annamite code, royal ordinances and local usages.

The Annamite law was common to most of the territories and it deeply differed from French law.[64] For instance, any buildings on someone else's land were considered as movable property, and good faith at the moment of cultivation was enough to become owner of the fruits produced by the land. Annamite law ignored acquisitive prescription. This had been acknowledged several times by courts and had been challenged by the enforcement of the French public order.[65]

Local issues had also been settled by numerous royal ordinances, and Boudillon produced a list of all those rulings, for example those implemented in Cochinchina.[66] The author claims that local legal sources are very difficult to gather, that the Annamite code provides insufficient rulings and that in order to complete the missing rules,

[56] P. Dareste, Traité de droit colonial, t. II, 1932, p. 241.

[57] Idem.

[58] Boudillon, 1915, pp. 14–98.

[59] Boudillon, 1915, pp. 99–139.

[60] Boudillon, 1915, pp. 140–166.

[61] Boudillon, 1915, pp. 167–206.

[62] Boudillon, 1915, pp. 207–211.

[63] Boudillon, 1915, pp. 212–215.

[64] Dareste, op. cit., p. 238.

[65] Dareste, op. cit., p. 239.

[66] Boudillon, 1915, op. cit., pp. 10–13.

he had to consult indigenous scholars ("lettrés") who had become very difficult to find.[67]

This set of rules wasn't structured enough to provide for a harmonized body with the capacity to address new challenges brought by the French occupation and eagerness to draw material interests from the colonization. Throughout the Union, land law claims were raised; this conflicting situation was huge and dangerous as it could bring local people to an uprising and revolt against the colonial power.

The French government decided to reform land law in the Indochinese Union and by this act to end definitively the basic stance of respect toward indigenous laws.

1.3.2 The Enactment of a New Colonial Land Law

In many respects, French law and indigenous laws were incompatible and difficulties were settled by the enforcement of a special colonial law. Two matters were of deep importance: categories of real property and its registration.

1.3.2.1 Categories of Real Property

Since the 1789 Revolution, French law acknowledges a comprehensive concept of state property: unoccupied land belongs to the State. In colonies, the country was considered as part and parcel of the French state and as a consequence all land previously under the king's property was considered as transferred to the French state.

Indigenous laws regarding state ownership were mostly unwritten and were recognized through case law from colonial courts. Boudillon mentions three types of owners: the Emperor, who receives all land that is abandoned or without owner; townships which hold communal property including land and paddy fields allocated by the Emperor; and private owners, with special laws governing family ownership.[68] As a result, there was a royal domain, a common domain and a private domain.

Regarding the royal domain, just as in all over Asia, legal scholarship considers that the monarch owns the whole land of the country and that he allocates rights over the land to private people. The King had the right to seize the land, but he would exercise it in rare occasions and he would reward it with indemnities. It mostly occurred when the owner didn't pay taxes or when he gave up his ownership. Many cases had enforced this law and judgments were based on Philastre's writings. Besides those exceptions, private owners were endowed with similar rights to the one granted by the Civil code.

In Cambodia, article 9 of the treaty of 1884 stipulated: "the ground of the kingdom, sole property of the crown until now, will stop being inalienable", and that "property

[67] Idem, p. 8.

[68] Idem, pp. 15–16.

will be settled by Cambodian and French authorities".[69] The governor of Cochinchina implemented this clause in many cases and it needed to be completed by several Royal orders.

In Cochinchina, an order as of August 22th 1882 organized land concessions. It divided land into three types: (1) wasteland in rural areas, (2) urban land, cultivated rural land, wasteland near Saigon and Cholon, (3) non-movable property dedicated to public services or for the public interest. Every type was governed separately: the first type of property was conceded for free; the third one was inalienable. The second one, by far the most important, could only be transferred through public auction and subject to the payment of land tax.[70] A major difficulty arising from this second category was to know if the property rights in land cultivated by non-owners could be sold.[71]

This wasn't the sole difficulty with land law; land registration was a very cumbersome problem.

1.3.2.2 The Reform of Land Registration

Land registration gave rise to numerous conflicts regarding land ownership and real property right such as mortgages. Local law in Cochinchina provided for a land registration system, which had been carefully established according to Royal orders. The legal meaning of the notifications mentioned in the register brought numerous disputes. The first goal of the register was to secure the payment of land taxes, and which legal scope had the mentioning of real property rights such as mortgage was unclear and heavily disputed.[72]

From the beginning of the occupation in 1862, some plots of land in the town of Saigon had been considered as wasteland by the colonial power and were put to sale. The French colonial administration decided to ensure this ownership and decided to implement French land law by an order of February 20, 1862.[73] Based on this enactment, any land sale had to be passed by a deed authenticated by the head of the civil affairs bureau and any other type of proof was considered void. When the registration was effective, mortgage registration could be preceded. But the 1862 order also stipulated that Annamite law should continue to govern local people.[74] The implementation of French metropolitan law had been expanded, but its transposition

---

[69]"le sol du royaume, jusqu'à ce jour propriété exclusive de la couronne, cessera d'être inaliénable" et qu' "il sera procédé, par les autorités françaises et cambodgiennes, à la constitution de la propriété au Cambodge".

[70]Boudillon, 1915, op. cit., pp. 60–61.

[71]Idem, p. 62.

[72]Idem, p. 30.

[73]Idem, p. 31.

[74]Idem, p. 32.

into the colonial legal order in Cochinchina was defective in many aspects and this legal environment resulted in insecure and expensive land law transactions.[75]

The Dia-bô, the Annamite register was maintained for local people as the quality of this institution had brought respect from the colonial administration. The legal consequence of the Dia bô registration was to build a presumption of ownership, which could be defeated by any type of proof against the registered ownership. A notification to the Dia-bô looked like any mention on a land register or a mortgage register. Consequently, the indigenous registration through the Dia-bô system was more of public notification of real rights, based on the object of ownership. This was contrary to French law, which was based on personal notification for mortgage registration, based on the person involved as the owner. Local administrators were ordered to keep Dia-bô registers and the legal conditions for its registrations had been cleared by the colonial power. As a result, mortgage registration was subject to Annamite law and case law.[76]

French authorities reformed the Dia-bô several times,[77] and the French system of mortgage registration, enacted by a law of 1855,[78] had been enforced in all colonial territories by 1921. Still, both systems couldn't exist at the same time, as they were based on conflicting principles. Furthermore, new rules brought by colonial law were severely defective for lack of preparation. This ended in the confusion between the two registers, French and Annamite.[79]

The question was to decide if registration should be entered twice, in both registers, or only one time, in which case the registers would be clearly separated, but users would have to check both for every single transaction.[80] In 1913 the Appeal Court of Saigon decided in favor of the first option, respecting the basic rule of the implementation of local law for local people. In later judgments, other courts opted for the second option, applying the law of the contract.[81] Besides this, the Annamite law wasn't enforced in Tonkin, where no Dia-bô had been introduced, and land sales had to be certified by the indigenous authorities.

In the end, the French government decided upon the general reform of land registration and it introduced a special land law for the Indo-Chinese Union. This came after similar reforms were implemented in the whole colonial empire.[82]

In the Indochinese Union, the reform was introduced by a series of governmental decrees based on both reports of Boudillon. On July 21st 1925, three decrees were

---

[75]Idem, pp. 33–35.

[76]Boudillon, 1915, op. cit., p. 63.

[77]Boudillon, 1915, op. cit., pp. 46 et s.

[78]Loi du 25 mars 1855 sur la transcription hypothécaire.

[79]Boudillon, 1915, op. cit., p. 35.

[80]Idem, p. 68.

[81]Feyssal, P. de, "Le service de la propriété foncière en Cochinchine", Phap-vien Bao, 1932, Janvier 1932, T. II, n° 1, pp. 3–11, Gallica.

[82]Cf. Dareste, op. cit., pp. 203–270.

promulgated, the first decree introduced land registration in Cochinchina,[83] which served as a model for the rest of the territories. The second one introduced the same law in the concessions of Hanoi, Haiphong and Tourane.[84] The third one organized registration in Laos.[85]

In order to enforce the new law, several reforms had to be first introduced. At first, the inventory of all the land in the country had to be fixed within a cadaster, personnel in charge with local responsibilities had to be nominated, etc. This was a long and complex reform. The governor of Indochina was able to enforce the two first decrees from 1927.[86] The reform was then introduced in Tonkin on April 1st, 1931 by an order of the Governor. But at the time of the publication of the Dareste Treaty on Colonial law in 1932, the reform hadn't reach Cambodia, Annam or the Kwang Tchéou Wan. It seems that the reform was never entirely implemented.

The new law created a uniform land law for the region. It was a special law, deeply diverging from French metropolitan law and it entirely reformed the indigenous laws. This was a very deep change for the local people; from then on, land registration was based on the law of the property, i.e. the law of the land, and not on the personal law of the owner anymore. It applied to all people, whether they were French, European, indigenous or foreigner. Real rights, among them mortgages, which had been heavily disputed, were once and for all legally settled. Acquisitive prescription, unknown by the Annamite law, was rejected.[87] The law was slightly adapted to indigenous customs. Inheritance law was adapted to the new legal context; the first spouse gained a right of usufruct on her husband's property. Special rules were dedicated to religious foundations, especially for ancestor worship.

As a result, private property was secured, thanks to the safety of registration; rights in rem could be established and transferred. The validity of contracts depended only on the concluding consent of both parties, but land notification could only be based on an authenticated deed. The form of the deed was governed by the personal law of the contractor, this meant that a notary deed was needed for Europeans and for local people, a deed written or authenticated by an indigenous authority of the contractor's domicile or of the land's location was required.

Title deeds were listed in a special sheet ("feuillet réel"), which created real rights. Registered real rights could not be challenged and real rights registration was the unique starting point for their establishment. Consequently, real right registration made all previous unregistered rights void. Claims for previous unregistered rights were not admitted and claims against infringed ownership could only seek indemnity.

In order to organize the land law register, an overall gathering of all real property documents was planned, putting together all of the dia-bô registers, official recogni-

---

[83]Décret, 21 juillet 1925 sur la propriété foncière en Indochine pour les trois concessions, R, 1926, 1, 182.

[84]Décret, 21 juillet 1925 sur la propriété foncière en Indochine pour la Cochinchine, R, 1926, 1, 129.

[85]Décret, 21 juillet 1925 sur la propriété foncière en Indochine pour le Laos, R, 1926, 1, 190.

[86]Dareste, op. cit., p. 244.

[87]Dareste, op. cit., p. 245.

tion of boundary markings, title deeds for real property, and any type of registration of real rights creation or transfer.[88] To complete this gathering, a comprehensive investigation was to take place for one year, and official advice had to be requested. In the end, individual notifiatcions for all were to be sent. At the end of this procedure, any owner could ask for the implementation of the new law in regard to his property. From the official delivery of the registered titles and sheet onwards, transfer of real property rights would only be valid after its entry in the land register.

1.4 Conclusion

As a conclusion, we can presume that if at first colonialism was based on the recognition of local laws applying to indigenous people, and that it intended to maintain local civil laws, it almost resulted in the vanishing of indigenous law. French law was deeply structured and enforced with the support of an overwhelming colonial power; to the contrary local laws were poorly structured and deprived of strength and dynamism due to the empowerment of a foreign authority. They couldn't adapt and resist against the introduction of colonial civil law reforms.

The example of real property shows that with the brutal introduction of a strongly framed and structured civil law, legal order was brought in one sense, but it relied on colonial values, defending first private commercial interests. For instance, common or collective property, deeply rooted in some indigenous traditions, decreased severely because of a lack of recognition by French law. In Annam, the land law reform resulted in the prevalence of private ownership and common ownership only lasted within minorities such as the Moïs.[89]

However, colonial private law was of secondary interest to the French government and its construction was fragmented without any general project or coherence.

References

Báo, P.-V. (1931a). *Revue judiciaire franco-annamite*. Hanoi: Gallica.

Báo, P.-V. (1931b). Question de droit usuel. *Première année*, (1), 396–398.

Bonhomme, A. (1931). Du droit applicable aux indigènes et des Juridictions le prononçant. L'Annam. In: Direction de l'administration de la justice. La justice en Indochine. In Organisation générale. La justice indigene, Section d'administration générale (Ed.), *Exposition coloniale, Indochine Française*. Hanoï: Imprimerie d'Extrême-Orient (available on Gallica http://gallica.bnf.fr).

Boudillon, A. (1915). *Le régime de la propriété foncière en Indochine. Ce qui a été fait – Ce qu'il faudrait faire. Rapport présenté à M. Le Ministre des colonies*. Gallica http://gallica.bnf.fr/ark:/12148/bpt6k751226.

[88]Dareste, op. cit., p. 248.

[89]p. 236.

Boudillon, A. (1927). La réforme du régime de la propriété foncière en Indochine. Rapport présenté *à M. le Gouverneur général de l'Indochine*, août 1924. Hanoï: Imprimerie d'Extrême Orient.
Bourgon, J. (2001). Le droit coutumier comme phénomène d'acculturation au Japon et en Chine. *Extrême Orient - Extrême occident*, (23), 125–143.
Bruschi, Ch. (1987–1988). La nationalité dans le droit colonial. *Procès, cahier d'analyse politique et juridique*, (18), 29.
Cressent, M. P. E. (1931). Le Laos. In: *Exposition coloniale, Indochine Française*.
Dareste, P. (1932). *Traité de droit colonial*.
de Feyssal, P. (1932). *Le service de la propriété foncière en Cochinchine*. Phap-vien Bao, Janvier, T.
Garrigues, A. F. (1931). Du droit applicable aux indigènes et des Juridictions le prononçant. La Cochinchine. In: *Exposition coloniale, Indochine Française*.
Godard, J. (1994). *Rapport de mission en Indochine du 1er janvier au 14 mars 1937*. Paris: L'Harmattan.
Habert, L. A. (1931). Du droit applicable aux indigènes et des Juridictions le prononçant. Le Tonkin. In: *Exposition coloniale, Indochine Française*.
Merle, I. (1999). La construction d'un droit foncier colonial: de la propriété collective à la constitution des réserves en Nouvelle-Calédonie. *Enquêtes, 7*, 97–126.
Nicolas, P. (1931). Du droit applicable aux indigènes et des Juridictions le prononçant. Le Cambodge. In: *Exposition coloniale, Indochine Française*.
Ortolland, A. (1993). *Les institutions judiciaires à Madagascar et dépendances*. Paris: L'Harmattan.
Phirun, K., & Crouzatier, J.-M. (1997). Les études sur le droit cambodgien. In P. Lamant (Ed.), *Bilan et perspectives des études Khmeres: langue et culture*. Paris: L'Harmattan.
Renucci, F. (2005). Le juge et la connaissance du droit indigène. Eléments de comparaison entre l'Algérie et la Lybie. In B. Durand, & M. Favre (Eds.), *Le juge et l'Outre-mer*. Lille: Centre d'histoire judiciaire.
Saada, E. (2003). Citoyens et sujets de l'Empire français, Les usages du droit en situation colonial. *Genèse*, *4*(53), 4–24.
Solus, H. (1927). *Traité de la condition des indigènes en droit privé*. Paris: Recueil Sirey.

Chapter 2
Contract Law in Myanmar: An Outcome of British Colonial Law

Yuka Kaneko

Abstract Myanmar has recently been the focus of investors, who have referred to the country as the final paradise for foreign investment entry. But its law adheres to the "Indian Code" that was transplanted during the British colonial era. For the future law reform, comprehensive systemization work is necessary. The contract laws around the world are struggling towards the same direction of contemporary modifications, while burdened with their different traditions, in the context of correcting the contractual asymmetry and making contractual freedom effective. Myanmar's future contract law reform must also accept the doctrines which are the consummation of current international trends, but it should be formed within the Myanmar's own terminology of jurisprudence.

2.1 Introduction

Myanmar has recently been the focus of investors, who have referred to the country as the final paradise for foreign investment entry. But the contract law system is archaic in its current adherence to the "Indian Code" that was transplanted when Myanmar was a province of India during the British colonial era. The "Indian Code" is generally explained as a series of attempts at codification of British common law, but in reality, the British common law was largely revised and structured to benefit the capitalist exploitation of the colonial economy. Within Myanmar's contract law also, the colonial law has been inherited word-for-word and the development of case law still cannot be seen today, while action accompanying the establishment of the ASEAN Economic Community (AEC) in 2015 has been limited to the enactment of a

Yuka Kaneko—Professor, Law and Development Program; Graduate School of International Cooperation Studies; Kobe University, Japan; LL.B. Tokyo University; LL.M., Georgetown University; LL.D. Kyushu University.

Y. Kaneko (✉)
Graduate School of International Cooperation Studies,
Kobe University, Kobe, Japan
e-mail: ykaneko@kobe-u.ac.jp

Y. Kaneko (ed.), *Civil Law Reforms in Post-Colonial Asia*,
Kobe University Monograph Series in Social Science Research,
https://doi.org/10.1007/978-981-13-6203-3_2

few laws such as a consumer protection law. Entities continue to flow into the country from around the world without regard to these stagnant conditions in the local law and each sign joint-venture contracts that specify their home country's laws as the applicable law, such that at present Myanmar's contract law is tending to be a melting pot in which the contract law cultures of various countries are competing with each other. The sovereignty and systematicity of the legal order is conspicuously involved in this chaos. However as an inverse concept, from within this confusion an advanced debate about contract law reform that includes many standpoints in comparative law has arisen, and with an attempt at a frontier experiment in the investigation of uniform contract law, which has been put on the backburner in Europe and also in Asia, the "benefit of late development" must be possible. The unification of contract law among developed countries has been derailed and British law itself, which is the source of Myanmar's contract law, has lost sight of common ground with the contract law culture of continental law despite being prompted by EU orders, and Britain is currently moving towards withdrawal from the EU. In the former colonies of Asia also, although there are calls for the creation of a uniform law unique to Asia in the era of the AEC, in reality each country still carries the burden of its colonial laws and if anything a proxy war is being fought between the laws of the former colonial powers with the AEC as the battleground. Under these conditions it is possible for Myanmar, the country to recently enter the era of regional integration, to stand at the front line and cast a light upon the future of uniform contract law in Asia. This paper aims to retrace the historical transition of Myanmar's contract law and unearth viewpoints that will contribute to future contract law reform and the involvement of international donors therein.

2.2 Historical Circumstances

In the field of contract law in Myanmar, the 1872 *Contract Act* prescribes the general laws of contract and the 1877 *Specific Relief Act* prescribes specific performance and injunctions as methods of equitable relief for breach of contract, and there are some specific provisions prescribed in the 1930 *Sales of Goods Act* and the 1881 *Negotiable Instruments Act*, while transactions for the sale, security or leasing of real property are prescribed in the 1882 *Transfer of Property Act*. These legislations, which were introduced by the Viceroy of India during the British colonial era as part of the "Indian Code", were automatically applied to Burma when it became a province of India in 1897 following three Anglo-Burmese wars that occurred from 1824, and when Burma became a separate British colony in 1937 the name was changed to the "Burma Code" but retained the same form. This area of contract law has not undergone any legislative amendments from independence until now. It is said that under the post-independence 1947 Constitution, there was some formation of case law during the period from 1948 until 1962 that referred to trends in British and Indian case law,[1] but a system of people's courts was established under the post-1962 Burmese Way to Socialism and the 1974 socialist Constitution and the formation of case law in effect stopped. The system of career judges was restored following the 1988 *coup d'état*, but the independent formation of case law and legislative amendment cannot be seen.

Modernization of the field of contract law is indeed a pressing issue that Myanmar law currently faces. Yet the "Framework for Economic and Social Reforms" that defines medium-term reform objectives under the current 2008 Constitution includes "improving contract enforcement" as a part of strengthening the "Rule of Law" (Article 116) but does not touch upon modernization of contract law itself. What is the reason for this?

Professor A. Burrows, who was involved in the British Oxford University's Myanmar Legal Support Program in 2015, was surprised at the differences in the contract law of both countries, and presumed the causes are first, that the drafters of the Indian Code drafted legislation quite different from the law in Britain, and second, that large changes occurred in British contract law throughout the 20th century yet were not reflected in Myanmar law, not only the reform of legislation but also in the formation of case law (Burrows 2015, pp. 2–3; Bringgs & Barrows 2017).

Regarding his first assumption, the drafting of the "Indian Code" was a large project conducted by the Government of India under the supervision of the historic legal scholar Henry J.S. Maine and purported to codify the essence of the British common law, yet it is clear from documents such as the memoirs of the legal officers involved at the front line of the drafting and the annotated versions of the Code that priority was given to the practical needs of the Viceroy and colonial courts.[2] The first Law Commission ordered by the Viceroy under the *Charter Act* of 1833 had a policy of "uniformity, diversity and clarity" as advocated by the Commissioner T.B. Macaulay and accepted the demands of the local courts that craved for development of substantive laws, not only in the field of criminal law but also civil law. The second Law Commission was moved to London and drafted civil and criminal procedural laws, but the calls for development of not only procedural law but also substantive civil law was strong from the Viceroy's side. The third Law Commission established in 1861 was inspired by the Government of India's advisor Sir Henry Maine and actively compiled draft substantive laws in each of the areas of civil law, including succession, contract law, negotiable instruments and the transfer of property. Based on these drafts, a series of civil legislation was enacted over a period of ten years commencing from 1865, including the 1872 *Contract Act*.[3] On the British side, there were historical legal scholars that strongly criticized this output on the point that

[1] All volumes of the English-language *Burma Law Reports* of Supreme Court judgments that were collated during this period are currently available on the Myanmar Supreme Court's website (http://www.unionsupremecourt.gov.mm/).

[2] This chapter mainly refers to the annotated versions of the 1872 Contract Act by Whitley Stokes, the legal adviser to the Viceroy's Council and drafter of the final version of the Act (Stokes 1887, 1887–8, 1891), and the annotated versions by Frederick Pollock and Dinshah Fardunji Mulla (Pollock and Mulla 1909, 1919).

[3] Based on the draft by F. Stephen.

it crossed the line of collating existing common law and introduced new codified norms,[4] while it was also criticized by those who supported codification, as they demanded a more comprehensive systemic structure.[5] After 1879 the Viceroy took over the task and established the fourth Law Commission and hurried the enactment of the remaining drafts. The policy of reconsidering the English common law where necessary and respecting local customs announced by the fourth Law Commission merits attention,[6] yet the events that actually occurred were the opposite, and the Indian Code can be thought of as a new set of legislation that was radically introduced as a method to improve the effectiveness of the Viceroy's management of the colony. Especially in the area of contract law, the application of the Hindi contract law and Islamic contract law that applied between Indian residents was abolished, and the 1872 *Contract Act* applied universally.[7] The scope of the 1877 *Specific Relief Act* was the same.[8]

Regarding Professor Burrows' second point, the apprehension that Myanmar law was not in any way concerned about the subsequent development of English contract law is correct. During the second half of the 19th Century when the Indian Code was being drafted, England was also in the midst of a dispute over legal codes, and the principle of a comprehensive code expounded by Bentham and Austin had influence. As a compromise, a series of legislation was enacted in the form of standalone statutes in the area of commercial trading, which included the 1893 *Sale of Goods Act*.[9] However, as stated in the preamble to the *Sale of Goods Act*, the legislation was intended as just a collation of present case law and the subsequent formation of case law did not cease; particularly in the context of consumer protection many revisions were needed to continually catch up with the case law. Following the enactment of a new *Sale of Goods Act* in 1979, the deepening of the contract law field continued and included the incorporation of EU directives, and has since expanded to the 2015 *Consumer Rights Act*. However during this time, contract law under the Indian Code has continued to be based upon the 1872 *Contract Act*, and the adoption of the English 1893 *Sale of Goods Act* was delayed until 1930. To somewhat compensate for this

[4]The 1872 Contract Act is strongly criticized by F. Pollock as being heavily influenced by the New York Civil Code. Pollock and Mulla (1909), p. 64.

[5]In an exchange of dispatches quoted in pp. xv–xvii of Stokes (1887), Lord Salisbury feared that "because of the fragmentation of the Indian Codes, it allows the arbitrary formation of law based on local customs by parties and first instances judges who do not understand English law" and argued the necessity of a more genuine codified system. The Government of India's response that "even if the law is partially codified, there is value in it providing a method to understand the obscure and contradictory English common law" is also provided.

[6]See Stokes (1887), pp. 19–20.

[7]See Pollock and Mulla (1919), pp. 5–9.

[8]During the process of drafting the specific relief law, the proposal that gave preference to specific relief over the payment of damages was applied due to the background of demands based on the sudden rise in economic power of the Indian people (the need to apply the law to breach of employment contracts against the background of the enhanced labor movement of dock workers), but eventually returned to a design that gave preference to the payment of damages over specific relief, as was the same in English law.

[9]Drafted by M.D.E.S. Chalmars.

blank period, the drafters of the Indian Code provided supplementary annotations on the latest trends in English case law.[10] The drafters of the Indian Code thought that the codification must be accompanied by continual re-enactment to prevent the hardening of the legal codes,[11] but in India itself legislative revision in the area of contract law was rare, even though Law Commission Reports occasionally called for it. As will be described later, the concept of undue influence that was introduced in the 1899 revision to the *Contract Act* drew attention, but subsequent radical revision of the *Contract Act* did not occur. England's 1893 *Sale of Goods Act* that took the initiative on the interventionist trend in contracts was inconvenient to India's vested interest class, and there is the possibility that the strong inclination towards contractual autonomy in the 1872 *Contract Act* better suited them. Also, it is possible that the hardening of legislation was preferable to the Indian government so as not to ignite debate about law reforms in the growing local judicial forum. The conservative trend continued after independence and although the 13th Law Commission Report in 1958 argued for radical reform of each section of the Act, no results were seen.[12] As a result, until now India has been left with a base that is a mutual contradiction between the inclination to diverge from the English case law faced by the 1872 *Contract Act*, and the 1930 *Sale of Goods Act* that is a copy of England's 1893 *Sale of Goods Act*. Meanwhile, legislative reform has been left on the shelf and subsequent case law and legislative development in England has been given a sideways glance while India has maintained addressing change through case law only.

Myanmar's contract law was constantly passive throughout based on this influence by the Indian contract law. Following defeat in the Anglo-Burmese War and annexation by British India in 1886, the 1872 *Contract Act* and 1877 *Specific Relief Act* as well as the 1930 *Sale of Goods Act* and other Indian legislation was automatically applied. Pursuant to the 1935 *Government of Burma Act*, from 1937 onwards Burma broke away from its position as a province of India and it was possible for

---

[10]In the first addendum (Stokes 1887–8), explanatory judgments on implied contracts, relaxation of consideration, restrictions on ascension clauses in bills of lading, disclosure obligations in insurance contracts, objective definition of the factual requirements of undue influence in Section 16, and unconscionable bargaining in Section 23 were introduced as the latest trends in English case law; this largely addressed the legal intervention in the freedom of contract that had become a problem. In the second addendum (Stokes 1891), the preface states that "many omissions were found particularly in the area of contract law" (p. 24), and the stance of analyzing the problems while using actual judgments from the Calcutta, Madras and Bombay High Courts as material is very interesting. Within these points of issue that have a practical concern are picked up, including an explanation of unconscionability, voidance of agreements in restraint of trade (Section 27), evidentiary requirements to prove commercial customs, validity of contracts by minors, capacity for wives to take independent action in India (which wives in England could not) and a high interest rate of 37% for breach of contract (Section 74).

[11]See Kusumoto (1970).

[12]The 1963 contract law revision was limited. However, the revision of the *Specific Relief Act* in the same year expanded specific relief.

Burma to embark on forming its own law, but not once was an opportunity such as a contract law reform commission established by the legislature or judiciary.[13]

The large difference between this passive stance with respect to the Indian Code and the feeling of vibrancy in the Burmese law that existed in Burma prior to British sovereignty attracts interest. In traditional Burmese law, while legal codes (Dhammathat) were relied upon, a system of legal precedents (Pyattons) developed through the flexibility of customary law, and the compilation of judgment annotations (Mahayazathat, etc.) also took place within the developing legal culture (Okudaira 2002). By just glancing at the contract law provisions of the Dhammathat, contract intervention rules devoted to the protection of weaker parties are of particular note. For example, concerning monetary loans, the *Wagaru Dhammathat*,[14] one of the oldest Dhammathat dating back to the 13th century, the first chapter deals with the law of debts, and the matters that are defined include formality such as witnesses at the time of entering a contract (Section 4), limits on interest (Sections 13, 17) and limits on debt servitude (Section 14). In the 18th century *Manugye Dhammathat*,[15] six categories of debt were more precisely classified (Chapter 3, Section 39) and interest constituted the planned damages for breach of a loan contract, which formed the basis for restrictions on interest rates and other debtor protection rules. Concerning sales contracts in the *Wagru Dhammathat*, Chapter seven corresponded to the trading law and included sophisticated provisions including formalities such as witnesses and a deposit (a type of consideration) at the conclusion of the contract (Article 85), the consent right of co-inhabitors in the purchase and sale of real estate that forms the basis of everyday life as well as the original owner's right of pre-emption at the time of reselling the property (Article 86), and the loss of title by a bad-faith buyer in the case of breach of contract due to deception and a good-faith buyer's right of resale (Article 87). The *Manugye Dhammathat* also had sophisticated contract rules that included principles of formality that made a witness mandatory at the time of concluding a contract and a seller's duty to compensate for faulty merchandise (Chapter 2, Section 4 R). In employment contracts, provisions similar to contemporary labor contract law, such as wage standards (Chapter 2, Section 10) and the employer's duty to consider safety (Chapter 8, Section 9) are also seen. Besides this, if the occasional precedent law and the administrative regulations (Yazathat) that were time-limited to the period of reign of one King were the subject of research, it would be possible to further follow the rich development of these unique laws. This dynamic legal system of legal codes and case law complementing each other in pre-colonial Burma also reminds us of the interactive development of common law and statute law in England following the 1893 *Sale of Goods Act*. However, it is difficult to say that the spirit of this Burmese traditional legal system was demonstrated at the time of the introduction of British colonial law. Was it a peaceful resistance as a form of sabotage against the forcefully imposed colonial law?

---

[13]Information confirmed in a research exchange meeting with contract law specialists under Dr. Mi Khin Saw Aung of the Dagon University Department of Law on 24 January 2017.

[14]With reference to Forchhammer's English version of King Wagaru's Manudhammasattham.

[15]See Okudaira (1986), pp. 114–124.

Despite the significant stagnation that even surprised Professor Burrows, the "Framework for Economic and Social Reforms" does not include contract law reform. The reason seems to be that no voices of reform were raised from the judiciary involved at the front line of application of laws.[16] They have devoted themselves to mechanically accepting the transplanted law for more than a hundred years. Professor Burrows believes that there must be an accumulation of Myanmar's own precedent law based on the transplanted English law, and the development of Myanmar's contract law will be encouraged through its rediscovery.[17] But is the Myanmar judiciary able to apply the contract law derived from colonial law in any way other than mechanical obedience? Based on a perusal of the post-independence English-language judgments that can be viewed on the Myanmar Supreme Court's website (contained in the 1948–1962 editions of the *Burma Law Reports*), in the area of contract law only English cases were mentioned as precedents and no references to Myanmar cases could be seen.[18] The post-1962 era of people's courts under the Burmese Way to Socialism was an era when People's judges wrote judgments in Burmese, so it is unlikely that there was technical deepening of the contract law. Against the expectations of Professor Burrows, Myanmar probably has not achieved the development of the colonial contract law that should have been seen. It seems to me that the future of Myanmar contract law requires overcoming the burden of the hardened colonial law and performing a process to "regenerate" contract law while recalling the memory of the dynamic pre-colonial law that was abandoned. Such opinions can also be found amongst the Myanmar judiciary.[19] There are more than a few hints to be drawn from the past (that is decended to now as living social norms) regarding modern revisions that cut into the stronghold of 19th-century style contract autonomy.

---

[16] In interviews with the Secretary-General of the Supreme Court and the vice-secretary of the Justice Ministry on 21–22 March 2016, contract law was not included in the priority list of reform.

[17] Otherwise, this will end in the unfortunate result of most investors selecting a foreign country's law as the applicable law in Myanmar courts. See Burrows *Id.*, p. 2.

[18] There were only 15 cases recorded in the Supreme Court judgments from 1948 to 1962 that concerned the 1872 *Contract Act* and 1930 *Sale of Gods Act*, and each of them delivered judgments based on English common law. However, there were examples of cases concerned with the 1892 *Transfer of Property Act* that referred to Myanmar's own precedents (for example, the 29 November 1959 Supreme Court judgment B.L.R. [1959] p. 179).

[19] Former Attorney General Hla Aung found that legislation borrowed from the West is not fixed within local society, and it is a good opportunity for legislative reform that systematically revises the shackles of English law. See Hla Aung (2008), pp. 95–97.

2.3 Regression of Consideration

2.3.1 Function of Securing Free Intention

As codified legislation of the general field of contracts which has not been codified within England itself, it is not unusual that the 1872 *Contract Act* draws interest as material for comparative law research. Particularly the fact that "consideration", which is regarded as a traditional feature of English contract law, largely became a mere shell in the 1872 *Contract Act* is a point that drew strong interest from Professor Burrows.

The principle of freedom of contract, which is the manifestation of the modern spirit, is that the formation of a contract is supposed to coincide with the free intention of independent parties, but in English common law "consideration" is added as an essential requirement of a contract. It is known that the role played by consideration, a relic from the pre-modern era, was questioned during the second half of the 19th century, the so-called heyday of modern contract law. The legal principle of consideration was also deemed an obstacle to be overcome by the drafters of the Indian Code, who placed importance on the convenience of managing the colony, and a bold reform path was intended while treating India's own precedent trends as a just cause.[20] As a product of such a periodic background, relaxation of consideration became the underlying trend of the 1872 *Contract* Act. However, with the regression of consideration, what other method could be substituted to serve the function that it had previously served?

It has been said that one function of consideration is to confirm the free intention of the parties. If the principle of freedom of contract is thoroughly implemented then contracts that lack free agreement would be invalid and unenforceable, yet because it is difficult to measure whether the subjective feeling of free intention exists, trade would be demurred. Therefore, in order to promote the safety of transactions, some objective indicator that evidences the true intent of free will is required even in modern law. In Japanese Civil Code, where German law was adopted, the concept of "legal action" is established, which makes a "expression of intention" via an external display of effective intention a requirement for an agreement. Similar to the *causa* of French law and *oorzaak* in the old Dutch Civil Code that derived from Roman law, it can be thought that "consideration" in English law also serves the function of ensuring the intention to contract that becomes the source of the power of enforcement. Many statues adopt a formalistic approach such as a notarized deed or registration in order to secure the intention to contract. In Burma also before British colonization, formalities such as witnesses were contract requirements dating back to the thirteenth century, as seen above. It is not possible to draw a line between the

[20]Stokes, *Id.*, p. 497; Pollock and Mulla (1919), pp. 16–32 explain the definition of "consideration" in Section 2(d)–(f) of the *Contract Act* and emphasize it is a requirement of business in advanced society.

modern and pre-modern eras on the point of requiring confirmation of the parties' intent in an agreement.

It can be said that with the application of the 1872 *Contract Act*, Burma abandoned the formal requirements of the Dhammathat as the means of securing intent and instead accepted "consideration". However, that concept of "consideration" diverged from the tradition of English case law and had a strong sense of radical relaxation of the requirement. First, concerning the requirements of a "contract" (the first line of Section 10), any "agreement" made by free consent of the parties with the competence to contract, for a lawful consideration, with a lawful object, is valid as a "contact." At first glance this seems to be the traditional rule. However, in the definitions of "agreement" and "consideration" there is an adaptation that deviated from tradition. That is, the "agreement" (Section 2(e)) is defined as "every promise and every set of promises, forming the consideration for each other"; in other words, it is not the exchange of promises with consideration which forms an agreement, but the party's promise itself is deemed to be consideration, making consideration in the traditional meaning of drawing the direct counterpart's promise unnecessary. This definition was that seen in the New York Civil Code of 1862 and was a daring venture of the drafters of the Indian Code.[21]

Furthermore, a "consideration" (Section 2(d)) is defined as an act or abstain or promise which "at the desire of the promisor, the promisee or any other person has done or abstained from doing, or does or abstains from doing, or promise to do or to abstain from doing, something." This act by "any other person" permits a third-party consideration. This allows situations in which there is no direct relationship between the direct parties to the contract and the consideration derived from the mutual promises. This was a conscious design by the drafters of the Indian Code.[22] At the time of enacting the *Contract Act* in the mid-19th century, English case law established the "privity of contract" doctrine that refused claims for execution by third parties who had not provided consideration. The drafters of the Indian Code intended to eliminate the doctrine through the operation of the definition of "consideration".[23] In England, although it has been relaxed in recent years by the *Contract (Rights of Third Parties) Act 1999*, the doctrine is still alive and execution of a contract is rejected unless the third party is identified in the contract or the contract is made for the benefit of the third party. In India, which has also maintained the 1872 *Contract Act*, the current trend in case law is to follow the English legislation. However, in Myanmar, not only are there the provisions of the *Contract Act*, but third-party enforcement provisions permitted by the civil execution process (*Civil Procedure*

[21] See Pollock and Mulla, *Id.*, pp. 29–32.

[22] See Pollock and Mulla, *Id.*, pp. 19–25.

[23] The drafters of the Indian Code planned an effective tax collection system so that the Zamindari, who were both landowner and tax collector, could jump across several levels of telescopic sublease and security relationships to directly claim from the actual holder of farming rights, which explains the relaxation of the doctrine. Pollock and Mulla, *Id.*, p. 22. However, in India there was no relaxation via statute like in England, so the privity doctrine was maintained via the operation of the case law.

Code, Order 21, Rule 16) are also adhered to and there are judgments that explicitly abolish the privacy doctrine in the actual practice of the courts.[24]

Secondly, the definition section of "consideration" recognizes "past consideration". The subsequent Section 25(2) is also to the same effect. Past consideration is when there is no present promise to be performed that provides a motivating factor for the promise. In British common law, past consideration was excluded both in the 19th century and also now. This was also an intention of the drafters of the Indian Code.[25]

Third, the definition clauses of "consideration" allow not only deeds but also omissions, i.e. forbearances such as waiving an outstanding debt upon receipt of partial payment and extending deadlines were also accepted as consideration. As a result, when such release or extension is granted, no additional consideration is required (Section 63, Illustrations). The same intent is also contained in 25(2) and (3) discussed below. 19th century British case law required additional consideration, a position which has been maintained until the present, which shows that this point was also a departure by the Indian Code's drafters.[26] However in Myanmar, if one reviews the *Burma Law Reports* from the post-war, post-independence era when the Supreme Court's decisions were published in English (1948–1962 editions), two judgments related to Section 63 of the *Contract Act* were published,[27] and in both cases the court denied the enforceability of the waiver/extension on account of the absence of explicit notification by the other party, and there was a tendency to adjust the interests of the parties by seeking an external representation separate from the consideration.

Fourth, consideration is sometimes replaced by formal requirements such as documentation and registration. In Article 25 of the *Contract Act*, while contracts lacking consideration are in principle invalid, contracts are effective without consideration in the following cases: (1) an agreement between closely related parties that is accompanied by formality such as documentation and registration, (2) a reward for a prior voluntary act, (3) a written agreement to repay a debt after the statute of limitation has passed. The contract requirement provisions (Section 10 onwards) do not prevent the establishment of formal requirements of the Statute of Frauds such as being documented, witnessed, and registration. Further, contracts that lack consideration are not automatically unenforceable, but it is a factor the court will consider when deciding upon the intent of the parties (Explanation 2). Here, though the drafters of the Indian Code displayed bold reform that makes substantive consideration unnecessary for the formation of a contract and broadens the definition of consideration, in a situation where it is difficult to confirm the intention of the parties, there is

---

[24] *Daw Po v U Po Hmyin* (1940) RLR 239, *Burma (Government Security) Insurance Co Ltd v Daw Saw Hia* (1953) BLRHC 350 and other cases referred to in Burrows *Id.*, p. 7.

[25] See Pollock and Mulla, *Id.*, pp. 26–27.

[26] See Pollock and Mulla, *Id.*, pp. 27–29.

[27] In a decision dated 24 June 1950 (B.L.R. [1950] p. 227), the Supreme Court questioned whether there was receipt and its effect concerning repayment via deposit of an equivalent amount in Japanese military currency. In a decision dated 29 March 1954 (B.L.R. [1954] p. 19), the Supreme Court questioned the effect of receipt when performance in installments was late.

an expectation upon the judges to conduct an individual examination based on the formalities such as documentation.

In this way, in the 1872 *Contract Act*, although consideration is formally one of the requirements for establishment of a contract, it lost its function of securing the intention of the parties, and how to fill this lost function remains as an issue. The skeptical attitude towards consideration is a reminder of the principle of liberal supremacy that has been continually quoted since the 19th century. The reform proposals by the United Kingdom Law Revision Committee established in 1937 and the anti-causalism in countries such as France and the Netherlands are also known.[28] The drafters of the Indian Code were in the middle of that tide. Also, the 13th Recommendation in the 1958 Contract Law Reform paper released by the Law Committee of India, which was established after India's independence, followed the recommendations of the United Kingdom's Law Revision Committee in calling for additions to Section 25 of the 1872 *Contract Act* (list of items not requiring consideration).[29] However, despite these headwinds, it is also true that consideration has survived until today. In the contemporary consumer society, where equality between contracting parties has been lost and the freedom of contract principle which presupposes the concurrence of free intention has been shaken, contract laws of many jurisdictions seem to be responding to the danger by utilizing traditional frameworks. One path to take is so to say the "substantiation of contract freedom" by refining the case law interpretation on the defective intention such as fraud, compulsion, misunderstanding and abuse of circumstances,[30] while the other route may be the strict pursuit of "formalization of contract freedom". The re-recognition of the function of contemporary consideration is this latter course. In countries such as India and Malaysia where the 1872 *Contract Law* was applied and continues to have force today like Myanmar, there is a trend for interpretation to place importance on the substantial function of consideration due to the influence of English case law.[31] In contrast to this, it is notable that the Myanmar case law applies the same law literally to relax the requirement (Burrows, *ibid.*, p. 7).

Then, in Myanmar law, what means have been used to fill the decline of consideration for securing free intention? development.

---

[28]Ohmura (1997), Uchiyama (2008), etc.

[29]The Law Commission of India (1958) added the release, concession, etc. of prior debts to the list of items not requiring consideration.

[30]The way that the Netherlands' 1992 Civil Code removed cause on the one hand, but also newly established a General Law of Property Law that introduced the abstract concept of legal acts and provided a better interpretive base for fair and equitable principles has been discussed long ago. Hartkamp (1994), Honduce (1994), etc.

[31]In *Kepong Prospecting Ltd v Schmidt* [1968] AC 810, the issue of the application of the privity doctrine in Malaysia was appealed to the English Privy Council, which confirmed the applicability of the doctrine. Malaysia removed the ability to appeal to the English courts in 1986 and the Federal Court of Malaysia became the final appellate court, but it still continues to refer to English law.

2.3.2 Function to Secure Legality

The function of securing legality can also be raised as one of the functions of consideration. Section 23 of the 1872 *Contract Act* states that the consideration and the object of an agreement that is forbidden by law, infringes the legal provisions, fraudulent, harm other persons or their property, or judged by the court to be immoral or against public order are illegal. Every agreement that has an unlawful object or consideration is void.

Upon review of the Burmese Supreme Court's *Burma Law Reports* (1948–1962 editions), of the 12 cases involving a dispute over the 1872 *Contract Act*, two of the cases relate to Section 23, with the judgments dated 4 April 1949[32] and 24 October 1951[33] respectively. In each case, the dispute contested the effectiveness of receipt of repayment (in Japanese military currency) from a Burmese resident borrower by an agent in Burma on behalf of a financier resident in India, during the period that Burma was occupied by the Japanese Army during World War II. One of the arguments put forward was the assertion that the agency contract had become straddled across the battle line between the Japanese and English at the beginning of Burma's occupation by Japan, which meant it became invalid due to violation of the "public policy" referred to in Section 23 of the *Contract Act*. In each case, the Supreme Court ruled that as there was a lack of explicit laws concerning commercial transactions straddling a battle line during wartime, the judges made discretionary decisions based on "justness, balance and conscience" in accordance with the general provisions of the 1898 *Burma Laws Act* (Section 13, (3)). Although the two cases were very similar in their background and issue in dispute and both resulted in the claim being dismissed, the Supreme Court's reasoning followed a totally different route in each case and can be considered an example that shows the versatile attitude of the court towards the interpretation of lawfulness.

In the first decision, the Supreme Court used its discretionary judgment based on Section 13(3) of the 1898 *Burma Laws Act* to interpret that the exception provisions of the prohibition against commercial transactions with the citizens and residents of enemy countries contained in the 1940 *Defense of Burma Act* applied, such that the receipt of repayment that was due was excluded from the prohibition clause and it was deemed legal. Therefore, violation of the "public order" referred to in Section 23 of the *Contract Act* had not occurred, and there was no need to consider the larger issue of the effectiveness of a contract that straddled a war front. In addition, regarding the governing law of the agent's actions, the plaintiff's claim of the law of the place where the contract was formed (i.e. Indian law) was rejected, and it was ruled that the law of the place where the agency was conducted (i.e. Burmese law) was the governing law, based on British case law precedents. However, on the other hand, the second Supreme Court decision did not refer to the first decision and started by addressing the issue of selecting the governing law, deciding to apply Burmese law based on Section 13(3) of the 1898 *Burma Laws Act*. Regarding the *Defense of Burma Act*

---

[32]B.L.R. [1949] p. 56.

[33]B.L.R. [1951] p. 25.

however, the court concluded that the Act did not apply as transactions within the British Empire did not fall under the Act's prohibition on transactions with citizens and residents of "enemy countries", and accordingly frustration under Section 56 of the *Contract Act* had not occurred. In addition, the court looked at the larger issue of the validity of an agency contract between parties on opposite sides of a battle front, which had been avoided in the court's earlier decision, and took a direct approach to developing an interpretation of "public order" in Section 23 of the *Contract Act*. While first confirming that the British case law is strict about prohibiting trade with enemy citizens and residents, the court turned to the continental law countries such as Germany, Austro-Hungarian Empire, the Netherlands and Italy and identified that, in these countries, trade that crossed over battle fronts is valid unless excluded by a special law. Further, the court returned to the situation in Burma and expanded upon the original argument of whether a general prohibition on trade during wartime contributes to the national interest of Burma, and drew the conclusion that such trade did not violate the "public order". Finally, concerning the supplementary argument about the choice of governing law, the court cited the theories of A.V. Dicey to reinforce the reason for choosing the law of the place where the act is conducted; it respected the parties' choice of governing law, but ultimately upheld the rejection of the claim as the burden of pleading had not been fully met.

Thus, the reasoning of the first decision and the second decision differed, which is clear from the description of the summary of the stare decisis (ratio decidendi) described in the General Index at the beginning of each issue of the *Burma Law Reports*. Yet the second decision makes no mention of the former decision, so there was a nonchalant change to the precedent. It appears that, for the judiciary also, the several years that followed independence from Britain was a period of confusion where the attempt to gain independence from English law continued. The first decision is based on English law, but while the second decision repeatedly refers to the English case law it was not bound by it, and extends the range of its comparative law examination to the continental law countries, which displays an attitude of attempting to build up Burma's own jurisprudence. The discretion based upon "justness, balance and conscience" permitted by the 1898 *Burma Laws Act* (Section 13, (3)) provided the grounds for the liberal statutory interpretation by these judges. However, this judicial activism, which tried to shape the substantive rules of contract law through the rough reasoning of the judges that questioned what was in the national interest, carried a risk of exceeding its authority, particularly under the 1947 Constitutional system that gave priority to the legislature.

Though these decisions are examples that convey the activist spirit of the Myanmar courts over the discovery of the substantial right of "public order" in contract law, the *Burma Law Reports* do not contain any other noteworthy precedents in the field of contract law.[34] The judiciary's power of statutory interpretation based on Section 13(3) of the 1898 *Burma Laws Act* is a last resort that has been rarely relied

[34] As other noteworthy Supreme Court decisions out of the few cases in the *Burma Law Reports* that concern contract law, there was a decision concerning the "substance of a contract" that determined whether delayed performance addressed in Section 55 of the *Contract Act* in a land transaction permitted a remedy of termination or damages (1 March 1950 decision at B.L.R [1950] p. 98),

upon to date, and instead the judiciary continues to obey the literal interpretation of the century-old colonial law. It seems that enhancing the legal basis for prescriptive judgments via the development of statutory law is essential in order for the court to regain the spirit that boldly embarked on the interpretation of "public order" and make use of it in the discerning pursuit of substantial contract rights without exceeding its discretionary power. As a legislative basis for the pursuit of such substantive contract rights, the 1930 *Sales of Goods Act* and the 2012 *Consumer Protection Act* will be considered later in Part 4 below.

2.4 Substantiation of Freedom of Contract

2.4.1 Breach of Contract Rules in the 1872 Contract Act

The reduced status of "consideration" in Myanmar's contract law raises the concern about the loss of the function of formally guaranteeing freedom of contract. When the consideration that evidences that a contract is based on a freely consenting agreement is lost, the court must engage in the difficult task of substantively verifying the intention of the parties to a contract, lacking the means of formalistically decide on a defect in the intension such as fraud or complusion. This will make the trends in civil lawsuits and enforcement obscure and unforeseeable. There is also a concern whether Myanmar's trial courts have a capacity to sufficiently verify whether there are any defects in the parties' intention. In that sense, the pursuit of formalistic requirements that guarantee freedom of contract may need to be reconsidered, which is possible under the "rediscovery of consideration" argument, or it may need a legal sociological exploration of the formal requirements or documentation and witnesses that were required by the contract law of the pre-colonial Dhammathat era and might still be seen in the towns today.[35]

Nonetheless, the 1872 *Contract Act* includes numerous provisions that can be grounds for judges to issue judgments that fill the gap left by the removal of consideration and realize freedom of contract. These provisions are detailed and have a strong impression of a judicial code that is advanced in its standardization based upon straightforward, formalistic elements. It also include an abundant number of the detailed illustrations and explanations that are characteristic of the Indian Code.

First of all, regarding competence to contract, there is a simple structure to decide whether a contract has been formed by determining whether a person is a minor or of

as well as decisions that recognized frustration (Section 56) and restitution (Section 65) in trade transactions that were hindered by the post-independence economic controls (24 October 1951 decision at B.L.R [1952] p. 65; 9 March 1953 decision at B.L.R [1953] p. 9), but in each of these the decision was based upon English precedents and there were no other cases showing an intention to form independent case law.

[35]For example, Bangladesh, which inherited the same 1872 *Contract Act*, added documentation, witnessing and registration as requirements of a contract (Section 10).

unsound mind (Sections 11 and 12) and is designed not to incorporate complicated rules such as cancellation and subsequent completion. A contract by a minor is voidable in English common law, and in India also there was a judicial trend that followed the English law at first. But from the beginning of the 20th century an independent trend based on the literal wording of the 1872 *Contract Act* was settled in India, which treated such contracts as being void and also established an interpretation that disapproved of cancellation and subsequent completion.[36] Policy decisions that gave priority to the protection of persons with limited capacity were seen in this judicial trend in India. Myanmar's judiciary can be thought of as also inheriting these precedents.

Next, coercion (Sections 14(1), 15), undue influence (Sections 14(2), 16), fraud (Sections 14(3), 17), misrepresentation (Sections 14(4), 18) and mistake (Sections 14(5), 20–22) are defined as causes for consent to not be free. The effect of each of these is different; in the case of coercion, fraud or misrepresentation, the contract will be void only if invoked by the counterparty (voidable), and especially in the case of fraud or misrepresentation, the counterparty can seek for the contract to be performed as if the relevant representation was true (restitution) (Section 19). The effect of undue influence is also that the contract is voidable at the counterparty's option, but the court also has a discretionary power to intervene and make appropriate changes to the terms of the contract (Section 19A).

The provisions regarding mistake are a distinctive feature. There are alternative provisions laid out for deciding that a contract is void or valid, depending on whether the mistake was one of a factual matter or a value, and whether the mistake was made by both parties to the contract or just one. The essence of the provisions is that an agreement is void when both parties are mistaken as to a matter of fact essential to the agreement (Section 20). The section's Explanation says that a value judgment is not a factual matter. A mistake about a domestic law does not void a contract, but a mistake about a foreign law is a mistake as to fact (Section 21). A mistake of fact by one of the parties alone does not have the effect of making a contract void (Article 22). But it does not mention what other additional condition (for example, a misrepresentation, malice or breach of a duty to provide information by the other party) must be met in order to be able to assert that a contract is void.[37] In other words, the situation this section addresses is the avoidance of an agreement due to a "common mistake", and not a mistake by one party in the manifestation of their intention, which is the question addressed by continental law systems including Japan. That a mistake by one party should be treated as a breach of a condition or warranty issue of a validly formed contract appears to be the thinking of the commentators of the Indian Code.[38] Particularly cases that include the culpability of the other party appear to be

[36]See Pollock and Mulla, *Id.*, p. 69. Also see the Law Commission of India's "13th Law Commission Report" (pp. 18–21, 35–37).

[37]Commentary on the Indian Code deals with a mistake by one party by simply stating that it was a debated point in the past, but currently "a proposition which no competent lawyer would think of asserting" (Pollock and Mulla, *Id.*, p. 142).

[38]See Pollock and Mulla, *Id.*, p. 134.

treated as a different type of breach, such as fraud or misrepresentation.[39] A mistake made by one party can be thought of as an issue that has generally been dealt with formalistically via "consideration" under traditional English law, and is possibly one of the areas at most risk of abuse due to the retrograding of consideration under the 1872 *Contract Act*. In that sense, what kind of relief has been provided by Myanmar's courts is of interest.[40]

As seen above, a contract is void if the consideration or the object of the contract that is unlawful, fraudulent or against public morals (Section 23), and the issues addressed by this section are not only the substance of the contract but also the breaches in the contract formation process that manifests as a problem with consideration.[41] Further, in contracts that do not require consideration also (Section 25), inadequate consideration alone does not immediately make a contract void, and the court must separately determine the validity of the agreement (Section 25, Explanation 2). We can understand that the regression of consideration, as seen in the relaxation of rules during contract formation and the promotion of business, also adds to the responsibility of the court during the enforcement stage.

Agreements that restrict a right to sue are void (Section 28). This is currently a point of debate in relation to the unfair contract terms discussed below. Further, agreements of uncertain meaning are void (Section 29).

2.4.2 Undue Influence—The Result of Indian Case Law

Even when looked at as an old law compiled nearly 150 years ago, the 1872 *Contract Act* can be seen as providing a certain base for legal interpretation aimed at the realization of freedom of contract. The section that defines undue influence (Section 16) and its Illustrations is the revised *Contract Act* incorporating new provisions introduced in India in 1899, and as well as a detailed explanation of the doctrine of undue influence from English equity precedents, has a unique apportionment of the burden of proof, and gives prominence to the point that asserting the doctrine is realistic. These new provisions have a similarity to the doctrine of "Unconscionability" that has attracted attention after it was defined in Article 2-203 of the US Uniform Commercial Code (UCC) published by the American Law Institute in 1952, and also overlap with the concept of "economic duress" which has been expanded upon in recent English case law.

Section 16(1) defines undue influence as "where the relations subsisting between the parties are such that one of the parties is in a position to dominate the will of

[39]The 1992 Dutch Civil Code, aware of Anglo-American case law, adopts this way of thinking in Article 6:228.

[40]As of 24 January 2017, the author could not receive an answer regarding case law on this point in an interview with six judges of the West Yangon District Court.

[41]Illustration (g) provides an example of an agreement being void due to implied fraud arising from insufficient provision of information during the contract formation process.

the other and uses that position to obtain an unfair advantage over the other". It can be said that it sufficiently describes the necessary essence of the English case law, where a "dominant position" is used for an "unfair advantage". The subsequent paragraph (2) is a presumptive provision regarding the "position to dominate the will of the other" that is the first requirement in paragraph (1); the presumption arises to reverse the burden of proof when (a) one party has real or apparent authority over the other or there is a fiduciary relationship, or (b) making a contract with a person whose mental capacity is temporarily or permanently affected by reason of age, illness, or mental or bodily distress. Paragraph (3) addresses the second requirement of unfair advantage in paragraph (1), stating that where a person in a "position to dominate the will of the other" contracts with the other party and the contents of the transaction appear unconscionable, either at first glance or based on the evidence, the presumption takes effect and the burden of proving that the contract is not due to the use of undue influence is reversed (paragraph (3)). According to Section 19A, the effect of undue influence is to render the contract voidable and the court can amend the contract to make it valid.

From the above, the distinctive feature of the section is that paragraphs (2) and (3) clearly identify the burden of proof to facilitate the realistic assertion of undue influence that is defined in paragraph (1). The other party only has to establish a fiduciary relationship or that the contract was entered under psychological distress as referred to in paragraph (2) and that the contents of the contract are unconscionable as referred to in paragraph (3); after that the party presumed to be in the dominant position has a burden to rebut that they used undue influence.

Although this undue influence clause is the codification of English case law, it is said that it is a remedy that was applied extremely positively in the Indian courts even before the enactment of the 1872 *Contract Act* by directly referring to English case law.[42] Furthermore, after the revision of the law in 1899, it seems that the development of India's own case law beyond the British case law started at the beginning of the 20th century; especially as seen in the case of high interest lending described in Illustration (c) that was introduced by the amendment of the law in 1899, where the unconscionability of a contract's contents was recognized, such as in the typical case of an unreasonably high interest rate, it seems that the attitude of the lower courts to immediately presume "undue influence" and reverse the burden of proof had strengthened.[43] In other words, among the requirements to be proven by the side claiming "undue influence", the requirement of a "dominant position" (the fiduciary relationship or psychological distress required by paragraph (2)) was gradually expanded and diluted in the judicial trends,[44] which suggests that the element to be proven converged upon the unconscionability of the contract's contents

[42]See Pollock and Mulla, *Id.*, p. 97 onwards.

[43]In Pollock and Mulla, *Id.*, p. 112, the authors strongly warn against the trend of lower courts departing from the strict application of Section 16.

[44]In Pollock and Mulla, *Id.*, pp. 99–106, a large number of Indian cases are discussed regarding the requirement for proof in Section 16(2) and introduces points of contention, such as Hindu women generally being psychologically weak and wealthy people generally being in a dominant position.

referred to in paragraph (3). Even though the commentators on the Indian Code saw it as a dangerous trend that hindered the freedom of contract, this development can be said to be an advanced trend that anticipated what is called the doctrine of presumed undue influence in current contract law and also touches upon the doctrine of economic duress that is influential in modern English law.[45]

Thus, if the element of "dominant position" is diluted within the constituent requirements of the doctrine of "undue influence", the court has gained a highly elastic basis for intervening in a contract that is not different from the United States doctrine of unconscionability. Unconscionability in United States law is not given a conceptual definition in Article 2-302 of the Uniform Commercial Code (UCC), but is a doctrine that allows the court to either refuse to enforce or to amend a contract or any of its clauses that are found to be unconscionable at the time the contract was made, for the purpose of avoiding "oppression and unfair surprise", while giving the parties the opportunity to provide evidence in rebuttal. It is given the same meaning in Article 208 of the Restatement of United States case law.[46] Generally, it is considered that both procedural unconscionability (a disadvantageous position during negotiation of the contract) and substantive unconscionability (unfair contents in the contract) are required. The constituent requirements of Section 16 of the 1872 *Contract Act* are not only remarkably similar to the United States doctrine, but rather proceeds the vague provision in the UCC as a legislative method of apportioning the burden of proof. The United States concept of unconscionability is considered not as an invention of Karl Llewellyn, one of the drafters of the UCC, but as having its beginning in the 18th century British case law.[47] Yet it has instead been identified that the gap is widening between the English law which adheres to the contract itself without going beyond the individual equitble relief and the law of the other Commonwealth countries that have been influenced by the UCC.[48]

The current Section 16 of the 1872 *Contract Act* is the basis for implementing substantial contractual freedom that was codified and built up through a large number of precedents by the Indian legal profession, while learning from the leading English case law, from the end of the 19th century to the beginning of the 20th century, much prior to the development of the United States UCC and the legislation based upon it in Commonwealth countries. This pioneering achievement was also inherited by Myanmar law.

---

[45] See Saintier (2016), p. 129.

[46] See American Law Institute (1981) *Restatement (Second) of Contracts*, Section 208. However, this doctrine only applies to consumer contracts.

[47] See Waddams (1976), p. 369.

[48] The doctrine of "inequality of bargaining power" developed in the 1974 case of *Lloyds Bank v Bundy* was rejected in the 1988 case *National Westminster Bank v Morgan*. See Zhou and DiMatteo (2016), p. 363.

2.4.3 *Legislative Modernization of the Rules on Defects*

There is a limit to the modernization of the rules on defects that can be achieved through the work of the judiciary alone, and there is no doubt that legislative reform of the more than century-old 1872 *Contract Act* is expected.

Yet action is slow. One reason that is given is that India, which has the same 1872 *Contract Act*, has not made any fundamental revisions to the Act since the 1899 revision mentioned above. Referring to the Law Commission of India's above-mentioned 1958 "13th Law Commission Report" which provided proposed revisions to the *Contract Act* in post-independence India, regardless of the ambitious general remarks advocating "modernization" of the *Contract Act* in the introduction, the specific proposals concerning each section were conservative throughout and considered favourable to the business world. Particularly concerning the series of sections on defects in the agreement, it was concluded that it was unnecessary to revise the law. For example, regarding undue influence (Section 16), it displayed a conservative attitude that criticised the judicial trend to rule contracts invalid for the reason of unconscionability alone in the absence of actual coercion and expressly renounced so-called presumed undue influence (p. 21, para 41). On the other hand, it stated that it was desirable to add a qualification to the restitution provision (Section 19) because of the difficulty in actually implementing it in cases of fraud and misrepresentation and that there were cases where it was substituted with damages (p. 22, para 44). Regarding the provisions concerning undue influence and mistake, which were the subject of the most movement within the doctrine of defects at that time, it was determined that there was no need for revision (p. 23, para 46). Realistically too, the 1963 revision of the Act in response to this report was generally lacking in fact and thereafter no further reform of these provisions has occurred until today.[49]

One feels that it is not easy for Myanmar to commence ambitious reform of contract law while the Indian 1872 *Contract Act* remains in an unchanged condition. However, it is possible for the country to enjoy the "latecomer's advantage" while skillfully utilizing the technical support provided by donor countries.

2.5 *Sale of Goods Act* and Consumer Protection—Realization of Just Contracts

2.5.1 *History and Overview of the* Sale of Goods Act

In Sect. 2.2 above, we saw that the drafters of the 1872 *Contract Act* had a policy that favoured the promotion of contracts and adopted bold reforms such making substantive consideration unnecessary in the formation of a contract and additional consider-

[49]The provision prohibiting the restraint of rights to commence legal proceedings was revised in 1997.

ation unnecessary upon amending a contract to waive a debt or postpone enforcement, in order to solve the burden of the doctrine of consideration that impeded the formation of contracts. In Sect. 2.3, we also saw the distinctive feature of the English case law principles on defective agreements, such as coercion, undue influence, fraud, misrepresentation and mistake being clearly set as realistic fundamental provisions by the courts to fill the role of securing a party's true intention, which was previously secured through consideration. However, consideration's formal procedural role was not just securing a party's true intention; it seems that substantial contemplation of consideration's role in securing the legality of an agreement is also necessary. The 1872 *Contract Act* contains Section 23 as a general provision, which entrusts the ultimate determination of the legality of the consideration and object of a contract to the discretion of the court based on public policy and morals. Precedents in which the Myanmar Supreme Court has boldly addressed the interpretation of "public policy and morals" were looked at in the previous sections, but the current situation where the determination of a contract's fairness is entirely left to the individual judge's discretion is excessively lacking in predictability. It appears that the creation of rules is a necessary issue.

In the area of sales contracts, the 1930 *Sale of Goods Act* provides certain rules, but its modernization is lagging. The act is almost a complete copy of the United Kingdom's 1893 *Sale of Goods Act* that was enacted nearly 40 years earlier and since then it has not been subject to any notable revisions in any of the former British Indian countries, including Myanmar.[50] In the meantime, the English case law saw major developments that led to the enactment of a new Act in 1979; the portion of the 1979 Act dealing with consumer contracts has since been replaced by the *Consumer Rights Act 2015*. This series of changes is the development of consumer contract law, but on the other hand, there have been no noticeable changes in the separated area of commercial contracts. For this reason, the fact that the 1930 *Sale of Goods Act* has remained unchanged in the countries of former British India suggests that the contract laws of these countries function to give priority to economic development, and the development of consumer law is therefore lagging. However, verification of this requires extensive examination of judicial rends in each country, which the author cannot conduct. Therefore, for the time being, this section will trace the changes to the sale of goods law in the United Kingdom and identify issues with Myanmar's 1930 *Sale of Goods Act,* with reference to the 2012 Consumer Protection Law recently enacted in Myanmar, so as to forecast the direction of future contract law reform that considers substantial contractual fairness.

In the field of sales contract law in the United Kingdom, the *Sale of Goods Act 1893* was enacted for the purpose of "collating the common law", and after that subsequent legislation which followed developments in the common law appeared in succession, including the *Law Reform (Frustrated Contracts) Act 1943*, the *Hire-Purchase Act 1964*, the *Supply of Goods (Implied Terms) Act 1973*, the *Consumer Credit Act 1974* and the *Unfair Contract Terms Act 1977*, before being incorporated into the new *Sale of Goods Act 1979*. Thereafter, a series of amendments were

[50]The Indian *Sale of Goods Act* was subject to minor technical revisions in 1963.

made based on European Union directives; a 1994 revision of the implied warranty provisions was based on EU Directive 1993/13/EEC on unfair terms, revisions to the Act's wording were made in 1999, a revision in 2002 was based on EU Directive 1999/44/EC concerning consumer goods guarantees, before finally, the EU directive 2011/83/EU on consumer rights led to the enactment of the *Consumer Rights Act 2015*, which superseded the *Sale of Goods Act 1979*.

By comparison, Myanmar's 1930 *Sales of Goods Act* has not undergone any revision since its introduction; while including some technical changes, it almost entirely follows the United Kingdom's *Sale of Goods Act 1893*, and the contents are generally advantageous to the seller. The provisions concerning formation of a sales contract (Section 4),[51] capacity to buy or sell (Section 2)[52] and the freedom of the form of contract (Section 5)[53] define rules that promote the valid formation of a contract by abandoning various issues such as consideration and capacity to contract. The provisions regarding conditions and warranties (Sections 11 to 17)[54] utilize a separation of the conditions from the seller's warranties to avoid rescission and rejection of the goods as much as possible. The timing of the transfer of risk (Section 26) follows the timing of the transfer of title (Sections 18 to 25, 27 to 30) and the seller's performance obligations are completed at an early stage by bringing forward the transfer of title.[55] Priority is given to the promotion of transaction in the defects of title.[56] In the performance of the contract (Sections 32 to 54), while incomplete performance by the seller is permitted, default by the buyer is pursued by all available means including the seller's liens on sold property.[57] Relief for

[51]Sales contracts are formed from the exchange of property for money. The phrase "money as consideration" used in the 1893 English Act (Section 1) has been removed.

[52]Myanmar's 1930 Act removed the provision of the 1893 U.K. Act (Section 2) that validated the sale of "necessities" to persons with limited capacity to contract. It would appear that it is treated as being void under the general principles of the 1872 Contract Act (Section 11).

[53]As an exception to the principle of freedom of the form of contract, the 1893 U.K. Act (Sections 4 and 5) requires an act such as documentation or part payment in the case of a high-value transaction. Myanmar's 1930 Act eliminated this special rule and makes freedom of the form of a contract uniform. The U.K. 1979 Act is of the same effect.

[54]The 1893 U.K. Act (Sections 11 to 14) is followed entirety. The 1979 U.K. Act revised these provisions as described below.

[55]In the 1893 U.K. Act, transfer of ownership occurs when the goods are identified by agreement (Section 16, Section 18 Rule 5), when delivered from the seller to a carrier (Section 32), etc. This is followed in the 1930 Myanmar act also (Section 18, Section 23(1), etc.).

[56]In the 1893 UK Act, although the sale of another person's property is invalid in principle (Section 21), a good faith buyer in a market transaction has priority (Section 22), a good faith buyer of a voidable title has priority (Section 23), the sale of stolen goods is invalid in principle, but if fraud is involved it returns to rule of giving priority to a buyer of good faith (Section 24) and a good faith buyer who trusted the long-term possession of the seller/former buyer will take priority (Section 25). Of these provisions, Myanmar's 1930 Act takes more simply seller-friendly stance, removing the provision on invalidation of the sale of stolen goods of the U.K. Act (Section 24) to make such sales valid, and adopted the other provisions.

[57]In the U.K. *Sale of Goods Act 1893*, in the case of incomplete performance by the seller, if the buyer voluntarily accepts the goods then the full amount must be paid (Section 30). Transfer of title and risk occurs when the seller delivers the goods to the carrier (Section 32). Criteria for inspection,

breach of contract (Sections 55 to 66) defines a limit on the seller's damages[58] and specific performance may be ordered at the discretion of the judge (Section 58). A miscellaneous provision (Section 62) stipulates that rights and obligations can be varied by agreement or by the course of dealing between the parties, which gives rise to the problem of unfair contract terms that still exists today.[59]

In this way, it can be said that Myanmar's 1930 Act inherited the orientation towards promotion of sales and security of transactions found in the United Kingdom's *Sale of Goods Act 1893* that represents 19th-century style of capitalism. In the face-to-face confrontation with this stronghold of commercial capitalism, the historical axis in which English 20th-century contract law was formed is brought to mind. Even after the *Consumer Rights Act 2015* was established in the United Kingdom and consumer contract law was removed, the remaining 1979 Act is marked by 20th-century style revisions and fulfills a role in adjusting imbalanced negotiating relationships such as with small and medium enterprises. Myanmar's contract law in the era of democratization cannot avoid taking this step when following the path to modernization.

In the following sections, I would like to address in particular the issues of implied warranties in Section (2) and consumer contracts in Section (3), which have undergone subsequent changes in English law.

2.5.2 Doctrine of Implied Warranties

The provisions on conditions and warranties in Myanmar's 1930 *Sale of Goods Act* are contract performance rules that fully adopted the United Kingdom's *Sale of Goods Act 1893*. The English law that advantages the seller does not require perfect tender and is aimed at maintaining the validity of a contract as much as possible, even in the case of incomplete performance. The essential feature is that the contractual provisions concerning the object of the contract are classified into "conditions" that are essential to the main purpose of the contract, and other provisions are classified as "warranties"; the buyer can rescind the contract in the case of breach of a "condition" (Section 12(2)), but cannot rescind or reject the goods for a breach of a "warranty",

---

notification and delay of acceptance by the buyer are detailed (Sections 34 to 37). The seller's lien in case of buyer's defaulting on the payment obligation and the seller's right of stoppage in the case of the in buyer's insolvency are described in detail (Sections 39 to 46), while these seller's rights are defeated if the buyer sells or pledges the goods to a good faith party for value (Section 47) and relief will be in the form of damages (Section 48). Myanmar's 1930 Act almost entirely follows these provisions.

[58]Under the U.K. *Sale of Goods Act 1893*, the buyer cannot reject the goods due to a breach of warranty alone, but is entitled to relief through reduction of the purchase price or damages (Section 53(1)) and the so-called "perfect tender" rule is not adopted. The grounds for calculation of damages are defined as limited to directly caused losses (paragraphs (2) to (4)).

[59]The U.K. *Sale of Goods Act 1893* (Section 55) states that contractual rights and obligations can be negative or varied by the express agreement or course of dealing between the parties. Myanmar's 1930 Act follows this. The U.K. 1979 Act revised the provision as described below.

which instead is resolved by an award of damages (Myanmar's 1930 *Sale of Goods Act,* Section 12(3)). Moreover, even if a "condition" is breached, if the buyer waives or accepts the breach, it becomes a breach of "warranty" and the validity of the contract will be maintained (Section 13).

On the contrary, "implied warranties" provided in Sections 14 to 16 of Myanmar's 1930 *Sale of Goods Act* is a distinctive development in English case law doctrine in the 20th century. Considering the overall tone of the Act that favours the seller, these provisions on implied warranties are exceptional in favouring the buyer and prescribe certain warranties that are imposed as mandatory statutory provisions even if there is no agreement between the parties in the written contract. Section 14 is a so-called implied warranty of title which, in the absence of an express intention by the parties to the contrary, implies provisions of (1) a legitimate right to sell the goods, (2) quiet possession of the goods, and (3) the absence of any third-party security interests that are not known to the buyer. Section 15 is an implied warranty that the goods correspond with the contractual description, however, Section 17 has an exception for contracts for sale by sample. Section 16 limits the scope of implied warranties and conditions concerning the quality or fitness of goods for any particular purpose to the following circumstances:

(1) Where the buyer informs the seller of the particular purpose of the goods, and the description is included in the scope of the seller's business, there is an implied warranty that the goods will be reasonably fit for such purpose. However, the sale of a specified article is excluded.
(2) There is an implied warranty that, where goods are bought by description from a seller who normally handles such goods, the goods shall be of merchantable quality. However, if the buyer performs an inspection, any defects that should have been found in the inspection are not subject to the implied warranty.
(3) An agreement clause based on business practice may be annexed.
(4) Express warranties and conditions do not restrict the warranties implied under the Act.

However, as the general provision of exemption through express agreement or course of dealing applies (Section 62), it is interpreted that the implied warranties can be contractually waived. In addition, concerning relief for a breach of an implied warranty, as it is a "warranty" and not a "condition", the buyer cannot rescind the contract due to a breach of warranty and must resort to a reduction of the purchase price or damages (Section 59).

These implied warranty provisions inherited by Myanmar's 1930 *Sale of Goods Act* from the United Kingdom's 1893 Act tend to be explained as reform legislation arising from the standpoint of consumer protection. However, from the historical perspective, it was a rule of commerce originally formed through the maturation of 19th century British colonialism. It is thought that as the economic influence of the difficult sellers in colonies who were able to compete on equal terms even within the court, the traditional doctrine of "caveat emptor" was shaken and promoted the formation of the theory of seller's warranties in the common law, leading to their incorporation in the United Kingdom's 1893 Act.[60] Even now, the implied warranty provisions are still within the range of rules to adjust imbalanced trade relations. From the perspective of consumer protection, the commencement of the transition in the doctrine of implied warranties that is described below is a 20th-century development. Although Myanmar's 1930 Act was introduced in the 20th century, it is a replica of the United Kingdom's 1893 Act and it is necessary to confirm that it has not undergone any revisions in a 20th-century sense.

But in the subsequent English case law, the doctrine of implied warranties showed evolution in the 20th century sense in the context of consumer protection. The following points can be noted:

(1) Interpretation of merchantable quality: The interpretation of the provision on the merchantable quality of goods contained in Section 14(2) of the England's Act, which corresponds to Section 16(2) of the Myanmar Act, was focused upon in subsequent case law. This is because the gap between the level of quality that merchants sell and the quality that consumers expect for their own consumption became a point of dispute in the context of consumer protection. A definition of "merchantable quality" was first provided in the 1973 revision of the Act, but was criticized for its ambiguity, such as the vagueness of the expression "fit for the purpose or purposes for which goods of that kind are commonly bought as it is reasonable to expect" and the width of interpretation that should be given to the phrase "all circumstances" upon which it is determined. This definition was retained in the new *Sale of Goods Act 1979*, but was replaced by a new definition in the 1994 revision of the Act. Through this revision, the term "merchantable quality" was abolished and a standard of "satisfactory quality" was adopted (Section 14), which is a standard that a "reasonable person" would regard as satisfactory taking into account all of the circumstances (Section 14(2A)); such circumstances being listed as including "fitness for all the purposes for which goods of the kind in question are commonly supplied, appearance and finish, freedom from minor defects, safety, and durability" (Section 14(2B)), which means that "satisfaction" not just in normal uses but in all uses has become the standard of the implied warranty. The *Consumer Rights Act 2015* (Section 9) abolished the traditional dichotomy of "conditions and warranties" and adopted the word "terms", but the criteria for performance of the contract remains as it was in the 1994 revision.

(2) Exemption due to buyer's inspection: The 1930 *Sale of Goods Act* (second paragraph of Section 16(2)) excludes the seller's implied warranty if the buyer performs an inspection. However, the United Kingdom's 1893 Act's provision (Section 14, (2)) was amended in the 1979 Act and restricted the exemption to cases where the buyer performed the inspection "before signing the contract". The seller's warranty over latent defects was maintained in Section 9(4)(b) of the *Consumer Rights Act 2015*.

[60]Zhou and DiMattea (*Id.*, p. 368) emphasize that the drafter Chalmers based it upon the codification of established case law only. Chalmers (1894), p. iv.

(3) Disclaimer: The 1930 *Sale of Goods Act* has a general provision (Section 62) that covers exemption and postponement by the buyer. In the commercial transaction of rights in English law, agreement clauses that expressly disclaimed all implied warranties based on the same section was frequently used, which was criticized as severely harming the rights of consumers. Therefore, in the United Kingdom, the *Unfair Contract Terms Act 1977* excluded consumer contracts from the application of the provision, which was succeeded by the *Sale of Goods Act 1979* (Section 55(1)). This was reflected in the list of invalid business liability exemption clauses in the *Consumer Rights Act 2015* (Section 31(1)).

2.5.3 Consumer Protection Law

External pressure from European Union directives has been behind these changes in English law in recent years. Likewise, Myanmar has been compelled to be involved in the movement of sharing consumer protection policy between the member countries that was aimed towards the establishment of the ASEAN Economic Community (AEC) in 2015. ASEAN has been influenced by the revision of the United Nations "*Guidelines for Consumer Protection*"[61] and has envisioned a scope of comprehensive commonality, from the establishment of consumer protection policy objectives to administrative and private law implementation methods.[62] Since around 2007, the development of a series of guidelines by the ASEAN Committee on Consumer Protection (ACCP) has been ongoing with the support of the Australian government and others.[63]

In relation to contract law, the direction the ASEAN guidelines will take is not visible yet, but some proposals have been attempted in the 2014 "*ASEAN Consumer Protection Digests and Case Studies: A Policy Guide I*" (Chapter 11, pp. 109–119) that was prepared with Australia support. While it refers to provisions on sellers'

---

[61]The *United Nations Guidelines for Consumer Protection* appeared in the 1980s and has since been revised, including a recent revision via a UN General Assembly resolution (70/186) in 2015. The general principles (Article 11) provide principles such as fair and equitable treatment as benchmarks in consumer protection, and the establishment of contract law and relief mechanisms as part of the obligations of the Member States (Article 14). As an approach to protecting the interests of consumers (Chapter C), it promotes the strengthening of private law responsibilities in the area of contract law (quality assurance in Article 23, unfair contract terms, etc. in Article 26) in addition to administrative regulations, backed up with a public quality standard certification system (Chapter D) and strengthening the judicial processes and alternative dispute resolution systems that ultimately realize the implementation (F Chapter).

[62]In addition to other topics such as consumer finance and debt collection (Chapter 1), safety regulations (Chapter 2), product liability (Chapter 6) and the interface with competition policy (Chapter 7), the *ASEAN Consumer Protection Digests and Case Studies: A Policy Guide (Volumes I and II)* published in 2014 deal with "statutory guarantees of quality in the supply of goods and services to consumers" (Chapter 11) as an issue related to the seller's warranties.

[63]The *Guidelines for Notification and Information Exchange on Recall/Banned Products* and *Guidelines for Selection and Implementation of Competent Redress Mechanisms* were published in 2013.

warranties established in Brunei, Malaysia, Singapore and the Philippines,[64] it does not provide a comparative examination; after providing a simple introduction to precedents from New Zealand and other countries on one or two issues such as "satisfactory quality" and "fitness for purpose", it comes to the easy conclusion that because the legislation of Malaysia and Singapore in the ASEAN region follows these international best practices, the other ASEAN countries should also follow (p. 119). But what Malaysia and Singapore have been studiously following is simply changes in the English law. Rather than deciding that it is best practice because it is close to trends in the English legal system, common rules arising from a closer analysis of the law of each country in the ASEAN region should be pursued, in view of the fact that many countries in the region have various legal systems, and based on the presumption that English law also has its own process of pursing change.

Nevertheless, prior to the launch of the AEC, a Consumer Protection Law, Law No. 10 of 2014, was hastily enacted in Myanmar also. The Law firstly defines an administrative organization that has jurisdiction over consumer protection, establishing a Central Committee chaired by the Minister of Commerce (Section 4) and defining its jurisdiction, including administrative supervision, authorization and support of the establishment of NGOs, consumer dispute resolution, and implementation guidelines of standards certification systems (Section 5). Secondly, it defines not only the rights but also the duties of consumers (Section 6), including a duty to comply with safe usage standards, a duty to comply with the decisions of consumer dispute settlement agencies, and a duty not to unfairly detriment businesses. Thirdly, it defines the rights and duties of businesses; rights include the right of defence in consumer disputes and the right to recover goodwill that is unfairly damaged in a consumer dispute (Section 7(a)). Regulations regarding the actions of businesses are divided into duties (Section 7(b)) and prohibitions (Sections 8 to 15); the former are private law duties that have been debated in the field of modern contract law described above, while the latter can be considered as administrative law obligations. "Businesses" includes individuals and corporations (Section 2(g)).

Among the private law duties of businesses, as well as mentioning the principle of fair and equitable treatment (Section 7(b)(iii)), quality warranty ((b)(iv)), opportunity for the buyer to perform a pre-contract inspection ((b)(v)) and subsequent defects ((b)(vi)) that have been issues in the aforementioned modern contract law, the scope includes not only goods but also service provision. As we saw in the previous section, since the principle of good faith is not specified in Myanmar's 1872 *Contract Act* and the 1930 *Sale of Goods Act* has only general quality warranty provisions, the provisions on the duties of businesses prescribed by the *Consumer Protection Law* exceed the existing contract law provisions. How the courts will read these new provisions in comparison to the traditional tendency to apply a literal interpretation of the contract law will attract attention.

---

[64]Referring to Section's 14–18 of Brunei's 1999 *Sale of Goods Act*, Sections 5–9 of Malaysia's 1999 *Consumer Protection Act* 5-9, Singapore's 1979 *Sale of Goods Act* and 2003 (revised in 2009) *Consumer Protection (Fair Trading) Act* and the Philippines' 1992 *Consumer Act*.

The categories of business acts prohibited by administrative regulation are the sale of mislabeled goods (Section 8), misrepresentation (Section 9), deceptive transactions (Section 10), deceptive inducement (Section 11), premium transactions (Section 12), inappropriate inducement (Section 13) and false advertising (Sections 14 and 15). The constituent requirements of the individual actions of these provisions are still unclear and it seems there is room for systematic improvement as it appears there is duplication or an aim to create overlapping regulation of different types of action within the same problematic situation. Especially regarding misrepresentation (Section 9), although the burden of proof is placed upon the business (Section 26), what particular requirements the reversed burden of proof applies to is unclear. As there is a concern that they will cause unnecessary hesitancy in business economic activity and impede transactions, refinement of the provisions seems necessary.

As a means of implementing the consumer protection provisions, consumer dispute settlement agencies are established at each level of the region or state, the district, and the township administrative hierarchy (Section 16), and "mediation" is conducted (Section 17). "Mediation" here is a quasi-judicial proceeding in which the dispute settlement agency conducts fact finding such as witness examination and issues a "decision" (Section 18). The agency also investigates violations of duties by businesses (Section 7) and labeling violations in the sale of goods (Article 8), and is responsible for administrative actions including warnings, severe warnings, relief, prohibiting distribution, recall order, destruction of dangerous goods and the suspension of business licenses (Section 19). An appeal against these actions must be made to the Central Committee within 60 days (Section 20), which issues a final judgment that is not subject to judicial review (Section 21). Further, the provisions of the Law are to be carried out only in accordance with this Law (Section 27), but is it the intention to apply the administrative dispute resolution to the contractual obligations of a business (Section 8), without going through the judicial process? In this quasi-judicial review process by the administrative dispute settlement agency, expert opinion from public certification bodies is referred to and such evidence is definitive (Section 29), and the dispute settlement agency is to cooperate with NGOs (Section 30).

The dispute settlement agency collects compensation from a business for a consumer who suffers loss (Section 22). Criminal penalties including imprisonment (3 years) are imposed for violations of the Law (Section 23). Consumers can also separately sue for civil damages (Section 24).

These regulatory tendencies of the *Consumer Protection Law* (e.g. Section 27) suggest that there is a plan for centralized implementation of the consumer dispute settlement by the Ministry of Commerce on every consumer problem, including the areas related to consumer contracts. The judiciary is only responsible for criminal punishment (Section 23) and claims for compensation due to illegal acts (Section 24), with an implication that the development of judicial doctrines governing sales contracts is not expected. Does it carefully avoid the introduction of international radical judicial trends through the courts? Or is it perhaps addressing the distrust that propelling the traditionalist Myanmar judiciary to the front of economic disputes will inhibit business activity? Nonetheless, if the "mediation" by the administrative dispute settlement agencies cannot secure transparent rules, the effect of inhibiting business activity will be the same, which can lead to consumer distrust of the administration. It is essential to revise constituent requirements that are clearer than the regulatory type and release detailed guidelines.

This orientation of Myanmar's *Consumer Protection Law* provokes consideration of the relationship that should exist between private contractual relationships and the government. The government's paternalistic contract interventionism, from intervening in private business relationships, providing for code-like contract conditions and the formalities, and leading towards dispute resolution, is also adopted by socialist countries in the ASEAN region such as Vietnam.[65] It seems that a national strategy for incubating infant industries is also intended, as it provides not only consumer protection but also import-substitution policy that cultivates the consumer market for local industries, and thereby functions as a legal system to protect small and medium enterprises in a weak bargaining position. However, in such contract interventionist countries, it is necessary to not only enact administrative regulatory laws, but to aim at constructing a complete set of a priori business rules such as an entire code system [66]; the endless pursuit of rule-making and systematization must continue, and corporate activities must also proceed within that orderly system. At the opposite end there is a preference for the unwritten laws and inductive rules based on the English common law system, where corporate activity is in principle entrusted to the autonomy of individual contracts, there is no action to have legislation that exceeds a "codification" of changes in the case law, where the interventionist consumer protection law is placed on the sideline of the main body of contract law via the *Consumer Rights Act 2015.* On the contrary, the Netherlands' new Civil Code has embarked on what can be called a systematic case law system, which places all civil, commercial and consumer contract matters under the name of the Civil Code, and trusts judicial interpretation that is based upon the general principles provisions. The United States' Unified Commercial Code (UCC), despite its creation being influenced by continental law codification principles, is falling into a detailed description of intricate and complicated rules with no systematicity visible. What path will Myanmar law take?

2.6 Future Issues

Contract law is in the midst of transformation, as seen in the doctrines of undue influence and implied warranties in English law. The tradition of English contract law, which held freedom of contract as a principle and respected the position of

[65] Vietnam's 2005 Commercial Law defines that transactions should be conducted using the contract forms provided by the administrative agency for each type of contract, and breaches are subject to severe administrative penalties.

[66] In Vietnam, support for drafting and implementing a Civil Code and other legislation by Japan's Official Development Assistance (ODA) has continued for more than 20 years from the mid-1990s until today.

literalism that minimizes judicial and legislative intervention in contracts, has been shaken by case law driven by social change in the era of globalization and by the external pressure of EU directives, leading to the creation of new contract norms. Though Myanmar has maintained the status quo, the 1872 *Contract Act* and the 1930 *Sales of Good Act,* which was uniformly applied to the British colonies in Asia and Africa, it will not suffice in this era of change in global contract law. As for the method of catching up, is it sufficient to borrow from the law of neighboring countries like Malaysia and Singapore, which continue to follow the latest trends in English law? It is not just about in what way the text of the English law should be copied. It will be difficult to effectively adopt legal doctrines that are borrowed from the English law without a debate that ventures into the essence of wide-ranging transformations in the English law and its reasons.

Moreover, the global economy that Myanmar is going to enter into in the future is not made up of only the British commonwealth countries. Even though the English legal system certainly maintains influence in the selection of governing law in international trade based in Singapore, within the ASEAN region there are several countries with civil codes based on the continental law system, including Thailand, Indonesia, Vietnam, Laos and Cambodia. Further, if it is planned to move trade promotion a step forward and introduce foreign capital, investors from various jurisdictions such as the United States, Japan, Korea, and China will bring their own contract culture, and will no doubt designate the law of their own country as the governing law in contracts such as joint venture agreements.

However, it is true that the contract laws of each country continue to struggle towards the same direction while burdened with their different traditions. At the very least, in the context of correcting the asymmetry in negotiating in the process of contract formation and making contractual freedom effective, and in the context of realizing contractual justice in the fulfillment of obligations and exercise of rights, the different traditions are disappearing and some things are being brought forth from the chaos. One symbol can be seen in the "principle of good faith" which has come to be treated as the basis for judicial discretion, sometimes in the continental law countries applied as a rule of contract performance (French *Civil Code*, Article 1134(3)), as a general principle of contract interpretation (German *Civil Code*, Articles 157, 242; Netherlands *Civil Code*, Article 3.12), or as an interpretation standard throughout a civil code (Japanese *Civil Code,* Article 1.2). In the United States' UCC (Article 1-304 etc.) as well, the principle of good faith has been stipulated as a principle of contract performance. English law was also pressed to adopt a legislative response to the EU Directive on Unfair Terms in Consumer Contracts (Article 4) with the 1999 amendment of the *Unfair Contract Terms Act 1977* and the principle has been adopted in the current *Consumer Rights Act 2015* (Section 62). In the main area of English contract law, there is considerable vigilance against the principle of good faith that allows discretionary judicial interference with contract autonomy[67]; the "principle

[67] While the contract interpretation rule expressed in the judgment of Lord Hoffman in *Investors Compensation Scheme Lit. v. West Bromwich Building Society* ([1998] 1 WLR 896 HL) was an opportunity to display the effect of "contextualism", the limited view is deeply-rooted that Lord

of good faith" has not been included in the *Sale of Goods Act 1979*, and it can be said that the response does not exceed it being separated as a special rule for consumer protection. However, in fact, in the process of the continental law countries taking the principle of good faith as the flagbearer of free-law (*Freirechtslehre*) in order to escape the yoke of 19th century legal positivism, English law also was attempting standardization through the individual development of the doctrines such as undue influence, economic duress and implied warranties. The future application of the principle of good faith in English law will likely be colored by traditional English legal terminology (reasonableness, commercially sensible, satisfactory quality, etc.), which is similar to other countries, so if justice as a conclusion is singular, it will be one form of achievement of contract law unification.

Myanmar's future contract law reform must also accept the doctrines which are the consummation of current international trends, but it should be formed within the Myanmar's own terminology of jurisprudence. It can be thought that comprehensive systemization work is necessary, in the form of a reorganization of general contract theory that fundamentally reviews the 1872 *Contract Act* engraved during colonial rule, partly incorporating the unique general contractual provisions such as undue influence that are in the 1930 *Sale of Goods Act*, and further incorporating the equitable relief rules defined in the 1877 *Specific Relief Act* that has not been discussed in this chapter.[68]

In that process, repositioning the pre-colonial Burmese legal norms that have been protected to the present day under the name of "customary law" as general principles that guide contract interpretation may also be useful.[69] Also during this work, as investors from various countries will bring different contract law cultures, it is desirable to invite the participation of the legal profession from those various countries and embark upon ambitious collaborative contract law development that cannot be captured in the single-country model. Also in the process of judicial application that follows the legislative reform, it is necessary that judges not use the introverted literal interpretation that has been deep-seated for a hundred years, nor the unruly discretionary interpretation brandished under Section 13(3) of the *Burma Laws Act*, but have a change of consciousness that requires the buildup of precise interpretive precedents within the statutory law. The involvement of legal technical cooperation from Japan will also be useful to support legal interpretation training for that purpose.

Hoffman's rule does no more than take into account the correction of harm caused by literal construction and restate the traditionally used standard of "reasonableness". In recent years there has been a case that expressly addressed the principle of good faith (*Yam Seng Pte. Ltd. V. International Trade Corporation* [2013] EWHC 111), but rather than imposing the principle of good faith as an implied rule in contracts, it stops at identifying it as being in the wording of the contract between the parties.

[68] According to the author's January 2017 interview of staff at the Ministry of Commerce, the Ministry is drafting new trade law legislation, but there are no lawyers in the drafting members and no consideration is being given to the 1872 *Contract Act* or the 1930 *Sale of Goods Act*. This is very problematic from a viewpoint of systemization of the law.

[69] See Hla Aung (2008), p. 96.

References

Aung, H. (2008). *Law and justice in Myanmar*. Yangon: Thida Press.

Bringgs, A., & Barrows, A. (2017). *The law of contract in Myanmar*. Hampshire: Ashford Colour Press.

Burrows, A. (2015). Understanding the law of contract in Myanmar. *Oxford Legal Studies Research Paper* No. 59/2015.

Chalmers, M. (1894). *The sale of goods act 1893 including the factors acts, 1889 and 1890*. William Clowes and Sons.

Hartkamp, A. S. (1994). Development of dutch private law—Viewed from European law. *Civil and Commercial Law Journal, 109*(4–5), 623–660.

Honduce, E. (1994). Protection of weak parties in contract law. *Civil and Commercial Law Journal, 109*(4–5), 661–691.

Kusumoto, H. (1970). Codification in 19th century India. *Waseda Comparative Law Journal, 6*(1), 79–109.

Law Commission of India (1958). *The 13th recommendation in the 1958 contract law reform.*

LSP Committee. (1922). Report of the committee appointed to examine the land revenue system of Burma (vol. 1). Superintendent Government Printing.

Niranjan, V. (2016). Specific and agreed remedies for breach of contract in Indian law: A code of English law? In M. C. Wishart, A. Loke, & B. Ong (Eds.), *Remedies for breach of contract.* Oxford University Press.

Ohmura, A. (1997). *Tenkei keiyaku to seishitsu kettei (type contracts and charactierization)*. Tokyo: Yuhikaku.

Okudaira, R. (1986). Burmese Dhammathat. In M. B. Hooker (Ed.), *Laws of South-East Asia* (Vol. I). Butterworths.

Okudaira, R. (2002). *Biruma hoseishi kenkyu nyumon—Dentoho no rekishi to yakuwari (introduction to Burmese legal history research—History and role of traditional law)*. Tokyo: Nihon Tosyo Kanko-kai.

Pollock, F., & Mulla, D. F. (1909). *The Indian contract act: With a commentary, critical and explanatory*. London: Sweet & Maxwell.

Pollock, F., & Mulla, D. F. (1919). *Indian contract act and specific relief acts: With a commentary, critical and explanatory*. London: Sweet & Maxwell.

Saintier, S. (2016). Defects of consent in English law: Protecting the bargain? In L. A. DiMatteo & M. Hogg (Eds.), *Comparative contract law*. Oxford University Press.

Stokes, W. (1887) *The Anglo-Indian codes*. Oxford: Clarendon Press.

Stokes, W. (1887–8). *A supplement to the Anglo-Indian codes*. Oxford: Clarendon Press.

Stokes, W. (1891). *The Anglo-Indian codes 2nd supplement*. Oxford: Clarendon Press.

Uchiyama, T. (2008). Oranda minpoten niokeru horitsu koiho no gendaika (modernization of the law of legal acts in the netherlands' civil code). *Waseda Hogaku Kaishi, 58*(2), 97–148.

Waddams, S. M. (1976). Unconscionability in contracts. *Modern Law Review, 39*(4), 369–393.

Zhou, Q., & DiMatteo, L. A. (2016). Three sales laws and common law of contracts. In L.A. DiMatteo & M. Hogg (Eds.), *Comparative contract law.*

Chapter 3
The Role of the Japanese Civil Code in the Codification in the Kingdom of Siam

Shiori Tamura

3.1 Establishing a Nation-State

The Kingdom of Siam and Japan were two of a few countries in the world which succeeded at the modernization by their own efforts. The both countries entered into the international relationship with the Western powers almost simultaneously; just one year later than the Convention of Kanagawa between the USA and the Tokugawa Shogunate, the Kingdom of Siam under the rule of *King Mongkut* (Rama IV.) signed the so-called "Bowring Treaty" in 1855 with the United Kingdom and allowed free trade and extraterritoriality to the foreigners. For the both countries, Siam and Japan, the second half of the 19th century was the dramatical period of the modernization.

However, the both countries showed significant dissimilarities in their modernization process. In Japan, its modernization policy proceeded at a quite rapid tempo. Japan has completely modernized its political and legal system and finished the industrialization of economic system by the end of the 19th century. On the other side, the Siamese society was still deeply affected by the feudalistic legacies from the time of the Ayutthaya dynasty ("Sakdina system" codified in the 15th century). The majority of the Siamese population ("Phrai") lived under the rigorous corvée system conducted by the feudal lords. The Phrais were main producing power for them and also military manpower in wartime. The rest of the population bought themselves as household slaves ("Thad") and were at the complete disposition of the feudal lords. Consequently, the large part of the population lived outside of the reach of the administration authorities of the Chakri dynasty in Bangkok:

> [T]here were over forty townships with varying degrees of autonomy and importance, on terms of both economic and political power [...] Bangkok exercised direct rule only over

Shiori Tamura—LL.B. Tohoku University; BA. Chuo University; LL.M., Waseda University.

S. Tamura (✉)
Faculty of Law, Thammasat University, Bangkok, Thailand
e-mail: shiori.tamura@gmail.com

Y. Kaneko (ed.), *Civil Law Reforms in Post-Colonial Asia*,
Kobe University Monograph Series in Social Science Research,
https://doi.org/10.1007/978-981-13-6203-3_3

> an area within a radius of two days traveling (by boat, cart, horse, or on foot) (Rajchagool 1994, p. 3).

When *King Chulalongkorn* (1853–1910) was officially crowned as Rama V. in 1873, the Kingdom of Siam still meant nothing other than a loose union of such independent townships ruled by the feudal lords. There was a high risk of possible military intrusion of the Western powers. Facing this reality, it was the supreme goal for the reign of *King Chulalongkorn* to overcome such a vulnerable situation and to establish a nation-state as soon as possible. In order to introduce a free status of citizens, the king started in 1874 a long-term project to abolish the corvée system and the debt slavery. Since 1860s, the legal system of private ownership of land was gradually formated. This process lasted until 1900s. In parallel, the tax farming system was introduced, and the tax personnel was appointed by the Bangkok authorities. As a result, the corvée labour was increasingly replaced with the wage labour and officially abolished in 1899. Many new types of free labouring occupations (carpenters, tailors, shoemakers etc.) sprang up in the changed Siamese society (Rajchagool 1994, pp. 64–69). In 1905, the slavery of all types was finally outlawed with the enactment of the "Slave Abolition Act" (Stearn 1997, p. 117).

In 1897, the hierarchical system of local administration was established ("Monthon System"), and the feudal townships and their rulers were successfully integrated into the central administration system in Bangkok. As result of the series of such reforms conducted by *King Chulalongkorn* ("Chakri Reformation"), the Kingdom of Siam has reached the stage of a nation-state at the beginning of the 20th century. The Siamese government was eventually ready for a comprehensive legal reform and codification.

3.2 Contribution of a Japanese Legal Adviser

During this transition phase, the Western countries and Japan were allowed to exercise consular jurisdiction. In the case of Japan, this privilege was granted in an additional agreement attached to the Siamese-Japanese Treaty of Friendship and Commerce in 1898. According to this agreement, the consular jurisdiction would expire in one year after the successful implementation of civil code, law of civil procedure, penal code, law of penal procedure, and law of court system. In coping with this situation, the Siamese government decided to invite a Belgian legal scholar named *Sir Gustave Rolin-Jaequemyns* (1835–1902) as General Adviser in order to complete the codification of required laws as soon as possible.

The Siamese government requested also another adviser from Japan. In 1898, on the recommendation of the Japanese government, the Siamese government appointed *Dr. Tokichi Masao* (1921–1922) as Assistant General Adviser. After the retirement of *Sir Rolin-Jaequemyns* in 1899, *Dr. Masao* succeeded to his post as legal adviser. He proposed to start with the codification of civil code. On the request from the Siamese government, however, he contributed mainly to the drafting of the penal code. At the same time, he was appointed as judge in the Central Court of Appeal in 1901 and then in the Supreme Court of Appeal in 1903. Through such legal practices in the court, he continued to contribute to the reform of Siamese law and the spread of the knowledge about Japanese law (Kagawa 2002, pp. 177–186).

The situation changed suddenly in 1904. On the occasion of the new treaty between France and Siam, the French government wished the Siamese government to hire French staffs for the codification projects. In 1905, the Siamese government appointed *Mr. Georges Padoux* as Legislative Adviser and commissioned him to revise the Draft Penal Code which had been already submitted to the government. As a result of co-operation between *Mr. Padoux* and *Dr. Masao*, the new Penal Code for the Kingdom of Siam was eventually promulgated in 1908 (Kagawa 2002, pp. 141–165).

The successful implementation of the penal code gave occasion to adoption of the additional French staffs. They were appointed as members of the Codification Commission. Under the direction of *Mr. Padoux*, they started the drafting of the Civil Code for the Kingdom of Siam. *Dr. Masao* participated actively in the discussion in the Revising Committee. They all agreed to an unified system of Civil and Commercial Codes modeled after the Swiss Civil Code and Code of Obligations. Regarding the whole framework of the code, the French advisers insisted in the Justinian system while *Dr. Masao* preferred the Pandectist system. *Mr. Padoux* made a compromise proposal of a six-books system (1. General Provisions, 2. Persons, 3. Real Rights, 4. Obligations, 5. Inheritance-Wills, 6. Provisions of Private International Law). According to this proposal, they at first finished the drafting of the Law on Obligations in 1912. Subsequently, they started the drafting of the Law on Persons. In the issue of marriage system, however, *Dr. Masao* came into serious confrontation with the French advisers; they intended to legalize the traditional practice of polygamy among feudal nobility. It was absolutely impossible for *Dr. Masao* to accept it. The codification project hat to be once suspended due to this conflict among the commissioners (Kagawa 2002, pp. 165–171).

3.3 Draft Civil and Commercial Code (1919)

In 1913, *Dr. Masao* resigned all his posts in the Siamese government and returned to Japan with the intention to contribute to the modernization of the Siamese society from the Japanese side.

Mr. Padoux left the Kingdom of Siam in 1914, too. Since 1916, the work of codification was continued under the direction of another French adviser, *Mr. René Guyon* (1876–1963), although with considerable delay. According to his report published by the authority of the Siamese government in 1919, the members of the Commission were said to have frequently referred to the French Code, English laws, the Swiss and Japanese Codes, the German Codes, the legislation of Italy, Belgium, the Netherlands, America, etc. However, *Mr. Guyon* described his basic policy for the drafting as follows:

> The aim of the members of the Commission has been above all to accomplish a work which would prove consistent with the requirements of the country. Consequently, they have, with the great care, avoided indulging in the too easy plan of copying any foreign Code, perfect as it might be, and of transferring their provisions (Guyon 1919, p. 187).

In other words, he rejected to draft the code based on any particular model law and insisted in his intention to develop an original concept of the whole civil law system. This persistent policy has, as of the state in 1919, resulted in the five-books system (1. Obligations, 2. Things, 3. Capacity of Persons, 4. Family, 5. Inheritance). Apparently, the Commission abandoned the initial plan to put a general part at the top of the code. Moreover, the part of the international private law should be detached from the code itself (Guyon 1919, pp. 199–211).

The uniqueness of the concepts of the French commissioners consisted not only in the overall framework of the code, but the internal structure of the each book showed also unusual features. *Mr. Guyon's* plan achieved its final goal with the "**Kingdom of Siam: Draft Civil and Commercial Code**" dated also the same year 1919.[1] The contents of this final draft are still available for us except the Books on Family and Inheritance. Its first part, Book on Obligations, has the following contents in its unusual order:

Preliminary		(Articles 1–39)
Division I	How Obligations Arise	(Sects. 40–137)
Division II	Of Some Particular Kinds of Obligations	(Sects. 138–199)
Division III	Transfer of Obligations	(Sects. 200–217)
Division IV	Effects of Obligations	(Sects. 218–305)
Division V	Rights of Creditors over the Property of the Debtor	(Sects. 306–349)
Division VI	Extinction of Obligations	(Sects. 350–387)
Division VII	Specific Contracts	(Sects. 388–1463)

Apparently, its composition conformed with neither the Justinian system nor the Pandectist concept. This originality, however, was just the ground for the intervention by *Phraya Manava Rajasevi* (1890–1984) into the work of codification. In the following years, it experienced a dramatic reorientation and proceeded toward the reception of the Pandectist system.

[1]Officially unpublished document. Fortunately, its copy was identified in the "Phya Manava Rajsevi Library" in the Main Library of Bangkok University in Bangkok on June 16th, 2013 (Signature 217 and 217.2 in the part of books in foreign languages).

3.4 Intervention by Phraya Manava Rajasevi

Phraya Manava Rajasevi in the title of nobility (*Plod Vichian na Songkhla* in his civil name) made his first commitment to the work of codification when he was, in the age of 18, appointed to the regular interpreter in the Codification Commission in 1909. The Minister of Justice at the time, *Prince Raphi Phatthanasak* (1874–1920), recognized his remarkable talents soon and allowed him to enter the Law School of the Ministry of Justice. He was certified as a Siamese Barrister at Law in 1911. Subsequently, he received the scholarship of the government and made a voyage to London. He was admitted to the Inner Temple and trained in English law.

Before his departure to London, he was granted an audience with *Prince Raphi*. At this opportunity, the prince disclosed his deep interestedness in the German civil law and gave *Phraya Manava Rajasevi* a secret instruction to go to Heidelberg and study the German civil law after the completion of the English law study (Thammasat 1982, pp. 19–20). Following this instruction, *Phraya Manava Rajasevi*, besides the study at the Inner Temple in London, gathered and studied the literature on the German civil law written in English.[2]

Moreover, he acquired another valuable advice from Attorney General for England and Wales at the time, *Sir John Simon* (1873–1954), who was a friend of *Prince Raphi* and arranged on the request of the prince the enrollment in the Inner Temple for *Phraya Manava Rajasevi*. At a certain opportunity, *Phraya Manava Rajasevi* showed *Sir Simon* one part of the Draft Civil and Commercial Code for the Kingdom of Siam prepared by the French advisers in Bangkok. *Sir Simon* saw in its unusual construction quite high risk of rejection by the Western counterparts in negotiation for the revision of the unequal treaties in the future. He strongly recommended following a widely acknowledged model law and named the Japanese Civil Code as a sample, which was considered as a successful adoption of the German civil law (Thammasat 1982, pp. 99–101). Following *Sir Simon's* advice, *Phraya Manava Rajasevi* gathered and studied also the literature on the Japanese law in English.[3] The Japanese Civil Code was for him an indispensable guideline and navigator to ensure WHAT and HOW to adopt from the German Civil Code.

In 1916, he obtained the qualification of English Barrister at Law. The outbreak of the First World War, however, made the German law study in Heidelberg unfeasible for him. He returned to the Kingdom of Siam instead. At that time, the considerable delay in the work of codification was already a critical issue in the Siamese government. In 1919, *King Vajiravudh* (Rama VI.) decided to send *Phraya Manava*

[2]According to his statement (Thammasat 1982, pp. 30–31), the following two publications were the most important sources for him: (i) Schuster, Ernest Joseph (1907). *The principles of German civil law.* Oxford London: Clarendon Press; (ii) Wang, Chung Hui (1907). *The German Civil Code, translated and annotated with historical introduction and appendices*. London: Stevens and Sons.

[3]The publications of Joseph Ernest de Becker (1863–1929) were the main sources for him (Thammasat 1982, p. 29). The most important ones were following two: (i) Id. (1909–10). *Annotated Civil Code of Japan* (3 volumes). London: Butterworth & Co.; (ii) Id. (1921). *The principles and practice of the Civil Code of Japan, a complete theoretical and practical exposition of the motifs of the Japanese Civil Code*. London: Butterworth & Co.

Rajasevi back to the Codification Commission as its secretary in order to accelerate the codification process. In the next year, he received a further task to translate the finished draft written in English into Thai language. During the revising procedure of his translation, he began insistently to complain about alleged inconsistency of the draft finished by the French commissioners and appealed for the need to revise the whole draft. Following *Sir Simon's* advice, he strongly recommended the adoption of the "Japanese method"; more properly, the reception of the German Civil Code in a similar manner to the Japanese Civil Code (Thammasat 1982, pp. 20–22).

3.5 Civil and Commercial Code of 1923–24 (Old Text)

His claim and proposal eventually motivated the Siamese government to the revision of the draft. Its procedure, however, could not be started immediately; the Siamese government had to once create an occasion for acknowledgement of the longtime efforts of the French commissioners in order to maintain a harmonious relationship with the French government.

For this reason, the Siamese government arranged a two-stage process; in the first stage, the main books of the "Draft Civil and Commercial Code" of 1919 should be officially promulgated, and then in the second stage, the freshly established code should be, before its implementation, replaced with its revised version. *Phraya Manava Rajasevi* often compared this plan to the historical happenings of the "Codification Controversy" in Japan and the promulgation of the "Revised Civil Code of Japan" in 1896–98 (Thammasat 1982, pp. 29, 60).

For the first stage, *Phraya Manava Rajasevi* and other Thai commissioners prepared three books (1. General Principles, 2. Obligations, 3. Specific Contracts). The plan to introduce a general part at the top of the code came to life again, and the first Book (totally 105 articles) was urgently composed mainly with the provisions from the "Book on Obligations" (Preliminary) and those from the "Book on Capacity of Persons" of the draft of 1919. The rest of the provisions from the "Book on Obligations" were divided into two parts; namely the general part (Divisions I–VI, totally 347 articles) and the specific part (Division VII, totally 845 articles).[4]

In 1923, the Codification Commission was, on the request of the French government, reorganized as "Department of Legislation" in the Ministry of Justice. On November 11th, 1923, *King Vajiravudh* promulgated the **Civil and Commercial Code for the Kingdom of Siam**, Book I (Preliminary, Sects. 1–3; General Principles, Sects. 4–105) and II (Obligations, Sects. 106–452).[5] These two books should be implemented on January 1st, 1924 (Sect. 2). On the day of implementation, however, *King Vajiravudh* issued the royal edict to postpone the implementation of Book I and

[4]For the details of the composition of the Code of 1923, Book I and II, see the tables of comparison among the draft of 1919, the codes of 1923, 1925, and 1992 prepared by the author (Tamura 2017a, pp. 5–20).

[5]For details of the Code of 1923, see its Japanese translation of the author (Tamura 2017b, c).

II. At the same time, Book III (Specific Contracts, Sects. 453–1297) was promulgated, and all the three books should be implemented together on January 1st, 1925. Subsequently, the Siamese government moved to the next stage of its plan.

3.6 Civil and Commercial Code of 1925–28 (New Text)

After the postponement of Book I and II, *Phraya Manava Rajasevi* was appointed to an ordinary drafting commitee member of the Department of Legislation. It was the beginning of the second stage of the plan for the revision of the code. There were other three Siamese drafters and *Mr. Guyon*. Presumably, they had planned to finish the work of the revision by the day of the implementation of Code of 1923–24 (January 1st, 1925). However, it was delayed until late of the same year.

On November 11th, 1925, *King Vajiravudh* issued the royal edict to completely repeal Book I and II of the Code of 1923. At the same time, Book I (Preliminary, Sects. 1–3; General Principles, Sects. 4–193) and II (Obligations, Sects. 194–452) of the **Revised Civil and Commercial Code for the Kingdom of Siam** were promulgated, which should be implemented on January 1st, 1926 (Sects. 2).[6] With the further delay of two years, the revised Book III was also promulgated on January 1st, 1928, and implemented on April 1st, 1929. This Revised Code was sometimes referred as to "New Text" while the original Code of 1923–24 was frequently called "Old Text".

Especially in the revising work of Book I and II, the drafting members applied the so-called "Japanese method" under the guidance of *Phraya Manava Rajasevi*. It should be repeatedly noticed that the work of revision was not any simple duplication of the German or Japanese code. The ultimate goal of the drafting members was surely the reception of the German Civil Code. In the actual situation of the Siamese world of legal profession at that time, however, almost nobody possessed sufficient knowledge about the German civil law. Its simplification or modification would be inevitable in order to find wide acceptance under judges and lawyers who were mainly educated in the English law tradition. This was probably the main reason why the Siamese drafters tried to follow the manner in which the Japanese drafters had adopted the German civil law into the Revised Civil Code of Japan (Thammasat 1982, p. 102).

3.6.1 Overall Framework and Composition of Book I (1925)

When we work out the details of construction of Book I and II in the Code of 1925, we could recognize certain common features and clear differences in their drafting policy. First of all, it is quite apparent that the Siamese drafters adopted the overall framework of the Revised Civil Code of Japan in the both Book I and II. The original

[6]For details of the Code of 1925 and model laws of each articles, see its Japanese translation of the author (Tamura 2017d, e).

version of Book I of the Japanese code was divided into six titles (1. Persons, 2. Juristic Persons, 3. Things, 4. Juristic Acts, 5. Periods of Time, 6. Prescription). In principle, the Siamese drafters followed this six-titles construction in its Book I, but they slightly modified it in the following three points.

Firstly, they decided to put the "General Provisions" at the top of Book I as a new "Title 1" and filled it mainly with the provisions of Book I of 1923 (Title 2. Application of Law, Title 3. Interpretation of Documents). Secondly, they combined the "Title 1. Persons" and "Title 2. Juristic Persons" to form a new single "Title 2. Persons" with two chapters. In this modification, the Siamese drafters followed rather the German manner of construction. Thirdly, they removed the "Chapter 3. Representation" from the "Title 4. Juristic Acts". The Siamese drafters probably intended to integrate this part into the part on the contract for agency in Book III.

According to the current recognition of the author,[7] the Siamese drafters filled such an overall framework of Book I with the provisions mainly from the Japanese, German, Swiss and French codes as well as those from the Code of 1923. The real numbers of provisions from these different origins could be summarized as shown in Table 3.1. Unexpectedly many provisions from the Code of 1923 (77 articles) survived the revising work especially in the titles on "General Provisions", "Persons", "Things" and "Periods of Time" as well as in "Prescription". Such provisions on the first four issues (53 articles) were adopted from the old Book I, and those provisions on the issue "Prescription" (14 articles) from the old Book II.

The second large group of the provisions (55 articles) was adopted from the Revised Civil Code of Japan. It is a multiple of the number of the provisions adopted directly from the German Civil Code (26 articles). Among these Japanese provisions, however, there are 24 articles which have their origin probably in the German civil law. The relation between the German and Japanese influence in the new Book I would be turned over if we would count them as German provisions. On the other hand, at least 21 articles among the other 31 Japanese provisions would belong to the "**Boissonade's Heritage**". It means, these articles have their origin in the Japanese Civil Code of 1890 which was drafted by *Prof. Gustave Émile Boissonade* (1825–1910), who was the French legal adviser to the Japanese government at the time of codification. Consequently, there are no comparable provisions in the German Civil Code. Obviously, *Phraya Manava Rajasevi* and other drafters must have been aware of this fact. Nevertheless, they decided to adopt them. It is true especially in the titles on "Persons" and "Juristic Acts". This circumstance would unveil their strong sense of trust and confidence in the Japanese Civil Code.

Quite roughly speaking, the revising work of Book I did not aim to replace the old provisions with new ones from foreign laws, but the drafters tried to save the core provisions of the old Book I, added new subjects (especially in the title "Juristic Acts") and complemented them mainly with the provisions from the Japanese and German civil codes.

---

[7]See the "Index" to the articles prepared by the Siamese drafters as well as the supplementary entries by the author (Tamura 2017h, pp. 3–7, 13–21).

Table 3.1 Book I, Code of 1925: its contents and origin of the provisions

Civil and Commercial Code of 1925	1923	Jp. (Gr. orig)[a]	Gr.[b]	Sw.[c]	Fr.[d]	Oth.[e]	Total
Preliminary	3	–	–	–	–	–	3
Book I General Principles							
I. General Provisions[f]	7	–	–	2	2	–	11
II. Persons							
1. Natural Persons	23	17 (4)	3	1	2	7	53
2. Juristic Persons	16	11 (5)	–	1	–	2	30
III. Things	4	–	3	2	–	5	14
IV. Juristic Acts							
1. General Provisions	1	1 (–)	1	1	–	1	5
2. Declaration of Intention	2	3 (2)	5	–	–	6	16
3. Void and Voidable Acts	3	5 (2)	3	–	–	–	11
4. Conditions, Time of Beginning or Ending	1	9 (3)	1	–	–	1	12
V. Periods of Time	3	3 (3)	–	–	–	1	7
VI. Prescription	14	6 (5)	10	–	–	1	31
Total	**77**	**55 (24)**	**26**	**7**	**4**	**24**	**193**

[a]Revised Civil Code of Japan (1896). The parenthesized number shows the number of the Japanese provisions which have their origin probably in the German civil law
[b]German Civil Code (1898)
[c]Swiss Civil Code (1907) and Code of Obligations (1911)
[d]French Civil Code (1804)
[e]Others means mainly the codes of Argentine, Brazil, Italy, Tunis or uncertain origin
[f]This chapter was inserted from the Code of 1923

3.6.2 Overall Framework and Composition of Book II (1925)

The circumstances in the revising work of Book II were quite different from the case of Book I. It would be correct to speak of "replacement". In any way, the Siamese drafters adopted the overall framework of the Revised Civil Code of Japan also in the Book on "Obligations". As is commonly known, the Japanese drafters had preferred the Civil Code for the Kingdom of Saxony (1863)[8] to the Draft Civil Code of Germany (1888/95) in certain points. The overall framework of the Book III on "Claims" of the Revised Civil Code of Japan was one of the Saxony legacies in the Japanese Civil Code. The Siamese drafters must have been aware of this fact

[8]Available at: https://archive.org/details/brgerlichesgese00kingoog [Accessed 11 March 2017].

when they compared the German and Japanese codes. Nevertheless, they preferred the Japanese Framework to the German one. In doing so, however, they strongly modified it in the following three points.

Firstly, Chapter 2 "Effect of Obligations" in Title I "General Provisions" was clearly divided into four parts ("Non-performance", "Subrogation", "Exercising of Debtor's Claims", "Cancellation of Fraudulent Acts") and extended it with further two parts ("Right of Retention", "Preferential Rights"), which were adopted from Book II on "Real Rights" of the Revised Civil Code of Japan. In the Draft Civil and Commercial Code for the Kingdom of Siam (1919) , these subjects were treated in the Division V of Book on "Obligations" in accordance with the French tradition. The Siamese drafters accepted this French concept, however, they almost completely replaced the original provisions of the draft with the Japanese provisions which are even the very important part of the "Boissonade's Heritage" in the Revised Civil Code of Japan.

Secondly, the Siamese drafters removed the provisions on the subject "Suretyship" in Chapter 3 "Plurality of Debtors and Creditors" of Title I "General Provisions" as well as the whole chapters on specific contracts in Title II "Contract", which should be separately provided for in Book III. Consequently, Title II contained only the general provisions on "Contract" which are divided into three chapters on the subjects "Formation", "Effect" and "Rescission" of contracts. Additionally, the Siamese drafters inserted the provisions on the subject "Earnest and Stipulated Penalty" from the German Civil Code between the subjects "Effect" and "Rescission". It should be noted also that the Siamese drafters preferred the German provisions to the Japanese concept in Chapter 3 "Plurality of Debtors and Creditors" of Title I "General Provisions".

Finally, the provision on the subject "Release" in chapter "Extinction of Obligations" in Title I "General Provisions" was placed at the second position in the same chapter next to the subject "Performance". In such a way, the Siamese drafters completed the five-titles structure of Book II on "Obligations" based on the overall framework of the Revised Civil Code of Japan.

According to the current recognition of the author,[9] the Siamese drafters filled this framework of Book II quite freshly with the provisions from the Japanese and German civil codes. Unlike in Book I, they preserved here in Book II only few provisions of the Code of 1923 (33 of totally 259 articles). It is the case for example in the part on "Exercising of Debtor's Claims" in chapter "Effect of Obligations" of Title I "General Provisions" and in Title VI "Undue Enrichment" as well as in Title V "Wrongful Acts". In the main parts of Book II, the Japanese and German provisions are quite dominant (respectively 104 and 94 of 259 articles) as shown in Table 3.2.

It would be quite difficult to identify the principles which the Siamese drafters applied when they selected particular provisions from the Japanese or German codes. Quite generally speaking, however, we could say that they preferred the Japanese provisions to the German ones in Chapter 2 "Effect of Obligations" and Chapter 5

[9]See the "Index" to the articles prepared by the Siamese drafters as well as the supplementary entries by the author (Tamura 2017h, pp. 8–12, 22–31).

Table 3.2 Book II, Code of 1925: its contents and origin of the provisions

Book II Obligations, Code of 1925	1923	Jp. (Gr. orig)	Gr.	Sw.	Fr.	Oth.	Total
I. General Provisions							
1. Subject of Obligations	1	2 (2)	6	–	–	–	9
2. Effect of Obligations							
(1) Non-performance	3	3 (–)	17	–	–	–	23
(2) Subrogation	1	1 (1)	2	–	1	2	7
(3) Exercising of Debtor's Claims	4	–	–	–	–	–	4
(4) Cancellation of Fraudulent Acts	2	1 (–)	–	–	–	1	4
(5) Right of Retention[a]	–	8 (1)	–	2	–	–	10
(6) Preferential Rights[a]	1	34 (–)	–	–	–	4	39
3. Plurality of Debtors and Creditors	–	1 (–)	12	–	–	–	13
4. Transfer of Claims	2	7 (1)	2	–	–	–	11
5. Extinction of Obligations							
(1) Performance	2	12 (3)	9	2	1	–	26
(2) Release	–	1 (1)	–	–	–	–	1
(3) Set-off	1	5 (4)	2	–	–	–	8
(4) Novation	–	4 (–)	–	–	–	–	4
(5) Merger	–	1 (–)	–	–	–	–	1
II. Contract							
1. Formation of Contract	2	4 (3)	9	–	–	–	15
2. Effect of Contract	–	5 (3)	2	1	–	–	8
3. Earnest and Stipulated Penalty[b]	–	–	9	–	–	–	9
4. Rescission of Contract	–	7 (7)	2	–	–	–	9
III. Management of Affairs Without Mandate	1	1 (1)	9	–	–	–	11
IV. Undue Enrichment	5	4 (2)	3	1	–	1	14
V. Wrongful Acts							
1. Liability for Wrongful Acts	5	2 (–)	4	2	–	5	18
2. Compensation for Wrongful Acts	–	1 (–)	6	4	–	–	11
3. Justifiable Acts	3	–	–	1	–	–	4
Total	**33**	**104 (29)**	**94**	**13**	**2**	**13**	**259**

[a]These parts were adopted from Book II "Real Rights" of the Revised Civil Code of Japan
[b]This part was inserted according to Book II "Obligations" of the German Civil Code

"Extinction of Obligations" in Title I "General Provisions" except in the part on "Non-performance". They eagerly adopted the Japanese provisions where the German Civil Code offered no comparable ones. It is the case especially in the parts on "Right of Retention" and "Preferential Rights" in Chapter 2 "Effect of Obligations". This is a massive bundle of the "Boissonade's Heritage" in Book II. On the other side, we could recognize that the German provisions are relatively dominant especially in Title II "Contract" and Title V "Wrongful Acts".

3.6.3 Uniqueness of the Part on "Non-performance"

Phraya Manava Rajasevi's motto was "*Follow the Japanese model*". The application of the "Japanese method", however, was not any "easy way" as he had initially expected. Indeed, the Siamese drafters must have faced a momentous and fundamental question in the core part of the law on obligations.

As commonly known, the German Pandectists in the 19th century developed a quite distinguishing theory on the issue "Remedies for non-performance of obligations".[10] Their starting point was the "Principle of Natural Fulfillment" (§241, German Civil Code of 1898). According to this principle, the primary effect of an obligation should be its specific performance. In other words, the debtor has to perform his obligation just as is specifically determined in the obligation, and the creditor may demand only such a specific performance from the debtor so long as it is possible for the debtor to perform his obligation in such a specific way. The both parties have no choice. The creditor may have his first opportunity to demand damages for non-performance when the specific performance has become definitely impossible. Accordingly, the concepts of "Impossibility of performance" and "Damages in lieu of performance" played central role in this Pandectists theory. It was the exact opposite of the Common Law which primarily allows the creditor only to demand damages from the debtor.

The drafters of the Revised Civil Code of Japan had rejected these two extreme positions and preserved the French scheme of the "Boissonade's Heritage" which left certain room for choice between claim for specific performance (compulsory enforcement) and damages. At the point, the Japanese scheme of "Remedies for non-performance" stood in a sharp contrast to the German scheme. This circumstance forced the Siamese drafters to make a very difficult decision; they were confronted with the choice between the German and Japanese schemes. *Phraya Manava Rajasevi* then devised a quite venturous method to overcome this dilemma; namely he preferred the German provisions, however, he completely rearranged them in accordance with the Japanese scheme.

Indeed, the most of the provisions in the part on "Non-performance" were directly adopted from the German Civil Code (17 of totally 23 articles). In principle, their original expression and wording were carefully preserved although some of them

[10]For the details, see Tamura (2013, pp. 905–911).

Table 3.3 Segmentation of the provisions of the German Civil Code (1898)

Segments			Targeted provisions (1898–2001)
1.	Scope of damages	**§§249–254**	249,[a] **254**
2.	Time for performance	**§271**	**271**
3.	Impossibility	**§§275–280**	**275, 278, 280**
4.	Debtor's default	**§§284–287**	**284, 285, 286, 287**
5.	Delinquency charge	**§§288–290**	**288, 289, 290**
6.	Creditor's default	**§§293–301**	293,[a] **294, 295, 296, 297, 298, 299, 301**

[a]These provisions were only taken into consideration as comparable ones

Table 3.4 Overall correspondency structure and rearrangement steps

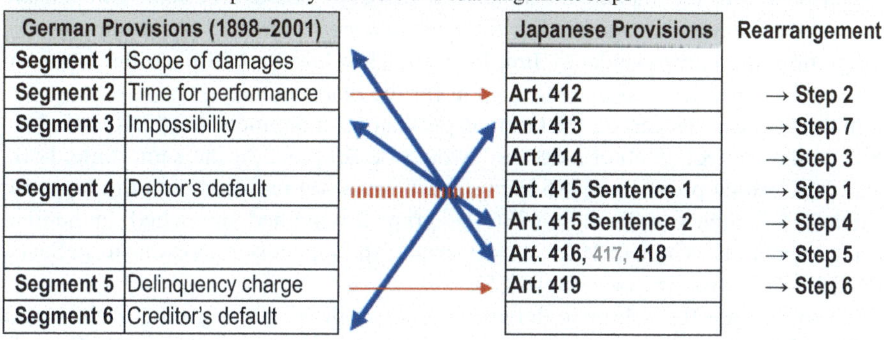

were slightly simplified. However, they stay in a "disturbed" sequential order (see the first column of Table 3.5). On the other hand, the Siamese drafters adopted only three provisions from the Revised Civil Code of Japan (Articles 414, 415 Sentence 1, 416). They stay in a quite ordinary sequence. Moreover, we could recognize here even the whole sequence of the Japanese scheme (Articles 412–419) if we would take also the comparability between the German-Siamese provisions and the Japanese ones in consideration (see the last column of Table 3.5).

3.6.3.1 Strategy for the Rearrangement

The procedure of this rearrangement of the German provisions is reproducible; according to the current recognition of the author, the targeted provisions of the German Civil Code could be segmented into following six sequences (Table 3.3).

Each of these segments could be linked to a comparable Japanese article on the corresponding subject. According to this "Correspondency Structure", the whole procedure of the rearrangement could be reconstructed in following seven steps (Table 3.4).

3.6.3.2 Procedure of the Rearrangement

Due to the essential difference between the German and Japanese schemes mentioned above, there was no similarly composed provision in this field which could serve as a starting point for the rearrangement. Even the central provision on the subject "Debtor's liability for non-performance" was quite differently composed; the German Civil Code (1898–2001) possessed the primary provision for this subject in its §280 on "Impossibility of performance" and the secondary one in §286 on "Damages from debtor's default" while the Revised Civil Code of Japanese has its single and general provision for the same subject in its Article 415. Nevertheless, a slight similarity could be recognized between the German §286 Paragraph 1 and the Japanese Article 415 Sentence 1; if we would replace the word "*default*" in the German provision with "*non-performance*", then we would have a virtually identical provision to the Japanese counterpart, namely "The debtor shall compensate the creditor for any damage arising from *his non-performance*". According to this recognition, the correspondency link between The German §286 and the Japanese Article 415 could serve as a starting point for the rearrangement.

In the first step, therefore, the German provisions in Segment 4 (§§284, 285, 286, 287) on the subject "Debtor's default" would be adopted. At the same time, however, the German provision §286 Paragraph 1 was soon replaced with the Japanese Article 415 Sentence 1. Though, §286 Paragraph 2 remained untouched. In the final arrangement of the Code of 1925, these German and Japanese provisions form Sects. 204, 205, 215, 216, 217 (see Table 3.5).

In order to put the debtor in default, of course, the beginning time of the effect of the obligation must be determined beforehand. In the second step, the German provision in Segment 2 (§271) was placed just before the provisions on "Debtor's default" (the top of them is §284). This positioning (Sect. 203 in the Code of 1925) exactly corresponded with that of the Japanese Article 412.

In the Revised Civil Code of Japan, thc provision to entitle the creditor to the claim for compulsory performance (Article 414) preceded the provision for damages due to non-performance (Article 415 Sentence 1). In the third step of the rearrangement, the Japanese Article 414 was adopted and located provisionally between §285 and Article 415 Sentence 1 in accordance with the Japanese scheme (between Sect. 205 and Sect. 215 in the Code of 1925).

Phraya Manava Rajasevi and other Siamese drafters probably recognized the Japanese Article 415 Sentence 2 as a provision on the subject "Impossibility of performance". In the fourth step, therefore, the German provisions in Segment 3 (§§275, 278, 280) were adopted and placed next to the German provisions adopted from Segment 4 (its last one is §287). In doing so, however, §280 was moved to the top position of the segment (Sects. 218, 219, 220 in the Code of 1925).

In the Revised Civil Code of Japan, the provisions on "Scope of damages" and "Contributory negligence" (Articles 416, 418) follow the Article 415 Sentence 2. In the fifth step, the German provisions in Segment 1 (§§249, 254) were adopted and placed provisionally next to the sequence of the German provisions adopted from Segment 3 (its last one is §278) in faithful accordance with the Japanese scheme.

Table 3.5 Final arrangement and origin of the provisions on "Non-performance"

Gr.	1923	a	Civil and Commercial Code of 1925		a	Jp.
§271		→	**Sect. 203**	Time for performance	≈	Article 412
§284		→	**Sect. 204**	Debtor's default through warning		
§285		→	**Sect. 205**	No default without responsibility		
	Sect. 327	→	**Sect. 206**	Debtor's default in tort cases		
§293	**Sect. 355**	→	**Sect. 207**	Creditor's default	≈	Article 413
§§294, 295		→	**Sect. 208**	Actual and verbal tender		
§296		→	**Sect. 209**	Cases where no tender is required		
§298		→	**Sect. 210**	Cases where creditor is not in default (1)		
§297		→	**Sect. 211**	Cases where creditor is not in default (2)		
§299		→	**Sect. 212**	No tender of counter-performance		
			Sect. 213	Compulsory performance	←	**Article 414**
	Sect. 373	→	**Sect. 214**	Objects of compulsory performance		
§286 (I)		≈	**Sect. 215**	Damages due to non-performance	←	**Article 415 S.1**
§286 (II)		→	**Sect. 216**	Damages in lieu of performance		
§287		→	**Sect. 217**	Strict liability during default		
§280		→	**Sect. 218**	Impossibility with responsibility	≈	Article 415 S.2
§275		→	**Sect. 219**	Impossibility without responsibility		
§278		→	**Sect. 220**	Vicarious liability		
§301		→	**Sect. 221**	No interest during creditor's default		
§249		≈	**Sect. 222**	Scope of damages	←	**Article 416**
§254		→	**Sect. 223**	Contributory negligence	≈	Article 418
§§288, 289		→	**Sect. 224**	Statutory interest for money debts	≈	Article 419
§290		→	**Sect. 225**	Interest upon lost values		

[a]Relationship between provisions: Adoption (→ or ←) or Comparability (≈)

At the same time, however, the German provision §249 was soon replaced with the Japanese Article 416 (Sects. 222, 223 in the Code of 1925).

The last provision in the Japanese scheme was the provision on "Delinquency charge" (Article 419). In the sixth step, accordingly, the German provisions in Segment 5 (§§288, 289, 290) were adopted and placed next to the German provision adopted from Segment 1 (§254). These are Sects. 224 and 225 in the final arrangement of the Code of 1925.

In the last step of the rearrangement, the whole bundle of the provisions in Segment 6 on "Creditor's default" (§§293–299, 301) was adopted and placed just before the provision on "Compulsory performance". This positioning (Sects. 207–212 in the Code of 1925) exactly corresponded with that of the Japanese Article 413. In doing so, however, there was fine-adjustment of several provisions. Firstly, the order of §§288 and 289 was turned over in order to put the provisions regarding exceptions of creditor's default together. Secondly, §301 was separated from the other provisions of Segment 6 and placed next to the provision on vicarious liability, which is the last position of the provisions on debtor's liability for non-performance (Sect. 221 in the Code of 1925). This separation was done probably because the Siamese drafters saw it rather as a provision to reduce the debtor's liability.

3.6.3.3 Final Arrangement and Its Achievement

After the rearrangement of the German provisions, several provisions were additionally adopted from the Code of 1923; namely Sect. 327 on "Debtor's default in tort cases" and Sect. 373 on "Objects of compulsory performance" (Sects. 206 and 214 in the Code of 1925). Furthermore, Sect. 355 on "Creditor's default" replaced the German provision §293 (Sect. 207 in the Code of 1925).

Regarding the final arrangement of the whole provisions on the issue "Remedies for non-performance" (see Table 3.5), it could be suffering from certain critical vulnerability to misunderstanding; *Phraya Manava Rajasevi's* idea to rearrange the German provisions in accordance with the Japanese scheme had lacked all the necessary theoretical prospects for its adequacy and functionality. It is quite uncertain how seriously he had considered the heterogeneity between the both concepts. Indeed, there are certain points which could cause doubts as to system consistency in the final arrangement.[11] First of all, Sect. 216 has remained in the original wording of the German §286 Paragraph 2 (on "default") even though its Paragraph 1 has been replaced with the Japanese Article 415 Sentence 1 (on "non-performance"). Moreover, several essential provisions in the German scheme have not been adopted into the Code of 1925, especially §276 on "Definition of debtor's responsibility" and §300 on "Effect of creditor's default" probably because such provisions are missing also in the Revised Civil Code of Japan. It would be a side effect from the "Japanese method".

In order to clean up such vulnerability and doubts, it would have been essential to closely investigate the theoretical backgrounds of the both concepts. However, the Siamese drafters had no opportunity to such a theoretical confrontation probably because the codification of the Code of 1925 was carried out without commitment of any German or Japanese legal advisers. Eventually, such an intensive and systematic assimilation of a foreign legal theory as the so-called "Theory Reception" of the German civil law in Japan (Kitagawa 2007) has never happened among legal scholars and practitioners in the Kingdom of Siam. Apparently, as *Phraya Manava Rajasevi* himself uttered (Thammasat 1982, p. 30), the language barrier was one of the reasons for such circumstances.

On the other hand, however, certain actual significance of this venturous arrangement in the Code of 1925 has been suddenly revealed since the promulgation of the "**Modernized Law on Obligations of Germany (2001)**".[12] Above all, the new Ger-

[11] See the consideration of the author on the "System Integrity Issue (1)–(5)" in Tamura (2017i).

[12] See the consideration of the author on the "Actuality Issue (1)–(4)" in Tamura (2017i).

man law has its core provisions on the issue "Debtor's liability for non-performance" in the modernized provisions §§280–283, and they stay in a sequential order which is just parallel to that of the provisions on the same issue in the Code of 1925; namely the basic principle of debtor's liability for non-performance (the modernized §280 to Sect. 215), damages in lieu of performance (the modernized §§281 and 282 to Sect. 216) and impossibility of performance (the modernized §283 to Sect. 218 and 219). This fact means that the conceptual difference between the German Civil Code and the Code of 1925 has been essentially reduced through the reform of the German law on obligations.

3.7 Outlook for the Future

In 1992, *King Bhumibol Adulyadej* (Rama IX.) issued the royal edict to promulgate the Revised Civil and Commercial Code of Thailand, Book I (see Tamura 2017f). In the new version, the expression and wording of every provision was purified from the language legacy from the time of the absolutism, and the whole book was rearranged. Moreover, the provisions on "Association" were removed from Book III and integrated into Book I, Title 2 "Persons", Chapter 2 "Juristic Persons". Nevertheless, the basic features and concepts of the original version were carefully maintained. The traces of the Japanese and German influence can still be clearly recognized even in this revised version. On the other side, Book II on "Obligations" has not experienced any such profound revision until today (see Tamura 2017g). A complete overhaul of Book II on obligations is still not in sight.

However, faced with the new development of the major two model laws—namely the implementation of the modernized German law of obligations (2002) and the Civil Code reform in Japan (2017), it would be highly desirable to critically review the conceptual commonalities and differences among the German, Thai and Japanese law of obligations from the viewpoint of comparative law. Such interactive exchange of legal theory and experience among these three systems would eventually contribute not only to clarification of identity of each law but also to achievement of common strategy for harmonization of law on obligations in the Asian region in the future.

References

Guyon, R. (1919). The work of codification in Siam [reprint]. In Traiveth, S. (2007). *Codification in Siam* [in Thai language] (pp. 188–229). Bangkok: Winyuchon.

Kagawa, K. (2002). *Biography of Masao Tokichi: Pioneer of international assistance for legal development*. Tokyo: Shinzansha (in Japanese language).

Kitagawa, Z. (2007). Japanese civil law and German law—From the viewpoint of comparative law. In K. Zentaro & R. Karl (Eds.), *The identity of German and Japanese civil law in comparative perspectives* (pp. 11–56). Berlin: De Gruyter Recht.

Rajchagool, C. (1994). *The rise and fall of the Thai absolute monarchy*. Bangkok: White Lotus Co., Ltd.

Stearn, D. (1997). *Chronology of South-East Asian History: 1400–1996*. Dee Why: The Mitraphab Centre Pty Ltd.

Tamura, S. (2013). The Thai civil law on non-performance in comparative, structural view—From past into its future. *Law Journal Thammasat University, 42*(2), 897–925.

Tamura, S. (2017a). "French advisers' heritage" in civil and commercial code, especially in Book I and II. As of February 3, 2019, from http://openlegaltextbook.info/Resources/01_French-Heritage_20161111.pdf.

Tamura, S. (2017b). The Japanese Translation of the civil and commercial code of 1923, Book I. As of February 3, 2019, from http://openlegaltextbook.info/Resources/01_OldText-B1-All_20140621.pdf.

Tamura, S. (2017c). The Japanese translation of the civil and commercial code of 1923, Book II. As of February 3, 2019, from http://openlegaltextbook.info/Resources/01_OldText-B2-All_20171113.pdf.

Tamura, S. (2017d). The Japanese translation of the civil and commercial code of 1925, Book I (original ver.). As of February 3, 2019, from http://openlegaltextbook.info/Resources/02_NewText-B1-V1-All_20170307.pdf.

Tamura, S. (2017e). The Japanese translation of the civil and commercial code of 1925, Book II (original ver.). As of February 3, 2019, from http://openlegaltextbook.info/Resources/02_NewText-B2-V1-All_20170307.pdf.

Tamura, S. (2017f). The German and Japanese translation of the civil and commercial code of Thailand, Book I (current ver.). As of February 3, 2019, from http://openlegaltextbook.info/Resources/03_NewText-B1-Current-All_20150507.pdf.

Tamura, S. (2017g). The German and Japanese translation of the civil and commercial code of Thailand, Book II (current ver.). As of February 3, 2019, from http://openlegaltextbook.info/Resources/03_NewText-B2-Current-All_20161120.pdf.

Tamura, S. (2017h). Reception of the Japanese civil code and "Boissonade's Heritage" in the civil and commercial code for the Kingdom of Siam, Book I and II (as of 1925). As of February 3, 2019, from http://openlegaltextbook.info/Resources/04_Index-Book1+2-V1_20161124_EN.pdf.

Tamura, S. (2017i). Basic view to reconstruction of the arrangement of the articles on "Remedies for non-performance" in the civil and commercial code of Thailand (1925). As of February 3, 2019, from http://openlegaltextbook.info/Resources/11_Reconstruction_20170310.pdf.

Thammasat University. (1982). The transcript of the interview with Phraya Manava Rajasevi [reprint]. In Thammasat University. (2014). *Phraya Manava Rajasevi (Plod Vichian na Songkhla)* [in Thai language] (pp. 11–138). Bangkok: Winyuchon.

Chapter 4
The Pathway of Civil Law Development in Indonesia: Laws on Land

Rudy

4.1 Introduction

The Indonesian legal system is inherited mostly from the Netherland legal system, while Netherland had been inherited the legal system mostly from French. The Indonesian Civil Code, as a concordant edition of Netherlands Civil Code, is a part of legal system that follows the Civil Law countries. Civil Code of Indonesia itself consists of four books namely Book I of Person, Book II of Property, Book III of Agreement, and Book IV of Statue Limitation. The discussion of civil law development can't be separated from the discussion of the civil code applicability and its changes.

The development of laws after independence has brought implication on the applicability of the civil code. The demand of institutionalization of Islamic law had pushed the Indonesian government to enact legislations in the foundation of Islam, such as Law No. 1 of 1974 on the Marriage and Law No. 7 of 1989 on Religious Court. By the enactment of those laws, Book I of Civil Code is only applied for non-Muslim in Indonesia. In its next development, the Law of Person regulated in the Indonesian Civil Code has been regulated specifically in the Population Administration Law and other related law.

In the other side, Book II on Properties of the Indonesian Civil Code divides properties into movable and immovable properties. The manifestation of immovable property is the land as the result of the property interpretation according to Article 506 paragraph 1 of the Indonesian Civil Code, it is stated that immovable properties

---

Rudy—Head of Constitutional Law Department at Faculty of Law University of Lampung; Director of Center for Law and Development University of Lampung; Expert Staff on Legislation Making in Indonesia Regional Representative Assembly.

Rudy (✉)
Faculty of Law, University of Lampung, Lampung, Indonesia
e-mail: rudy.1981@fh.unila.ac.id

Y. Kaneko (ed.), *Civil Law Reforms in Post-Colonial Asia*,
Kobe University Monograph Series in Social Science Research,
https://doi.org/10.1007/978-981-13-6203-3_4

are yard and everything built on them. The development of property law as part of civil law system then very connected with the land law regulation in Indonesia. The Basic Agrarian Law in 1960 (here in after called BAL) had been annulled mostly by the applicability of the book II of Civil Code on property. BAL stipulated that all property rights except hypothec in the Book II of the Civil Code had been annulled and replaced by the land rights stipulated in BAL. By the enactment of BAL and various land law related such as the Security Law in late nineties, the development of law has gone to undirected direction.

In addition, Book III of the Civil Code, specifically regulate the contract, had less importance since the enactment of the 1967 Foreign investment law and other regulation on the specific contract. However, basic principles of contract in the civil code had been remained applicable such as freedom of contract and validity of contract (Sunaryati Hartono 2001). There was a draft of contract law prepared in 1960, but faded away as the result of regime changes during sixties (Lev 1965).

In sum, very few provision of civil code is applicable and civil law has been developed in many laws and regulation, enacted especially during the developmental state. Among the huge area of the civil law development above, this article focuses on the land law development as the main part of the property law. The discussion on the land law is very important especially after the independence. Post independence Indonesia saw huge developments, arising from internal and external influences. Beside the internal need for economic development and political stability, Indonesia is witnessing profound changes of the international legal system that imposes so-called international requirements to comply (Kadelbach 1999). Those internal and external dimensions are related with the land use and utilization for economic development.

To achieve the goal of discussion, the next section will trace back the development of law during the colonial period. It is important to see the root of civil law development in Indonesia and the problem during the first engagement between local and western law. After that, the Sect. 4.3 of this article will provide the analysis of the effort to construct unified legal system after independence and how the land law development was used as tools of economic development. The Sect. 4.4 of this article provides analysis of huge development after the democratization of Indonesia. The last section analyze the direction of law development especially development of land law.

4.2 Civil Law Construction in Colonial Period

Indonesia civil law development in colonial period may be staged into three periods of law development: VOC period; British period; and Netherland Indies period. This section will describe and analyze the development of civil law especially land law during the period.

4.2.1 VOC Period

VOC officially started the economic activity on 1602 in Indonesia (De Kat Angelino 1931). The VOC legal system was aimed mainly at the coastal towns and suburbs under its direct control and rarely reached the rural hinterland. Thus, the records of legal development of the Dutch East Indies only came from the travel records of the Governor General at the time. Legal needs were met by making special rules. Regulations had been in the form placards (Soepomo and Djokosutono 1955). In the field of land law, the placard dated 18 August 1620 required the registration of land within VOC occupation (Handoko 2014).

The compilation of placards and customary law had been started during the Governor General Van Diemen authority. He had instructed to collect and compile all placards of law. In 1642, in Batavia, the placards had been systematically compiled and published under the name "van Batavia Statutes" (Statute Batavia) and updated in 1766 with the name "Bataviase Niewe Statuten" (New Batavia statute) (Soepomo and Djokosutono 1955).

In 1747, VOC issue order to make a codification of Java criminal law for a new court in Semarang. The result of the command was Mogharrar Book, which was an overview of Islamic law. At the same time, Boschennar Jan Dirk van Clootwijk took the initiative to record customary law contained in the royal palace of Bone and Gowa. In 1760, DW Freijer made a short essay or a compendium of the laws of marriage and inheritance law of Islam. In 1768, on the initiative of resident Tjirebon, a book named "Tjerebons rechtboek" has been compiled (Soekanto 1958). At the end of the 18th century around the year 1783, there was book titled History of Sumatera that showed the reviews and inspection on customary law was published by Marsden. Marsden investigation centers are Redjang, Pasemah, Lampung, Korintji, Minangkabau, Siak, Batak, and Aceh (Soepomo and Djokosutono 1955).

The research of the old documents finds that the VOC was not eager to make huge development of the law in Indonesia. The activities of the law development were limited to the compilation of local law.

4.2.2 British Period 1811–1816

When the British came in 1811, their first concern was directed at the issue of how the treasury of the government may be filled up. After seeing varieties of natural resource and its potential, the British government was determined to improve the conditions as had been done in India. British Governor General, Lord Minto, had been ordered to perform all corrective measures as quickly and effectively as possible, starting with gathering information about the farmers, the land, and all related information, before they can make something new legal improvement (Raffles 2014). The result of the research was the policy of land rent of which the farmer may rent the land directly to government.

Land rent system was made as follow: First, elimination of feudal services, and provided freedom for the farmer planting. Second, the government must supervise all farms, including the process for collecting the crops and land rent. Third, land rent should be calculated based on the actual conditions and how big the land was, with a fair calculated time (Raffles 2014).

This article finds that the British Government didn't intend to make the comprehensive development of law. It is argued that land rent policy didn't give legal certainty of ownership of the local people and regarded as the quick way to collect the money from local people.

4.2.3 Netherland Indies Government Period

British government was giving back the East Indies in 1816 to Netherland Indies Government. The period of Netherland Indies Government saw the emergence of western law transplantation in East Indies or Indonesia. The transplantation during the period could be seen from the enactment of several law codifications in accordance with concordance principle such as Civil Code in the form of Burgerlijk Wetboek, Commercial Code or Wetboek van Kophandel, and Criminal Code or Wetboek van Strafrecht.

Those codes are specifically applied for Netherland people or European people in Indonesia. The enactment of Civil Code raises question on the applicability of the code for the Indonesian people. In this regard, the General Provisions of 1847 maintained the old principle of *corpus juris civilis*, that the natives of the archipelago would was permitted to live according to their own laws and traditional institutions (Vollenhoven, in Holleman 1981). Thus, unwritten adat law was applied to Indonesian people. This dualism policy was strengthened in the establishment of the court for Indonesian people, for example *Pradoto* Court to adjudicate based on the law of the king, *Surambi* Court to adjudicate based on religion, and *Padu* Court to adjudicate the case based on the customary law (Vollenhoven, in Holleman 1981).

In the field of land law development, this period marked the beginning of land law development in Indonesia by the enactment of 1870 Agrarische Wet (Agrarian Law). In fact, 1870 Agrarian Law was enacted to give the Netherland Indies Government the ability to lease the land to foreigners under Civil Code. What was important in this Agrarian Law was the creation of Domein Verklaring stating that all land without the evidence of civil law ownership of property rights shall belong to the state. Thus, land under communal property or other traditional forms were not acknowledged against the state since the communal rights never have the civil law ownership evidence.

4.2.4 Legal Dualism Legacy

The colonial policy on development of law has left the legacy of legal dualism. Legal dualism provides the dual application of the law for each category of the people. Western law had been constructed for the western people and the local law in the form of adat law had been preserved for Indonesian people. In the field of land law, the dualism made the problem of ownership rights since the application of adat rights for local people didn't lead to ownership security. The policy, in the other side, gave benefit for Western Corporation and western people for the strong ownership of right under Civil Code.

In this regard, the registration of the land ownership under Civil Code had become powerful document and had been acknowledged as the legal document for the land registration in the post independence. This led to more land conflict in the post independence since many Indonesian people didn't have the strong document of ownership under civil code.

4.3 Development of Land Law After Independence

This section discusses the effort to construct the national law after independence during the Old Order and New Order. The period saw the two contrasting development of radical effort to re-create the new civil code during the Old Order and steady movement of law development to support economic development during the New Order.

4.3.1 The Constructing of National Law and Its Implication to Civil Code

When Indonesia became independent, its founding father was trying to develop its own national law. The difficulty arises not only because of the diversity of the legal system, but also because of the legal system had been already created as a result of long time transplantation since colonial time. The other problem was the creation of national law could not be achieved in a quick and short way. Thus, to fill out the vacuum of law, 1945 Constitution stipulated that all laws and legislation existing under the Netherland Indies Government became the laws and legislation of the Republic of Indonesia, until repealed, revoked or amended or found to be contradictory to the Constitution. Therefore, the laws and regulations in Indonesia after independence remained the same as the legislation enacted in colonial times, such as Civil Code, the Commercial Code, Criminal Code, and the other colonial laws.

The effort to unify the legal system was continued with slow start. After more than 10 years from Independence, in 1958, National Legal Development Agency (LPHN), which main task was to seek the design of national legal system fit with Indonesia characteristic, was established. In this regard, there was debate on the applicability of the Civil Code inherited from the colonial government and the Agency started thinking on the drafting new civil code. In 1962, the idea of drafting new civil code got support from Minister of Justice and Chief of Justice. Minister of Justice at this point, made proposal on the abolishment of Civil Code and Commercial Code as the starting point for the new draft. In 1963, Circular Letter of Chief Justice voiced the same idea with the Minister of Justice and declared the Civil Code as no longer in force (Lev 1965).

The drafting idea for new civil code involved the abolishment of Commercial Code and integrated the substance of Commercial Code into Book III of Contract. Chief Justice itself had prepared the draft on Contract Law based adat law, national sense of justice, and western principle. The draft was general and short, consisting of sixteen parts divided into a total of 93 articles. Many scholars had attacked this draft at that time saying that it was not complete (Lev 1965).

Other important development for the unification of law was the creation of Basic Agrarian Law (BAL) in 1960. The 1960 BAL was the first national agrarian law that intended to replace Agrarian Law of 1870 and land rights under Civil Code. The enactment of BAL had been used as argument by the LPHN to focus on the drafting of contract law in 1963. This argument based on the legal fact that BAL enactment had abolished the most part of applicability of Book II on Property and paves the way of property law unification. The basic problem remained that even though the intention of BAL creation in the beginning was the abolishment of the colonial legal system, the drafter in the end could not use or find the legal argument for the Indonesia's land title based on adat law. Therefore, in the end, BAL drafter could not accommodate the communal rights based on adat law instead using the principle of western rights.

Indonesia experience show that drafting the civil code is very difficult, especially when the legal system is pluralistic. The debate on amendment of new civil code during sixties revolved around the kind of system shall be adopted among adat law system, Islamic law system, and western law system. It is different with French who found the way in integrating the old customary law of French society into the code since the beginning. This difficulty led to the enactment of separate laws during the period of developmental state or New Order.

4.3.2 Developmental State and the Fallen of Adat

With the advent of New Order authoritarian regime since 1968, a basic understanding of the law for economic development has found its place. The regime changes brought new perspective on the development of civil law. Thus, new regime had overthrown many works of old regime including the draft and idea of new civil code. New Order put priorities on the foreign investor entry into Indonesia and all institutions and laws shall support this policy. This period saw the birth of Laws No. 1/1967 on Foreign Investment Law, Law No. 5/1967 on the Basic Forestry Law (hereinafter BFL) and Law No. 11/1967 on Mining, etc. For New Order, drafting the individual law would be convenient rather than drafting the new civil code that would take a long time.

Throughout the New Order, 1960 BAL Principle State Control had been used to achieve the developmental goals, coupled with formulation of other natural resources related laws. Authoritarian government took control of the nation's resources and directs them towards the benefit of economic development. Since the resources always related to the land, it brings tension to many people who have legal relation with those lands. The result of this tension is creation of many injustices to many people upon their property rights especially to people who only had the traditional title based on adat law against the legal document registered under Civil Code during the colonial period.

The unification the nation-state continued with the enactment of Law No. 5/1979 on Village. The Village Law had big impact on the fallen of adat community and law because the Law established uniform village structures in Indonesia with the model of Java Regions. Thus, they destroyed the structure of adat in all over the country. The fallen of adat structure was one of structure and systematic movement by authoritarian government to achieve unification and homogenization in Indonesia. While many land concessions were coming from adat property rights, the disappearance of adat system and structure had made the legal ground for claiming adat rights will be lost in front of the formal law. This condition is true in case of Indonesia where the adat community had been decreasing all over the time. In the late nineties, the new Land Registration Law was enacted but it failed on giving legal title on the traditional right.

In sum, laws, government regulation, president instruction, ministerial decrees, and local regulations related to land affairs and exploitation of other natural resources have been formulated to create a more conducive environment for foreign investment and market creation activities. Those legal instruments then ignore the existence of other systems that live in the community such as indigenous people have the right to land, which is called the land titles of indigenous peoples and the property rights of the people who inherited the land from the past. The period fit with Kennedy (2006) description on the instrumentalism of law as the agent of politic and economic agenda through legislation and administrative action during the second period of law and development agenda.

With the enactment of law and regulation covering the land, Book II of the Indonesian Civil Code was applied only for several provisions on movable property and security rights. The latter covers property and individual security. The property security covers the privileged debts, pawn and hypothec, while individual security covers personal guarantee. In their development, the Security Law has been standing on their own apart from Book II of Civil Code. By the enactment of Security Law, Book II of Civil Code had been abolished, leaving the principle of the movable property.

The period saw the diminishing of Civil Code application in Indonesia. Related to enforceability in Indonesia, there was consensus among the scholar in Indonesia to use the Civil Code rules and principle only but not as codification of law. It is concluded that the codification system had been faded away in the mind of legal architect in Indonesia in the late nineties. The instant thinking for economic development pursue had made the Government of Indonesia prefer to leave the codification system.

4.4 Post Reform and New Development of Land Law

The end of 20th century marked the huge changing of legal political system especially in Indonesia. Thus, they have very huge implication on the development of law in Indonesia. The post reform for Indonesia could be illustrated, not only as the period of constitutional and democratic consolidation, but also the period of legal rush. In addition, Indonesia law development has been under pressured by legal standards commonly featured in democratic modern states thorough legal assistance and law transplantation, even though this assistance may not solve the problem.

4.4.1 The Period of Legal Rush

After New Order had fallen in 1998, there was a force to reform all aspects nation life including the law. This led to many formulations of new laws and the ratification of many international law instruments. The development of law during the post reform has been directed through the National Legislation Program in accordance to Law on Legislation Making. National Legislation Program is a list of future national legislation that should be formulated and enacted during the five years legislator period.

However, the absence of the grand design of legislation development makes the development of legislation is nowhere to go, instead of being an instrument of economic development and democratization. The condition is worsened through the effects of globalization, which has presented with of international obligation in the form of formulation of domestic law (Burke-White and Slaughter 2006). Indonesia in this case is required to observe its obligations in line with the international direction in order to prevent the risks of isolation from international order (Capaldo 2003).

Therefore, during a decade after reform, Government of Indonesia under the direction of IMF and World Bank enacted many economic laws related such as the Mortgage Law, the Company Law, the Capital Market Law, the Bankruptcy Law, the Fiduciary Transfer Law, and the Arbitration Law as well as several Intellectual Property laws including laws on Copyrights, Patents, Marks, Industrial Designs, Integrated Circuits, and Plant Varieties. All these law had been projected to support the economic activity and to find the international standard.

In addition, the post reform saw the proliferation of many legislations. During 1997–2017, more than 500 laws had been enacted. This number is far bigger than legislation enacted during New Order regime. The number shows that Indonesia

Table 4.1 Indonesia legislation enactment by years

No	Year	Number
1	1945–1950	140 Law and 30 Martial Law
2	1951–1960	133
4	1961–1965	10
5	1966–1970	85
6	1971–1977	43
7	1977–1982	55
8	1982–1987	45
9	1987–1992	55
10	1992–1997	45
11	1997–1999	75
12	2001–2005	151
13	2005–2010	192
14	2011–2015	127
15	2016	22

Source Compiled by author from many sources

which is in the path of legal rush stress on quantity of legislation. Number of legislation enacted since independence can be seen from Table 4.1.

In the field of civil law and economic law during 2000–2016, this article found more than 40 legislations had been enacted. In same period, this article also found that there are 23 land related legislations had been enacted.

The quantity of legislation enacted by the legislation maker is not followed by the quality of the legislation. The low quality of legislation evidenced by the many laws that were reviewed in the Constitutional Court. During the period 2003–2017, there were more than 500 laws were reviewed in the Constitutional Court, and most of them is related with land law. It proves that the legislation was not formulated in accordance to the constitutional provision. In fact, sectoral interests and ego of each ministry and political parties influence legislation development, led to disharmony of the provision among many laws.

4.4.2 Recent Development on Land Law

Many problems have occurred as the result of long time injustice upon the property rights in Indonesia. From the reports coming to parliament, land problems may be classified into several problems such as land ownership, wasteland problems, land grabbing, land management, spatial planning management, customary rights acknowledgement, land compensation, and the problem as the result of decentralization authority.

One of the sources of problems is the law and regulation on land itself. Within the field of land law, author research on Synchronization and Harmonization of Regulations on Land Registry led to the conclusion that there has been a massive development of legislation but not directed, it caused overlapping arrangement and substance. In addition, our research on spatial planning in several regions has a result in a similar conclusion.

The massive regulation and overlapping provision in the field of the land law are the result of the legal rush activities by legislation maker. While the 1960 BAL is still applicable, the period saw the enactment of Law on Forestry, Law on Water Resources, Law on Environment, Law on Oil and Gas, Law on Geothermal, Law on Coastal and Small Island Management, Law on Spatial Planning, and Law on Fishery. These laws have been regulating the same issue and have their own technical regulation for the enforcement. The technical regulations are in conflict or incomplete.

In addition, the law enacted above had been reviewed in front of the Constitutional Court and several laws such as Law on Water Resources, Law on Forestry, and Law on Oil and Gas had been regarded as unconstitutional. The judgment saw that the provision of unconstitutional laws has benefit not only for the corporation but also put the limitation of access upon property rights by the ordinary people in Indonesia.

The period also saw the emergence of customary rights. The Asian Crisis brought back the customary identity-giving rise to local rights including adat rights within decentralization policy. In addition, The Constitutional Court, in its decision No. 35/PUU-X/2012, acknowledged the customary forests that are located within the forest zone. The Court ruled that customary forests should not be classified as state forest zone. It constitutionally gives indigenous and local communities the right to manage their customary forest. A problem is that there is no legislation on adat communities yet in order to enable them to claim their forests as customary forests. Official from National Land Agency explained that technical regulations are needed to make Constitutional Judgment applicable.

In addition, BAL and its implementing regulations have set out clear form of land rights that are applied in Indonesia, as well as subjects of law to obtain rights to land. But there is no explicit provision in the law that set out the form of land rights can be granted to indigenous peoples that fit with customary land rights characteristic. In addition, customary community is not an individual or a legal entity incorporated under positive law in Indonesia. As a result, there is a difference of interpretation of legal experts and officials National Land Agency to the rules governing what kind of titled rights granted to indigenous people.

The General Assembly in this regard has passed a Decree IX/2001 on Agrarian Reform and Natural Resources Management to solve the problems. The Decree instructed following legal reforms such as reviewing relevant laws related to land and natural resource; providing the national budget for agrarian reform; and resolution of agrarian conflicts. The first thing to do is reviewing the law and regulation on land and make a reform on land and regulation on land.

4.5 Reconstruction of Legislation Development

The discussion on the recent development of the land law and land related law indicates the need of formulation and improvement on the reconstruction of land law and regulation. The reconstruction shall be directed to the harmonization of the law as the roots of land law problem.

In this regard, overlapping provision and disharmony are actually an anomaly for a country with Civil Law tradition that is very conscious on systematization of legislation in the form of codification. I argue that following our long tradition of codification may be fruitful for the future development of land law in Indonesia. We can learn from success of Netherland on revising the Civil Code after more than 100 years in 1992. Therefore, the codification of the land law shall be considered as the solution for the future development of land law.

This solution is may be effective because we are in the state of formulation of Law on Land, Law on the Land Rights, and Law on the Land Special Court, Law on Agrarian Conflict Resolution, Law on The Customary Rights Recognition in the same time. Those Laws had been listed in the National Legislation Program. It means that those Laws have been listed to formulated and enacted in near time by the parliament.

Thus, it will be best to integrate all the laws regulating the land in the form of codification. The author itself had suggested this solution during the hearing with Indonesia Parliament. The integrated codification maybe started with using the BAL principles in Book I of General Principles, followed by the Book II on Land Rights, Book III on Land Registration, Book IV on Dispute Resolution and Land Court. In the process, the careful attention should be directed to type of land rights covering the traditional rights and its registration.

We have been leaving the codification model for legislation development, but the movement is already started in other field. The codification model has been started within the field of election law this year, initiated by NGO and supported by International Donors and General Election Commission. Tripartite model of collaboration is truly working. This is evidenced by the Parliament positive respond on starting the discussion and formulation of Election Law Codification. The same strategy may be used in Land Law Codification initiative. The tripartite initiative from NGOs, International Donor, and Government may become a catalyst for the initiation of Land Law Codification in the Parliament.

4.6 Conclusion

The land as main part of property rights in Indonesia has long history of problems, created from the colonial time and accumulated through long period of time until present. In its path, civil code as the first source of property rights had been left behind if not forgotten, replaced by many national laws. The paper suggests that the initiation of land law codification is able to integrate all the land law systematically as discussed above. It may take tremendous efforts and consistency, but it is worth to settle the legacy of land conflict in Indonesia.

References

Capaldo, G. Z. (2003). *Implementation of international treaties and the Italian constitution. A priority reform in the globalization era* (Attuazione dei trattati internazionali e Costituzione italiana. Una riforma prioritaria nell'era della comunità globale). Naples: ESI.

De Kat Angelino, A. D. A. (1931). *Colonial policy, volume II: The Dutch East Indies*. The Hague: Martinus Nijhoff.

Djokosutono, R., & Soepomo, R. (1955). *Sedjarah Politik Hukum Adat*. Jakarta: Djambatan.

Handoko, W. (2014). *Kebijakan Hukum Pertanahan*. Yogjakarta: Thafa Media.

Holleman, J. F. (Ed.). (1981). *Van Vollenhoven on Indonesian adat law*. The Hague: Martinus Nijhoff.

Kadelbach, S. (1999). The transformation of treaties into domestic law, 42 GYIL.

Kennedy, D. (2006). 'The Rule of Law', political choices, and development common sense. In D. M. Trubek & A. Santos (Eds.), *The new law and economic development: a critical appraisal* (pp. 95–128). New York: Cambridge University.

Lev, D. S. (1965). The lady and the banyan tree: Civil-law change in Indonesia. *The American Journal of Comparative Law, 14*(2), 282–307. https://doi.org/10.2307/838638.

Raffles, T. S. (2014). *The history of Java*. Yogyakarta: Narasi.

Slaughter, A.-M., & Burke-White, W. (2006). The future of international is domestic. *Harvard International Law Journal, 47*. https://doi.org/10.1093/9780199231942.003.0006.

Soekanto, R. (1958). *Meninjau Hukum Adat Indonesia*. Jakarta: Soerungan Petjenongan.

Sunaryati Hartono, C. F. G., Setiawan, & Taryana Sunandar. (2001) *The Indonesian law on contract*. Japan: Institute of Developing Economies (IDE-JETRO).

Part II
Outcomes of Contemporary Legal Reform Assistance

Chapter 5
A Study on the Civil Code Revision: The 2015 Civil Code of Vietnam

Hong Hai Nguyen

5.1 Introduction

The Socialist Republic of Vietnam promulgated the Civil Code three times in 1995, 2005 and 2015. There were general approaches which are inappropriate leading to the fact that they are not truly the civil codes in essence. Majority of the contents of this article touches upon the reforms of the 2015 Civil Code against the versions of 1995 and 2005. The 2015 Civil Code consists of 689 articles, and is structured into 5 parts with 27 chapters. It retains 81 articles, inherits and amends 573 articles, adds 70 articles, and annuls 123 articles, as compared to the 2005 Civil Code.

For the purpose of revision of the Civil Code, the Government and Ministry of Justice have carried out theoretical and practical reviews of the enforcement of the 2005 Civil Code at the Supreme People's Court, Supreme People's Procuracy and 19 ministries, sectors and other central organizations ad in all 63 provinces and centrally run cities; and organized hundreds of seminars at different scales and with different participants (scientists, judges, notaries public, lawyers, registrars, businesses, banks, socio-professional associations, people, etc.); many foreign organizations and experts from Japan, France, Germany, etc., have made important contributions to formulating policies and making and improving the draft of the Civil Code (of which knowledge, theoretical achievements and practical experience of Japan, and assistance from the Japanese Ministry of Justice, Japan International Cooperation Agency (JICA) and Japanese professors and experts are of special importance).

Hong Hai Nguyen—Deputy General Director, Department of Civil-Economic Laws, Ministry of Justice Drafter of 2015 Civil Code of Vietnam, 2014 Law on Marriage and Family of Vietnam Lecturer (1996–2010), Faculty of Civil Law, Hanoi Law University LL.B. Hanoi Law University; LL.M., Hanoi Law University.

H. H. Nguyen (✉)
Department of Civil-Economic Laws, SRV Ministry of Justice, Hanoi, Vietnam
e-mail: nhhai@moj.gov.vn

Y. Kaneko (ed.), *Civil Law Reforms in Post-Colonial Asia*,
Kobe University Monograph Series in Social Science Research,
https://doi.org/10.1007/978-981-13-6203-3_5

This article will introduce the main features of this attempt of code drafting by the author who was directly in charge of the drafting process.

5.2 Fundamental Legal Philosophies

5.2.1 General Approaches

The following is the general approached taken by the drafting team:

(1) Ensuring that the Civil Code is a law of respect for and protection of civil rights, and a law of market relations.

(2) Ensuring the most fundamental two values of the market economy society, namely the subjects are equal and have freedom and voluntariness in private relations; the State and state agencies, when participating in private relations, are equal with other subjects; and the State's intervention in private relations is minimized.

(3) The revision of the Civil Code must be placed in the existence and operation of the entire system of market economic institutions, system of documents of private law[1] and in the diversified and unceasing socio-economic development. Of which, the Civil Code has the position and role as a legal fundament, the "Constitution" of the private law system. The Code's provisions must be general, stable and feasible in order not only meet the present practical requirements but also give proper forecasts to catch the continuous changes of reality, creating a foundation for building and improving the private law system in the future. Specialized laws have the role to concretize equality and freedom-voluntariness in private relations in different socio-economic spheres with detailed provisions.

(4) Conflicts in private relations will be settled based on solutions which are closest to justice. People's rights to civil requests and access to justice must be guaranteed. The court, in the capacity as the body exercising the judicial right and protect justice, may not refuse to settle civil cases or matters for the reason that there is no law to apply. It is necessary to diversify sources of civil law and order of priority of these sources so that arbitration institutions can have sufficient necessary legal tools for promptly responding to people's requests.

(5) Inheriting and developing regulations which still suit reality as well as fine cultural values, customs and ethics of Vietnam; and learning international experience, especially experience of countries that have legal traditions similar to Vietnam's.

[1] Vietnam has a system of very diverse specialized laws in almost other socio-economic areas.

5.2.2 *Structure of the Civil Code*

The following is the idea on the structure of the Civil Code chosen by the drafting team:

(1) That the Civil Code follows the structure of Institutiones of the French Civil Code or structure of Pandekten of the German Civil Code is not a novel choice for Vietnam, because, in history and at present, both structural systems of Civil Law had and have significant influence on the civil law of Vietnam.[2]
In the process of revising the Civil Code, there existed many scientific arguments about what structure of the Civil Code to choose and, the Pandekten structure was chosen by Vietnamese lawmakers. This choice not only avoided big structural changes against the 2005 Civil Code but also was based on advantages suitable to Vietnam's contexts below:

   (i) Different law sources are unified in a sole legal system without causing big changes to the current legal system;
   (ii) Ensuring that the Civil Code is stable and well adaptable to fast changes of reality in Vietnam;
   (iii) Ensuring that the Civil Code has general legal standards of the humanity and has the specific identities of Vietnam; and does not give rise to high costs in time and resource thanks to the knowledge, theoretical achievements and practical experience of other countries;
   (iv) Creating a basis for a dynamic, practical and toward-justice private law system, thus helping build a scientific argument environment for the courts, judges, lawyers, notaries public, researchers and law trainers, etc., thereby contributing to the formation and development of legal behavioral standards recognized by the society.

(2) The new Civil Code is structured into five parts below:

   - *Part One. "General provisions"*: which includes general provisions which are effective not only for the entire Code but also for the entire private law system, such as basic principles of private law, legal status of natural persons and legal persons, property, legal acts, representation, time limit, and statute of limitations;
   - *Part Two. "Ownership rights and other rights over property"—Real Rights*: defining the relationship between humans and property;
   - *Part Three. "Obligations and contracts"—Claims*: defining the human-to-human relationship;

[2]The civil codes of Vietnam were affected either by the structure of Institutiones of the French Civil Code (e.g., the 1931 Civil Code of Northern Vietnam, the 1936 Civil Code of Central Vietnam and the 1972 Civil Code of the Republic of Vietnam) or by the socialist legal viewpoints of the former Soviet Union and countries of Eastern Europe and the Pandekten of the German Civil Code (e.g., the Civil Codes of 1995 and 2005). The 1995 and 2005 Civil Codes, although affected by the structure of Pandekten, were written rather simply in a way of Institutiones which is understandable for everyone; they lack essential abstracts and have no links between the parts, chapters and articles.

- *Part Four. "Inheritance"*: defining the transfer of property and obligations left by the deceased person;
- *Part Five. "Law applicable to civil relations involving foreign elements"*: defining legal conflicts.

  So, basically, the new Civil Code of Vietnam has the structure of the civil codes of the Pandekten system, but it has two specific characteristics (See the chart below):
  - The part "Family" is not included in the Civil Code[3];
  - The provisions on legal conflicts are included in a separate part in the Civil Code.[4]

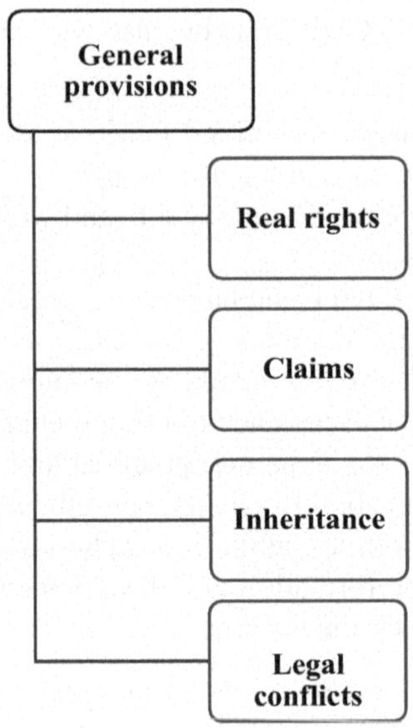

(3) The Civil Code, though having the Pandekten structure, is not "closed" but "open", and accepts specialized laws having provisions which are different from

[3]Affected partly by the laws of the former Soviet Union and countries of Eastern Europe and partly by the nature of families in Vietnam, Vietnam has a separate law on marriage and family enacted in 1959, 1986, 2000 and 2014. The 1995 and 2005 Civil Codes also have no part "Family".

[4]The 1995 and 2005 Civil Code had this part. The Civil Code of Louisiana State (USA) made according to the structure of the French Civil Code has the part on legal conflicts. The author holds that legal conflicts are only a special case when either subject or both subjects are foreigners or when a legal event occurs in a foreign country, so reserving a part on this issue is inappropriate for assurance ò the abstract, generalization and consistency of the Civil Code, especially when it is already stated basically in the part "General provisions". When necessary, civil relations involving foreign elements should be regulated by a separate law on international justice.

those of the Code,[5] and is also opened for the amendment, supplementation and improvement of the Code's provisions to meet changes in reality.[6]

(4) The Code's provisions are general provisions for the entire private law system and are generalized and abstracted. However, the Code also contains specific provisions on principles of application, exceptions, and limits of general provisions[7]; and typical and stable relations of private relations.[8]

(5) The Civil Code has some provisions with specific cultural identities suitable to a nation with multiple ethnicities and different cultural identities and customs like Vietnam, such as rights to first name, name, nationality, guardianship, common ownership, and inheritance, etc.[9]

5.2.3 Fundamental Principles of the Civil Code

The following is the fundamental principles drafted by the drafting team:

(1) **Principle of equality**[10]

All natural persons and legal persons are equal and may not, for any reason, practice discrimination, and are equally protected by law regarding personal rights and property rights. The Socialist Republic of Vietnam and central and local state agencies are equal with other subjects in private relations.[11]

(2) **Principle of free will**[12]

The subjects may establish, exercise and terminate their civil rights and obligations on the basis of freedom, voluntary commitment and agreement, and accountability. They may exercise their civil rights at their own will, and the non-exercise of civil rights is not a basis for terminating the rights, unless otherwise prescribed by a law. For instance:

---

[5] Articles 3 and 4: If not contrary to the fundamental principles of private law.

[6] "Openess" can be seen in Articles 4, 5, 6, 9, 13, 18, 37, 39, 75, 76, 131, 149, 160, 161, 246, 247, 258, 259, 268, 269, 197, 298, 405, 406, 418, 431, 442, etc.

[7] For example: Articles 2, 4, 10, 13, 14, 15, 74, 97, 98, 99, 106, 117, 160, 466, and 468 …

[8] The provisions on act capacity of individuals, guardianship, legal acts (civil transactions—the Civil Code), representation, statute of limitations, purchase and sale contracts, property borrowing contracts, outside-contract compensation for damage, inheritance, etc.

[9] For example: Articles 5, 7, 26, 29, 52, 53, 231, 603, 644, 645, 651, and 654, …

[10] Clause 1, Article 3, and Articles 97 thru 100.

[11] The Code also abolishes the provisions creating the State's "exclusive rights" in private relations which are rather common in the 2005 Civil Code, for example, the Civil Code has the tasks to protect the interests of the State (Article 1); the principle of equality does not cover the content that the State is equal with other subjects in civil relations (Article 5) …

[12] Articles 2, 3, 9, 10, 117, 138, 160, 163, 171, 186, 398, 418, 420, 624, 626, 631, and 644 …

- The owners may perform all acts at their own will over their property, and the subjects having other claims may perform all acts within the ambit of their rights prescribed by a law;
- The subjects may freely enter into contracts and reach agreement on contractual terms;
- If the subjects reach agreement on compensation for damage in contracts, such agreement shall apply[13];
- The subjects may freely enter into cooperation in order to establish and exercise civil rights[14];
- Natural persons have free will in transferring their property to others after they die.

In addition, free will is also subject to law-prescribed limits, such as not violating prohibitions by law, not contravening social ethics or limits of real rights, ensuring performance of civil obligations, performance and termination of contracts, interest rate, designation of heirs, or deprivation of the heirs' right to inherit, etc.

(3) **Principle of abstracting-separating**

In order to separate real rights and claims in a civil transaction, the Code sets three legal time points, namely (i) Effective time of a contract; (ii) Time of transfer of ownership rights and other rights; and (iii) Time of effect to a third party.[15] In which:

> The effective time of a contract gives rise to obligatory relations between the parties from the time of contract signing, unless otherwise agreed upon or otherwise prescribed by a relevant law.[16]

The time of transfer of ownership rights and other real rights will be determined under the Civil Code or a relevant law (e.g., land law, real estate business law, housing law, marriage and family law, law on securities etc.)[17]; if such time is not prescribed by law, it must comply with agreement of the parties; if such a law and agreement are not available, such time will be counted since the property is transferred to the obligee.[18]

The time of effect for a third party will be established from the time of registration or the time the obligee holds or seizes the property. Concerning this issue, the Code

---

[13]Articles 13 and 360.

[14]In ownership relationship, the owner may agree to permit another subject to establish easement, usufructuary and right of superficies on the former's property (Articles 246, 258 and 268); in contract relationship, the subjects may reach agreement among individuals and legal persons on joint contribution of property and efforts to perform a certain task and on joint benefit and responsibility (Articles 504 thru 512) …

[15]However, the new Civil Code still fails to properly deal with separating the transaction that establishes other rights in rem from the time when other rights in rem become effective in a public manner.

[16]Article 401, Clause 1, Article 310, and Clause 1, Article 319.

[17]For instance, the Land Law prescribes that the time of transfer of land use rights is counted from the time of registration.

[18]Article 161.

states: (i) If a civil transaction is invalid but the property has been registered at a competent state agency then transferred to a bona fide third party through another civil transaction and that party has based himself/herself/itself on such registration to establish and perform the transaction, such transaction will not be invalid[19]; (ii) If a security measure becomes effective for a third party, the security-accepting party may reclaim the collateral and is entitled to the payment priority under the Civil Code or a relevant law.[20]

(4) **Contract-bound principle**[21]

From the time a contract becomes effective, the parties must exercise the rights and perform the obligations toward one another as committed; the contract may only be modified or cancelled as agreed upon or prescribed by law.

The parties must take self-responsibility for their non-performance or improper performance of civil obligations. The cancellation or unilateral termination of performance of the contract will be considered breaching the contract if it is not agreed upon or prescribed by a law. If the contract is for the benefit of a third party, when the third party agrees to enjoy the benefit, then the parties may not modify or cancel the contract although the contract has not yet been performed, unless such modification or cancellation is consented by the third party.

(5) **Goodwill and honesty principle**[22]

An subject must establish, perform and terminate his/her/its civil rights and obligations in a goodwill and honestly and may not abuse his/her/its civil rights to cause damage to another person, breach his/her/its obligations or illegally realize other purposes. For instance:

- The obligee must apply necessary and reasonable measures in order to prevent damage from occurring or limit damage to himself/herself/itself.
- In case the circumstance sees a fundamental change but one party does not show a goodwill or cooperate in remediating the consequences, the other party may request the court to modify the contract.
- Before realizing the collateral, the security-accepting party must give a written notice to the securing party within a reasonable time limit.

(6) **Fault**[23]

(i) The fault of the obligation-breaching party (under or outside the contract) will be determined by inference. If the obligation-breaching party commits an illegal act causing a consequence unbeneficial to the obligee, the former will be inferred as being at fault and have to perform civil liability toward

[19] Article 133.

[20] Article 297.

[21] Articles 401, 417, 423, and 428; Clause 2, Article 436, and Clause 2, Article 427 …

[22] Clause 3, Article 3, Articles 10, 300, 362, and 420, and Clause 5, Article 585.

[23] Articles 360, 364, 584 and 585 …

the obligee.[24] However, there is also an exception that the civil liability still arises regardless of whether there is a fault[25] or the civil liability will only arise when there is a ground to believe that the obligation-breaching party is at fault.[26]

(ii) If the obligee does not apply necessary and reasonable measures, thus letting damage occur, or does not limit damage to himself/herself/itself, he/she/it will be regarded as being at fault and may not request compensation for damage which he/she/it could have prevented or limited.

(iii) In case of breach of obligation and the damage is caused partly due to the fault of the obligee, the obligation-breaching party will have to pay compensation in proportion to his/her/its fault.

(iv) The obligation-breaching party will not have to bear civil liability if the breach is due to a force majeure event or entirely due to the obligee's fault.

(v) The person responsible for paying compensation may have such compensation reduced if he/she is not at fault or if his/her fault is unintentional and the damage is too big compared to his/her financial capacity.

(7) **Property**[27]

(i) Property includes immovable property and movable property. Immovable property and movable property may be present property or future property.[28]

(ii) Property rights mean rights that can be monetarily valued, including land use rights, property rights over subject matters of intellectual property rights, and other property rights.

(iii) It is necessary to clarify the relationship between land under ownership by the entire people and land use rights of organizations and individuals, and offering more options in exploiting land and land-attached property and exercising land use rights (land use rights are property rights, right of superficies, etc.).[29]

---

[24]This provision means that the breached party needs only to prove that damage is real and caused by the illegal act committed by the breaching party without having to prove the latter's fault. However, there are also exception like in Footnotes 19 and 20.

[25]For example, compensation for damage for polluting the environment (Article 602).

[26]For example, Article 605 prescribes the fault of the construction executor for letting houses or other construction works cause damage; Articles 460 and 461 prescribe the fault of the donor of property causing damage to the donnee.

[27]Articles 105 thru 115.

[28]See also Article 108.

[29]The new Civil Code does not include the provisions "Transfer of land use rights" in a separate part because it determines land use rights as property and transactions related to land use rights as civil transactions. The specific issues will be given in the Land Law. Also, property referred to in this Code may be the object of a purchase and sale contract. If, as prescribed by a law, property is banned or restricted from transfer, the property being the object of a purchase and sale contract must comply with such law; the property to be sold comes under the ownership of the seller or the seller has the right to sell it (Article 431).

(iv) Property registration must be made public.

(8) **Principle of settlement of private relations by solutions close to justice**[30]

(i) The court may not refuse to settle a civil case or matter for the reason that there is no law to apply.

(ii) The court may only apply the provision on statute of limitations when so requested by the subject involved. The person who benefits from the application of the statute of limitations may refuse to apply such statute of limitations, unless such refusal aims to shirk performing his/her obligations.

(iii) A decision on settlement of a case or matter according to administrative procedures may be re-considered at the court. When settling a request for protection of civil rights, the court or another competent agency may cancel a specific decision issued by the agency, organization or person.

(iv) To diversify law sources and order of priority of application of law sources:

- Other relevant laws regulating private relations in specific spheres may not contravene the fundamental principles of civil law[31]; otherwise, the provisions of the Civil Code will apply;
- If there is no law and the parties have no agreement, customary practices will apply; if customary practices are not available, the provisions of the law regulating similar civil relations will apply; if there are neither customary practices nor similar provisions, the court or judge may choose one of the legal tools below: "fundamental principles of civil law", "court precedents" or "justice" to settle civil cases or matters.[32]

5.3 Some Fundamental Regulations

5.3.1 Real Rights[33]

The relationship between humans and property under the new Civil Code is re-designed in both structure and content on the basis of the theory of real rights. Specifically as follows:

---

[30]Articles 4, 5, 6, 14, 15 …

[31]Article 3.

[32]The application of court precedents is realized in proceedings activities in Vietnam. The Supreme People's Court has a portal on publicization of court judgments and rulings and a portal on court precedents.

[33]Part Two "Ownership Rights and Other Rights Over Property (Articles 158 Thru 273).

(1) The Code distinguishes the real relationship and legal relationship between humans and property.[34]

(2) For the real relationship between humans and property, the Code adds regulations on possession independently from ownership rights and other rights over property, instead of prescribing that possession is the result of ownership rights, a power of owners under the 2005 Civil Code.[35]

(3) For the legal relationship between humans and property, besides ownership rights, the Code adds other direct rights over property of persons other than owners (collectively referred to as "other rights over property") as a component of real rights of which ownership rights take the central position[36] (See the chart below).[37]

[34]However, in addition to regulations on possession (practical relationship), the new Civil Code still has the contents of ownership rights, including the right to possession (legal power), leading to confusing in conception and application of law.

[35]See Articles 179 thru 185. The possession by the person other than the owner cannot be a basis for establishing ownership rights, except the cases specified in Articles 228, 229, 230, 231, 232, 233 và 236 of the Civil Code. However, possession gives rise to legal effect like a relationship between the possessor and property recognized and adjusted by law and has the effect of right inference (inferred as bona fide, in case of a dispute over rights to property, the possessor will be inferred as the person having such right).

[36]These three rights are the result of separating part of ownership rights to create an independent right. Specifically as follows:

- Easement (servitudes): restricting part of use rights of owners from their immovable property to serve the exploitation of one or more other immovable property under others' ownership;
- Usufructuary: separating use rights (including the right to use and collect yields) from ownership rights;
- Right of superficies: being established by "slicing" an immovable property into small spatial levels and establishing separate ownershiprights over the part of immovable property attached to each of these levels.

[37]The provisions on property (definition and methods of classification of property) are transferred to Part One "General provisions". The 2005 Civil Code only acknowledges the owner as the person having direct rights over property.

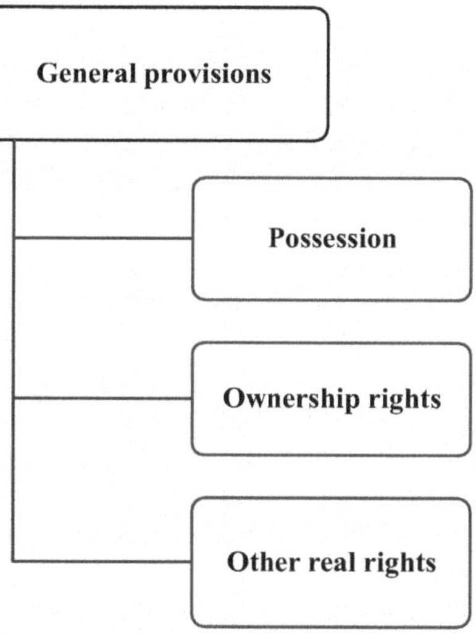

(4) The Code recognizes three other rights over property (also known as other real rights), namely easement (servitudes),[38] usufructuary,[39] and right of superficies,[40] and also specifies legal signs of real rights of these three rights and their relationship and ownership rights. Specifically as follows[41]:

[38]Articles 245 thru 256. Rights exercised on an immovable property (servient estate) aiming to serve the exploitation of another immovable property under another's ownership rights (dominant estate). Servitudes still exist with the existence of relevant immovable property items and the demand for enjoying rights still exists although dominant estate and servient estate have been transferred to another subject.

[39]Articles 257 thru 266. The right of a subject to exploit the utilities of, and enjoy yields and profits from, property under under ownership of another subject within a specified period, which will last until the first usufructuary being an individual dies or until the first usufructuary being a legal person ceases its existence, which must, however, not exceed 30 years. Before the new Civil Code was enacted: Vietnam's Law on Forest Protection and Development has acknowledged the right to use forests as the right to exploit utilities of and enjoy yields and benefits from forests, and to lease the right to use forests under contracts in accordance with this law and civil law; Restriction of the division of inheritances was provided in the 2005 Civil Code, and the right to stay of a spouse upon divorce is recognized in the 2014 Law on Marriage and Family.

[40]The right of a subject over ground, water surface, space above the ground or water surface and subsoil which the right to use belongs to another subject. The subject having the right of superficies may own the property formed. If this right is transferred in part or in whole, the transferee may inherit the right of superficies under the conditions and within the scope corresponding to the transferred part of this right.
In a certain aspect, it serves as a legal basis for making clearer the relationship between land under ownership by the entire people and land use rights of organizations and individuals, and offering more options in exploiting land and land-attached property and exercising land use rights.

[41]Ownership rights naturally have these legal signs which are more adequate and stronger against other rights in rem.

(i) The subject having other real rights directly holds and controls the property under the ownership of another subject[42];
(ii) Other real rights will be established and exercised under law; no one may be illegally restricted in or deprived of other real rights; the subject having other real rights may take measures not contrary to law to protect himself/herself/itself and prevent any person who commits an act infringing upon his/her/its rights.[43]
(iii) Other real rights may be established according to law, agreement or testament (or according to natural geographical positions, for servitudes). Other real rights become effective for all individuals and legal persons, unless otherwise prescribed by a law.[44]
(iv) Other real rights still become effective in case ownership rights are transferred, unless otherwise prescribed by a law; the owner may not claim property possessed by the subject that has other real rights over such property.[45]
(v) The subjects having other real rights may perform all acts within their scope of rights prescribed by a law without causing damage to or affecting the national interests, people's interests, public interests or lawful rights and interests of owners of property or of other persons.[46]
(vi) The subjects having other rights will have to bear risks to the property within their scope of rights prescribed by a law, unless otherwise agreed upon with the owners of the property or otherwise prescribed by a law.[47]

(5) Ownership rights and other real rights will be restricted in emergency circumstances to protect the environment, ensure social order and safety, or put up boundaries or boundary markets for immovable property, etc. In case of extreme necessity for the reason of national defense and security or for the national interests, in emergency state or for disaster prevention and control, the State may compulsorily purchase or requisition property of organizations and individuals with compensation at the market price.[48]

---

[42] Article 159.1: Although this provision is used to define other rights over property and does not cover ownership rights but in legal nature, the ownership rights already have such characteristics, which are even more adequate and stronger than any other right over property.

[43] Articles 160.1 and 163.1.

[44] For example, the Land Law prescribes that land-related changes must be registered, However, the way the Civil Code gives provisions still fails to ensure transparency and publicity of other rights in rem. According to the Ministry of Justice of Vietnam, other rights in rem established according to law or natural geographical positions (for servitudes) are not required to be registered because the law (or natural geographical positions) already ensure publicity of rights; while other rights in rem established under agreement or testatement need to be registered to publicize the establishment of rights according to the will of the subjects and the effective time arises from the time of registration of the rights.

[45] Articles 160.1 and 166.2.

[46] Article 160.3.

[47] Article 162.2.

[48] Articles 2.2, 163.2, and 171 thru 178.

(6) Form of ownership is defined based on the difference in the way of exercise of the power of owners but not based on the "subject" factor as stated in the 2005 Civil Code.[49] Three forms of ownership defined in the Civil Code include ownership by the entire people, private ownership and common ownership.

5.3.2 Security for Performance of Obligations[50]

(1) The Civil Code acknowledges nine measures to secure the performance of civil obligations[51] according to two approaches: (1) law-prescribed security[52] and agreement-based security[53]; (2) and security without property[54] and security with property.[55] The Code has developed and reserved ownership rights into a measure of agreement-based security with property on the basis of the provisions on reservation of ownership rights under property purchase and sale contracts; and developed lien on property into a measure of law-prescribed security with property on the basis of inheriting the provisions on lien on property in performance of bilateral contracts.

(2) Secured obligation may be part or the whole of an obligation, a present obligation or a future obligation. Future obligation is an obligation that is formed in the security time limit, unless otherwise agreed upon by the parties. The parties need not to reach a specific agreement on the scope of the future obligation and time limit for performance of this obligation; when a future obligation is formed, the parties are not required to re-establish a security measure for such obligation.

(3) A third party[56] may reach agreement with the obligee (creditor) or with both the creditor and obligor (debtor) on the third party's commitment to take a trust-based security measure (guaranty or pledge of trust) or a property-based security measure (mortgage or pledge) to secure the performance of the debtor's civil obligation. This security may take the form of the use of the third party's property to secure the performance of the debtor's civil obligation or the form

---

[49] State ownership, collective ownership, private ownership, common ownership, and ownership by political organizations, socio-political organizations, organizations of socio-political-professional organizations, social organizations, and socio-professional organizations.

[50] Articles 292 Thru 250.

[51] Pledge of property, mortgage of property, deposit, security collateral, escrow account, retention of title, guaranty, pledge of trust, and lien on property.

[52] Lien—a security measure not arising from transactions bur arising from specific circumstances.

[53] Pledge of property, mortgage of property, deposit, security collateral, escrow account, retention of title, guaranty, and pledge of trust.

[54] Guaranty and pledge of trust.

[55] Pledge of property, mortgage of property, deposit, security collateral, escrow account, retention of title, and lien.

[56] One or more than one individual and legal person.

of the guarantor's use of his/her/its property to guarantee his/her/its guaranty obligation.

(4) Collateral may be movable property or immovable property, present property or future property. Immovable property may be an object of pledge if it is prescribed by a law.[57] The mortgage of land use rights with land-attached assets will be determined based on the criterion that land use rights and land-attached assets belong to the same owner or different owners.[58]

Collateral must come under the ownership of the securing party; collateral may be described generally but must be the one that can be determined; collateral may be present property or future property; the value of collateral may be larger than, equal to or smaller than the value of the secured obligation.[59]

(5) In the agreement-based measure of security with property, there is the difference between the effective time of a security contract and the time when the security measure becomes effect.[60]

(6) A security measure becomes effective for a third party from the time it is registered[61] or from the time the security-accepting party holds or seizes the collateral. When the security measure becomes effective for the third party, the security-accepting party may claim the collateral and is entitled to payment priority among the parties that receive collateral as prescribed by a law. If the security-accepting parties agree to change the payment priority order for one another, the subrogor is entitled to payment priority only within the scope of security of the subrogee.[62]

(7) The security-accepting party may realize the collateral only when there is a ground as agreed upon or prescribed by a law and must comply with the process of realizing collateral. In case a party is holding collateral for the security-accepting party, the latter may request the court to settle the case and may not seize the collateral, unless otherwise prescribed by a law.[63]

The method of realizing the pledged or mortgaged property must be agreed upon by the security-accepting party and securing party; if no agreement is reached, the property will be auctioned, unless otherwise prescribed by a law. If the collateral's

---

[57] However, the current Land Law does not allow pledge of land use rights yet.

[58] Articles 318, 325 and 326.

[59] However, in case it is not agreed upon or not otherwise prescribed by law, one property used to secure performance of many obligations must have the value at the time of establishment of the secured transaction larger than the total value of the secured obligations.

[60] Articles 310, 319 and 331.

[61] A security measure is registered as agreed upon or prescribed by a law.

[62] Articles 297 and 308.

[63] The National Assembly'd Resolution No. 42/2017/QH14 of June 30, 2017, on pilot handling of non-performing loans of credit institutions, permits credit institutions to seize collaterals if such seizure is agreed upon under security contracts, security measures have been registered and the collaterals do not come under dispute being settled by the court. The Resolution also permits the court to apply summary procedures to settle disputes related to the obligation to hand over collaterals or disputes related to the right to realize collaterals.

value is not large enough for payment for the obligation of the securing party, the part of the obligation for which payment has not yet been made will become the unsecured obligation.

5.3.3 Contracts[64]

(1) An offer to enter into a contract is an explicit expression of the intention to enter into a contract and to be bound by such offer made by the offeror for a given party or to the public (below referred to as the offeree).[65]

(2) In case a party has information that may affect the acceptance to enter into the contract by the other party, it must notify such information to the other party; in case a party knows about secret information of the other party in the course of entering into a contract, he/she/it must keep such information confidential and may not use such information for his/her/its own purpose or for another illegal purpose; any party that violates the obligation relating to information in the entry into contracts, thus causing damage, must compensate therefore.[66]

(3) The silence of the offeree will be considered his/her/its acceptance of the offer to enter into the contract, if it is agreed upon or it is a habit established between the parties.[67] If the offeror does not specify a time limit for reply, an acceptance reply will be valid only if it is made within a reasonable time limit.[68]

(4) The time of entry into a written contract is the time when the last party signs the contract or otherwise expresses his/her/its acceptance in writing. In case a contract is verbally entered into then established in writing, the time of its entry will be determined according to the time of entry into a verbal contract. If the parties have agreed on a time limit within which silence means acceptance to enter into the contract, the time of entry into the contract is the final time of such time limit.[69]

(5) The contractual parties may reach agreement on the contract contents. In case the contract-drafting party (that has the active role in interpreting the parties' will in entry into the contract) inserts the contract contents which are unfavorable to the other party, the contract will be interpreted in a manner favoring the other party.[70]

(6) Standard-form contracts and general transaction conditions must be made public for the offeree to know or be obliged to know the contract contents, general

[64] Articles 385 Thru 569.

[65] Article 386.

[66] Article 387.

[67] Article 393.2.

[68] Article 394.1.

[69] Article 400.2.

[70] Articles 398 and 404.6.

transaction conditions; the order and methods for such publicization must comply with law.[71]

(7) In case a third party under a contract waives his/her/its benefit after the obligor has performed the obligation, the benefit derived from the contract will belong to the party that should have been the beneficiary if the contract is not performed for the benefit of the third party, unless otherwise agreed upon.[72]

(8) Penalty for breach of contract will be applied as agreed upon. The penalty level will be agreed upon by the parties, unless otherwise prescribed by a law. If the parties have an agreement on payment of penalties for breach of contract but have no agreement on payment of both penalties and compensation for damage, the breaching party will only be liable to pay penalties.[73]

(9) The obligee may claim compensation for the loss of benefits which he/she/it would have enjoyed from the contract. The obligee may also request the obligor to pay expenses arising due to the non-fulfillment of contractual obligations which are not covered by the compensation payable for the loss of benefits which should have been brought about from the contract; at the request of the obligee, the court may order the obligor to compensate for the spiritual damage caused to the obligee. The compensation level will be decided by the court based on the contents of the case.[74]

(10) In case of a fundamental change of circumstances, the party whose benefits are affected may request the other party to re-negotiate on the contract within a reasonable time limit. If the parties cannot agree on modification of the contract, either party may request the court to: (i) terminate the contract at a specified time; or (ii) modify the contract to balance lawful rights and interests of the parties in the context of a fundamental change of circumstances. The court may only decide to modify the contract in case the damage to be caused by the termination of the contract will be greater than expenses for performance of the contract once it is modified.[75]

(11) One party may declare to cancel the contract if the other party seriously breaches the contractual obligations. Serious breach means one party's failure to properly perform his/her/its obligation to an extent that the other party cannot achieve the purpose of entry into the contract.[76]

[71] Articles 405 and 406.

[72] Article 416.2.

[73] Article 418.

[74] Article 419.

[75] Article 420.

[76] Article 423.

Chapter 6
One Aspect of Civil Procedure Reform in Asia: Placing the Focus upon Vietnam

Shiro Kawashima

6.1 Introduction

In recent years there has been significant economic development in Southeast Asia. The rapid development of the market economy unavoidably demands the sharing of common rules that cross national borders and the development of systems to meet those needs.

Southeast Asia consists of several countries that have different races, histories and political systems, and although there are differences in the speed of economic development, each country is currently working towards the advancement of not only the economic and social development of their own country, but also the welfare and happiness of the citizens under the country's basic policies. The development of laws is essential to maintain and improve the development of economic activity and social stability. The development of laws which form the basis for social and economic activity is necessary to build an affluent and stable society based on the principles of respect for the individual and democracy. The rational modernization and visualization of the civil law system, even if it is based on the history and traditions peculiar to a country, is inevitably required in order to create and establish a social safety net through the law. While being awash with globalization, for the purpose of social and economic development the country must provide an after-the-fact remedy

---

This article is part of the research results of the research fund led by Professor Ph.D. Yuka Kaneko of the Kobe University Graduate School of International Cooperation Studies. I would like to give my heartfelt thanks for receiving the opportunity to gain valuable knowledge through this research, which could not have been gained by only researching civil procedure law within Japan or comparative research with Western civil procedure laws.
S. Kawashima—LL.B. Waseda University; LL.M., Hitotsubashi University; LL.D. Kyushu University.

S. Kawashima (✉)
Department of Law, Doshisha University, Kyoto, Japan
e-mail: skawashi@mail.doshisha.ac.jp

Y. Kaneko (ed.), *Civil Law Reforms in Post-Colonial Asia*,
Kobe University Monograph Series in Social Science Research,
https://doi.org/10.1007/978-981-13-6203-3_6

redress system for the appropriate and prompt resolution of civil disputes through impartial institutions; the completeness and accessibility of the system guarantees the free and open economic activity of individuals and businesses.

At the centre of such a legal redress system is the law of civil procedure. In the area of this basic procedural law, since the start of this century each Southeast Asian country has seen major reform of the processes that were formed and utilized under the historic background of each country. For example, new civil procedure laws were established in Vietnam in 2004 and Cambodia in 2006. In both cases the new laws were promulgated as a result of the support for development of laws in foreign countries.[1] A fundamentally "adversary system" is adopted within the legislation, which is a basic form in a modern code of civil procedure.

Japan participated in the support for development of laws for each country as the legal technical assistance, but remarkable differences can be seen in the enactment process of these two civil procedure codes. Differences are also seen in the specific contents of the established codes. The enactment process for the codes itself appears to be having an effect upon the realistic utilization and operation of civil procedure in the future, as well as its future development.

This article will be limited to a discussion of Vietnam because I could engage myself in the reform process after the promulgation in 2004.

As an aside, Japan's legal system development support is being implemented as a part of the new form of the Official Development Assistance (ODA), but also has the aspect of being a visible implementation of the principle of international cooperation and harmonization that is called for in the preface of the Japanese Constitution of 1946. Further, legal system development support was one of the detailed proposals in the "Recommendations of the Justice System Reform Council; For a Justice System to Support Japan in the 21st Century" published in 2001. Specifically, "Promotion of Legal system development support" was provided as one of the "Responses to

---

[1]There are many works available on the topic of legal system development support, but for an example, I would like to offer as a high-level introductory text that reviews the entire topic Kagawa & Kaneko (2007) *Houseibi Shien Ron*; *Seido Kouchiku no Kokusai Kyouryoku Nyuumon* (*Legal System Development Support Theory*; *Introduction to International Support of System Development*).

According to the Ministry of Justice's Research and Training Institute, "'Legal system development support' can be described as 'activities to support the development of legislation and the system which implements it by a developing country' … which includes not only the provision of advice and participation in the drafting of specific legislative bills and nurturing the people responsible for drafting the laws, but also widely includes the development of systems to apply and execute the legislation as well as supporting the development of human resources that specialize in the law and will work within these systems" and "research of the necessary legal systems within the country receiving the support, their implementation and circumstances, and the social, economic and political circumstances that form their background, which is necessary in order to effectively provide this type of support, is an important part of the activity." Ozaki (2002) Houmusho Sougou Kenkyuusho Kokusai Kyouryoku-Bu ni okeru Min-Shouji Hou wo Chuushinn ni Shita Houseibi Shien Katsudou ni tsuite (Legal System development Support Centered upon Civil and Commercial Law by the International Cooperation Department of the Ministry of Justice's Research and Training Institute), *Hou no Shihai*, 126, 5.

internationalization" for the Japanese justice system.[2] Furthermore, legal system development support activities within Japan go beyond supporting the drafting of legislation in other countries; depending on the form of support, retrospectively it can be thought of as providing an opportunity for self-examination of Japanese law itself.[2,3] It is not the unilateral transplanting of a legal system and instruction, but the joint consideration of formulating and improving the system, while the sharing of information is also of significance.

Generally, the area of civil procedural law is an important area of legal system development support. Apart from the legal system development support for civil procedure, Japan's legal system development support in the area of civil procedural law provided through the Japan International Cooperation Agency (JICA) and the Ministry of Justice's Research and Training Institute is extensive and wide-ranging as well as progressive in form[4]; there is currently, for example, civil procedure development support in China, support for establishing settlement and mediation i.e. conciliation systems in Indonesia and East Timor, and support for establishing bankruptcy law systems in several countries including Vietnam. As this article cannot include everything, it will provide some examination of the support given to establish a civil procedure law in Vietnam.

In the case of civil procedure as a procedural law, promoting integration between the form and the practice is required. Although civil procedure itself, as the most serious, deliberate and formal civil dispute resolution process, has a deep sense of being a specialized field, it also has an aspect of expressing in detail the country's governing policies and is an important element of a democratic nation. This is not just the formal manifestation of formal legislation, but from the perspective of the

[2]The "Recommendations" document stated that "legal system development support for developing countries should be promoted" and Japan has, until now, "implemented legal system development support that makes use of Japan's experience of inheriting modern legal systems from various countries while establishing legal systems and operations in keeping with the state of affairs within the country, and has accepted trainees from Asia and other developing countries, dispatched experts, conducted local seminars, etc. in the fields of civil and commercial law and criminal justice". The incorporation of this support has the position of being important for Japan to fulfill a proactive role as a member of international society, as well as facilitating the development of smooth civilian economic activity as the globalization of the economic society advances. Regarding legal system development support, it has been proposed that it should be continued to be proactively promoted with planned coordination between the government, lawyers and bar associations, with even greater provision and sharing overseas of information regarding judicial systems, etc. It has also been proposed that law schools accept exchange students as a part of legal system development support.

[3]For example, Kaino (2001) Houseibi Shien to Hikakuhougaku no Kadai (Legal System Development Support and Comparative Law Issues), *Asia Keizai*, 42(1); and Kawashima (2001) Houseibi Shien to Sono Purosesu wo Tsuujita Naisei-teki Shiza no Kakutoku; Minji Soshou Hou Kenkyuusha no Shiten kara (Acquisition of Introspective Viewpoints from Legal System Development Support and its Process; Viewpoint from a Civil Procedure Law Researcher), *ICD News*, (48), 1. Of course, this depends upon the fundamental idea and basic position of the legal system development support (and the specific individuals it comprises).

[4]For legal system development support provided by Japan listed in an annual format, there is, for example "Houseibi Shien Katsudou Nenhyou" (Annual Table of Legal System Development Support) (2005) *ICD News*, (20), 196 (however, this is current as of 14 January 2005).

processes used in actual operation, definite democratic legal practices that respect the autonomy of the parties are also desirable.[5] This is a question of realizing a procedural law that is an organic integration of theory and practice, quickly responds to social needs, and can be easily used, understood and relied upon by the people. It is the same on the court's side also. The ultimate goal of legal system development support in the legal area of civil procedure can be thought of as establishing an institutional environment throughout the country such that people and businesses can make use of the civil process and obtain legal relief at any time. This is an issue for civil procedure in Japan also, as an ideal that should be realized in the future, and in any event, I would like to examine the legal system development support by having a glance at the interesting drafting and legislative process for civil procedure and the process that followed.

6.2 2004 Civil Procedure Reform in Vietnam

6.2.1 Background History of the Civil Procedure Revision

6.2.1.1 The Previous Law and the Path to Revision

Vietnam was the first country to receive legal system development support from Japan.[6]

First I would like to take a concise look at the background history that led up to new promulgation of Vietnam's civil procedure law.

Vietnam adopted the Doi Moi Policy in 1986, which is the Vietnamese new economic program. This aimed to change the planned economy and promote market-oriented economic reform under socialism. In accordance with this basic policy, a constitution that recognized private property rights was enacted in 1992 and the country had to establish definite legal systems that could accommodate a market economy by way of constitutional revisions in 2001.

In 1993, a civil procedure code compilation committee was established in the Supreme People's Court, and the "Communist Party of Vietnam Central Committee Politburo Resolution" (08-NQ/TV) issued on 2 January 2002 demanded that a civil procedure law be promptly enacted.

During this era there were three orders regulated by the National Assembly's Standing Committee that regulated civil court processes, namely the Order of Civil Case Resolution Procedure Regulation in 1989, the Order of Economic Case Resolution Procedure in 1992 and the Order of Labor Case Resolution Procedure in 1996.

---

[5]See also Kawashima (2007) Nihon ni okeru Houseibi Shien no Kadai to Tenbou ni tsuite (Issues and Views regarding Japanese Legal System Development Support), *Housei Kenkyuu*, *73*(4), 685–714, Kyushu University.

[6]Inaba (2008) Houseibi Shien Jigyou no Ima (Current Legal System Development Support Projects), *Jurist*, (1358), 2–8.

At the time these Orders were planned to be revised as laws passed by the National Assembly in later years.

There were several differences in the regulations of these Orders, but they had the following basic proceedings in common.[7] That is, for the most part, the procedural characteristics included a wide scope of subject-matter; a wide scope in the judgment that was rendered, which was not limited to the subject matter as the applied claim i.e. there was no principle of restriction of the judgment to the applied subject matter; the principle of ex officio examination of evidence was adopted; a detailed examination of evidence was performed in the absence of the parties as preliminary examinations prior to the trial; the time for the trial was in principle limited to once only in order to allow the prompt conclusion of the procedure; and the effect of the judgment can spread wide beyond the plaintiff and defendant. Further, socialist legal characteristics of the provisions included separate procedures for economic and civil cases, the public prosecutor's ability to commence a suit, the trial panel structure of the courts that includes citizen lay judges called people's jurors, the public prosecutor's authority to attend trial, the public prosecutor's right of appeal, the existence of a cassation instance system and provisions for rehearing a case in the retrial system on the ground of newly found fact.

6.2.1.2 Support from Both Japan and the United States

It is general that, Japan's legal system development support for Vietnam in the areas of civil and commercial law commenced in 1994,[8] but after the aforementioned Resolution in Vietnam, Japan's legal system development support towards drafting a new civil procedure code in actuality commenced in 2002.[9] Writing of the draft law was based upon two fundamental policies. One aim was to respond to the demands of contemporary Vietnam and the other was to make the continual development of the civil procedure possible, that is, the aim to establish a civil procedure code that measured up to the tides of internationalization.[10]

It was the United States that presented the requirement for internationalization to the Vietnamese government, and it was the United States that gave a direct opportunity for the enactment of a new civil procedure code in Vietnam in a concrete form.[11]

---

[7]Regarding the following see Masahiro Iseki "Betonamu Minji Soshouhou" (Vietnam's Civil Procedure Law), Kagawa and Kaneko, supra note 1 at 85–86.

[8]Ozaki, supra note 1 at 8.

[9]Maruyama (2005) Betonamu Minji Soshouhou Seitei; Waga Kuni no Kisou Shien (Vietnam's Civil Procedure Law Enactment; Japan's Drafting Support), *ICD News*, (21), 5–9.

[10]Dang (2005) Betonamu Minji Soshouhou no Seitei to Shikou ni okeru Betonamu Saikou Jinmin Saibansho no Yakuwari (Role of the Supreme People's Court in the Enactment and Operation of Vietnam's Civil Procedure Code), *ICD News*, (20), 32–38 (Mr. Phuong is a deputy chief justice of Vietnam's Supreme People's Court).

[11]Kaneko (2010) Betonamu Minji Soshou to Saiban Doutai; Kihan Taikei no Mosaku (Vietnam's Civil Procedure and Trial Dynamics; Search for Standard Criteria), in Yuka Kaneko, *Ajia no House-*

In 2001 the "U.S.-Vietnam Bilateral Trade Agreement" was signed between the United States and Vietnam. Chapter 2, Articles 11–13 of the agreement defined details of procedural regulations concerning civil procedure and civil preservation that the signatory countries were required to establish for the protection of intellectual property rights within both countries. Chapter 6, Article 3 provided that both countries are able to submit comments on the formulation of laws concerning economic activity. It was on that basis that the United States was able to request the establishment of a civil procedure code under certain conditions.

Support for drafting was performed as a part of the STAR Project (Support for Trade Acceleration Project) by USAID (the United States Agency for International Development).[12]

The aims of the drafting included (1) introduction of emergency preservation measures (civil preservation) in order to strengthen the protection of intellectual property rights, (2) strengthening the "independence of the judiciary" by removing the public prosecutor's right to commence actions, and (3) a dramatic transition from an inquisitorial system to an adversary system, in order to strengthen the rights of parties and lawyers, and so that trials are conducted based upon only the evidence that was introduced in open court.

This support for drafting a civil procedure code bill that was provided by the United States' STAR Project was identified as differing from the support provided by Japan.[13] That is, the "support" offered by the United States regarding the civil procedure code had the character of protecting the United States' own interests based upon the bilateral agreement. The STAR Project conducted seminars about the drafts and submitted written comments, the contents of which mainly corresponded with the comments submitted by Japan, such as protecting the procedural rights of parties and the fairness of processes and so on. However, the "support" was not continual support as provided by Japan, but was sporadic and the contents of the United States' comments were the same as the contents of American law. For example, the structure of the code was not separated into volumes such as general provisions, trials, appeals, non-contentious cases, etc., but instead the form of a structure of 25 chapters was recommended, as was the civil preservation seen in American law.

Incidentally, Vietnam did not allow foreigners to be directly involved in the legislative process.[14] Vietnamese bureaucrats researched foreign legislative materials and experiences, and protected the principle of drafting legislation with contents that were the most suitable to Vietnam's circumstances. On that point, Japan's legal system development support was limited to providing reference materials and advice for that purpose. Three Japanese specialists who were professors of Civil Procedure

---

ibi to Houhatten (Asian Legal System Development and Legal Development), University Education Press, 79, 81 (originally published in 2009).

[12]The following is according to Kaneko, supra note 11 at 81, 85. In the U.S.-Vietnam Bilateral Trade Agreement, legal system reform objectives were raised as a condition of Vietnam's entry into the World Trade Organization, in particular a requirement to strengthen the civil and commercial processes as part of strengthening the implementation of intellectual property law. Id.

[13]Regarding the following, see Iseki, supra note 7 at 90.

[14]Regarding the following, see Maruyama, supra note 9 at 8–9 and Iseki, supra note 7 at 86.

were assigned to provide support, which was performed by providing comments and advices on the drafts written by Vietnamese officials. In response to this, the Vietnamese side referred to the comments and revised the drafts in turn. The Vietnamese side requested comments on specific points which they took particular interest in, but the Japanese side did not limit themselves to those points and provided comments and suggestions on points that they thought necessary throughout the entire drafts.

Most of the comments were adopted into the new code, but Japan generally did not comment on Vietnamese constitutional provisions such as the cassation instance system and trial panel members, which proceeded on the premises of the Vietnamese side's revision policy.[15]

In a short period of approximately two years, the draft civil procedure code was prepared and in June 2004 the new Civil Procedure Code was enacted by the National Assembly. With the Civil Procedure Code coming into force, the aforementioned three Orders were repealed.[16] However, because another new Civil Procedure Code was enacted as a revision of this code in 2015, this code is called the 2004 Civil Procedure Code from now on.

6.2.1.3 Specific Issues in the Enactment of the Civil Procedure Code

According to the explanation from the Vietnamese side, the specific issues in the enactment of this Civil Procedure Code are as follows.[17]

The first issue was the "covering scope of the civil procedure code provisions". There was the question of whether to include several special types of cases in the Civil Procedure Code, namely, cases related to electoral enrollment in a public case, domicile registration in a family and administrative case and labor strikes in a labor case.

The second issue was the "rights and obligations of related parties with an interest in a case". Namely, there was the question of whether related parties could apply to a court to protect their rights or interests, whether the public prosecutor could do so, etc.

The third issue was the "party's right of self-determination", that is, the principle of procedural jus dispondi. The question related to what extent a party's right of self-determination should be recognized from the aspect of commencing or ending a lawsuit. The issue was whether to recognize the rights for a government institution or other organization (for example, organizations to protect the rights of women and

[15]Iseki, supra note 7 at 87.

[16]It has been pointed out that eventually, Vietnam did not incorporate the United States' particular civil procedure law; Iseki, supra note 7 at 90. However, because Vietnam subsequently realized entry into the World Trade Organization (WTO), it can be thought that the 2004 Vietnam Civil Procedure Code cleared the conditions set by the United States. This fact reflects the fundamental principles that should be contained in a modern civil procedure law (the fundamental elements that support modern civil procedure law), which suggests that whether it is Western law or continental law, or capitalist law or socialist law does not matter, and is very interesting.

[17]Phuong, supra note 10 at 34–38.

children, labor organizations, etc.) to commence a lawsuit in order to protect the rights or interests of an individual. Further, whether to adopt the principle of restriction of the judgment to the applied subject matter was at issue. These are problems of an adversary system generally.

The fourth issue was the "party's obligation to submit evidence". Here, the questions included whether to place time limits on the parties' submission of evidence and in what circumstances should the court be permitted to gather evidence ex officio. These were issues of the principles of advocacy principle under which parties have authority and responsibility to produce relevant facts and evidences that become foundation of judgment, and they come from thought of adversary system.

The fifth issue was "emergency provisional measures (civil preservation)". This was an unavoidable issue particularly due to the requirements of internationalization as a condition of Vietnam's entry into the World Trade Organization (WTO).

The sixth issue was "procedural determination of approval of settlement and compromise etc." This issue related to the process of the parties reaching an agreement and its contents on the base of procedural jus dispondi principle.

The seventh issue was "securing the effectiveness of a judgment's effect". This issue relates to compulsory execution (judgment execution law). The Code of Civil procedure in Vietnam didn't include provisions of enforcement of judgment unlike in Cambodia.

The eighth issue was the preparation of "guidance documents". This issue related to detailed "guidance documents" that embody contents of the legislation, for example, the format of written judgments, that are prepared by the judicial council of the Supreme People's Court following the establishment of the Civil Procedure Code.

Although it was thought to provide provision of res judicata, it was not included in the issues in the drafting process.

6.2.2 Establishment of the 2004 Civil Procedure Code: Overview of the Code

6.2.2.1 Adoption of the Principle of the Adversary System

A thorough examination of the 2004 Civil Procedure Code must be left for a later date, but as an overview, the comments from Japan were largely adopted in the area of respecting the autonomy and right of self-determination of parties.[18] This

[18] The following is according to Iseki, supra note 7 at 87–88. Regarding the support for the drafting of Vietnam's Civil Procedure Code, it can be seen that the just three Japanese special participants made great efforts over the short period, and fortunately, each of them left us with papers including the following. Yoshimura (2005) Betonamu Minji Soshouhou Seitei; Seiritsu no Haikei to Tokuchou: Dai-Ichi Shin ni okeru Shinri Tezuzuki wo Chuushinn toshite (Establishment of Vietnam's Civil Procedure Code; Background to Realization and its Features, Focused upon the Trial Process at First Instance), *ICD News*, (21), 10 later published in Yoshimura (2011) *Hikaku Minji Tezuzukihou (Comparative Civil Process Law)*, 369; Yoshimura (2006) Betonamu Minji Soshouhou no Kongo

demonstrates the fundamental adversarial structure of the Civil Procedure Code. However, rules that are strongly reminiscent of the prior fundamental structure can also be seen.

(i) Adoption of the procedural jus dispondi principle respecting the self-determination of parties
The principle of restriction of the judgment to the applied subject matter under the procedural jus dispondi principle was not adopted in the civil procedure of the old law era. For example, in the procedure for a claim of vacancy by the owner of a house, the court could also order people other than the defendant i.e. third parties who were living in the house to vacate. In these circumstances, even if there was not a counterclaim filed by the defendant, the court could order the plaintiff to reimburse the beneficiary expenses incurred by the residents. Under the old law, as there was no restriction of the judgment to the applied subject matter under the procedural jus dispondi principle, it can be thought that the procedure operated on the basis of an authoritative and custodial procedure oriented towards complete resolution of a dispute, where the role of the court was to capture the social conflict in the subject of the lawsuit and resolve all of the legal problems that were included.[19]
Regarding this, a provision was established within the 2004 Civil Procedure Code that limited the court's judgment to the scope contained in a lawsuit's petition or written request. This is a adoption of principles of restriction of the judgment to the applied subject matter (Article 5 of the 2004 Civil Procedure Code (hereinafter referred to as the "2004 Code")), as well as provisions regarding a counterclaim and its process (2004 Code, Articles 172–178).[20]
Through this, the scope of a court trial and judgment became limited, the self-

no Kadai: Nihon Minji Soshouhou tono Hikakuhouteki Shiten kara (Future Issues for Vietnam's Civil Procedure Code: From a Comparative Law Viewpoint of Comparison with Japan's Code of Civil Procedure), *ICD News*, (*26*), 2 later published in Yoshimura (2011) *Hikaku Minji Tezuzuki-hou (Comparative Civil Process Law)*, 439; Iseki (2005) Nihonhou to Hikakushite no Tokuchou; Saibankan, Kantokushin, Kinkyuu Hozen Shobun (Features Compared to Japanese Law; Judges, Cassation and Emergency Preservation Disposition), *ICD News*, (21), 58; Iseki (2006) Betonamu Minji Soshouhou no Shourai no Mondai (Future Issues for Vietnam's Civil Procedure Code), *ICD News*, (26), 13; Sakai (2005) Betonamu Minji Soshouhou Seitei; Hishou/Kokusai Minji Soshouhou oyobi Hanketsu Shikou Tezuzuki no Gaisetsu (Establishment of Vietnam's Civil Procedure Code; Outline of Non-Contentious Cases, International Civil Procedure Law and Judgment Execution Processes), *ICD News*, (21), 85, Sakai (2006) Betonamu Minji Soshouhou no Shourai no Kaisei Mondai (Future Revision Issues for Vietnam's Civil Procedure Code), *ICD News*, (26), 27.

[19]The above is according to Iseki, supra note 7 at 87. In Iseki's essay, this is called a "social welfare view of civil procedure". Also, in Kaneko, supra note 11 at 92, it is called a socialist-style public benefit "social dispute resolution view".

[20]Apart from this, the Japanese side recommended that the judgment text which is requested of the court be included in the complaint, but the portion regarding the claim to be described in the complaint is defined as "the specific clauses that the court is requested to impose against the defendant" (2004 Code, Article 164). The comment "It is currently unknown how this provision will be implemented" was made. See Iseki, supra note 7 at 87.

determination of parties in the area of the civil dispute resolution process is respected, and autonomy is recognized by the court.

Further, provisions including the right of self-determination of parties regarding bringing an action (2004 Code, Article 5) and concluding an action under the intent of the parties (procedural conciliation, etc. 2004 Code, Articles 10, 180–188; regarding appeals, Article 270) were also provided. These are all related to the principle of procedural jus dispondi, expressed as the principle of no adjudication without prosecution, but it means that the basic foundation common to modern civil procedure that western countries have was adopted in the 2004 Code (refer to Section 1(3) above).

(ii) Partial adoption of the principles of advocacy, specially both principle of prohibiting ex officio examination of evidence and the principle of admission

Under the old law, the principle of ex officio examination of evidence was present and judges examined the case in detail under their own authority in the stage of preliminary examinations so as to prepare with the trial.[21] In a sense, it was a process like a "preliminary hearing" in a criminal case.

Regarding this, the 2004 Civil Procedure Code provides that the collection and submission of evidence is within the authority and responsibility of the parties, and the consequences of insufficient evidence is the responsibility of the parties (2004 Code, Article 84; see also Article 7). However, there is a provision that, limited to the circumstances where a party cannot collect evidence itself and upon application by the party, the court can summon a witness or order the submission of documents (2004 Code, Article 85). This adopts the principle of the submission of evidence by parties as a rule, and allows supplementary limited ex officio examination of evidence. This corresponds to the third principle of the principles of advocacy in Japan.

Further, there is a provision that where a party makes an admission the fact does not need to be proven by the party (2004 Code, Article 80(2) and (3). This corresponds to the second principle of the principles of advocacy under Japanese law).

These regulations have the stated aim of reducing the burden of the court, but imply the recognition of the right to self-determination of the parties and the allowance of the parties' autonomy. However, that the discovery of new evidence after final judgment is a reason for reopening and reviewing a case (2004 Code, Article 304) and offering incompatibility of a judgment with the objective facts as a ground for applying for cassation review (2004 Code, Article 283(1)) shows that there still remains an aspect of giving priority to orientation towards absolute truth of fact, rather than the stability of the position of the parties based on a final judgment.[22]

---

[21] In the process of drafting Vietnam's Civil Procedure Code and in the Japanese translation also, the expression "public trial" like a criminal procedure is used, but the civil procedure's central trial process is referred to as open court trial of oral pleadings in the same manner as in Japanese law.

[22] Iseki, supra note 7 at 88.

However, the principle regarding "facts" (the burden of fact-pleading principle, where a fact in issue not argued by the parties cannot form the basis of a judgment), which is the first principle of the principles of advocacy under Japanese law,[23] is not specified within the legislation.[24]

(iii) Retention of broad scope of a judgment's effect
The effect of a judgment is related to the procedural structure and particularly the structure of the parties and the trial. The Japanese side suggested drafting provisions regarding the effect of a judgment, but the 2004 Civil Procedure Code does not go beyond retaining the provision that all citizens, government agencies and organizations must observe legally effective judgments (2004 Code, Article 19), which is similar to Article 136 of the Constitution. Because government agencies in this context may include a court hearing a subsequent case, this can be thought of as being similar to the principle of res judicata. There are no provisions in the 2004 Civil Procedure Code that specify limits on the objective and subjective scope of the res judicata of a judgment.
Because this sort of legislation has the meaning of wide acceptance of the effect of a judgment delivered by one of the nation's courts, provisions regarding related parties (2004 Code, Article 56) and procedural participation (2004 Code, Article 61) have been prescribed on the premise that the effect of a judgment spreads to other people beyond the plaintiff and defendant, as well as provisions that presume the effect of the judgment can derive from any part of the reasons for the judgment (2004 Code, Article 80(1)(a)).

6.2.2.2 Establishment of Detailed Procedural Provisions

In the area of procedural operation, it was found that most of the comments submitted by the Japanese side were adopted.[25]

As an example, provisions regarding jurisdiction have been established, including the scope of the civil jurisdiction (see Section 1(3) above), subject-matter jurisdiction, geographical jurisdiction, and transfer of a case (2004 Code, Articles 25–38).

Further, provisions regarding emergency provisional dispositions (civil preservation, see Section 1(2) above also) that were insufficient in the old law have been provided, as have provisions regarding providing bond in such instances and regarding appeals (2004 Code, Articles 99–126). The primary utility of these emergency preservation dispositions is demonstrated by being able to use them before commencing a lawsuit, but the emergency provisional dispositions in the 2004 Civil Procedure Code can only be used after commencing a law suit (see Section 1(3) above) also.[26] So

[23]For example, see Kawashima (2013) *Minji Soshouhou (Civil Procedure Law)*, 431.

[24]Kaneko, supra note 11 at 97.

[25]Iseki, supra note 7 at 88.

[26]The following is said in Iseki, supra note 7 at 88 regarding the emergency preservation disposition provisions in the 2004 Civil Procedure Code. Namely, "Many issues remain. As civil preservation was not really used previously, our advice ended up not being digested. The intellectual property

the system of emergency preservation dispositions has been insufficient in Vietnam yet.

Also, provisions which did not exist under the old law regarding the various restraints on the examination of evidence (measures against the obstruction of evidence collection, giving testimony, etc.) and the maintenance of order in court have been newly provided under the Chapter titled "Handing Acts of Obstructing Civil Proceedings" (2004 Code, Articles 384–390). In particular, the provisions regarding orders to submit documentation, etc. (2004 Code, Article 389) have stronger coercive power than those in Japan (also see 2004 Code, Article 7).

Concerning the trial, the central process of trials conducted under the civil procedure, a basic structure is defined for the examination of evidence such as the examination of the parties and witnesses and the presentation of closing arguments (2004 Code, Articles 213–235).

However, the process at the stage of preparing for the trial (preliminary examination stage) is generally not defined (see 2004 Code, Article 179 onwards). Therefore, although the examination of evidence at the preparation stage was not transparent and there was a problem with the involvement of the parties in the process, as there are methods of limiting the use of the results of examination of evidence during the preliminary examination process, even though the methods are not always sufficient, it has been found that there are provisions of sorts concerning the matter (see 2004 Code, Articles 227, 236).[27]

Additionally, the contents that should be included in a written judgment have been established and are comparatively detailed (2004 Code, Articles 238, 279, 301). The provisions are thought to be more specific than the regulations in Japanese law, but this is a characteristic of Vietnam not having a Federal Rules of Civil Procedure in the United States and Japanese Civil Procedure, and everything being defined within the one civil procedure code in Vietnam; they probably also serve as guidance for judges when writing judgments up. Moreover, what should be included in a written judgment is related to the course of the civil procedure, that is, what was examined and tried in the preliminary examinations and the trial processes and how it was examined and tried, as well as what and how it should be certified in the judgment, but the provisions provide fixed guidance to the trial process and the judge's procedural directions.

law enacted in 2005 has a portion regarding preservation dispositions, which is better developed than in the Civil Procedure Code. However, it is primarily thought that it should be developed in the general Civil Procedure Code rather than the intellectual property law." We can expect that the results of the intellectual property law will be refined and turned into general law. However, for that purpose, civil preservation must only be a provisional disposition, and it is necessary to sufficiently understand the meaning that it is a temporary relief order that differs from a judgment following a procedure.

[27] Iseki, supra note 7 at 88.

6.2.2.3 Socialist Law Matters

As stated above, during the drafting of the 2004 Civil Procedure Code, the Japanese side generally did not provide comments regarding systemic matters such as cassation instance, retrial and judgments by trial panels including peoples' jurors.[28] These systems have been retained in the Code.

The ex officio cassation system is peculiar to socialist law. The purpose of cassation instance is that when there is an error in the application of the law in the final judgment, upon an objection by the Chief Justice of the Supreme People's Court or the Prosecutor-General of the Supreme People's Prosecutors, the judgment is annulled, the effect of the annulment extends to the parties, and the correct decision is provided. Vietnam's civil procedure has a two-level adjudication regime (2004 Code, Article 7), but cassation instance has the role of ensuring the correctness of a final judgment.

The cassation instance system itself has its basis in the Constitution (Constitution, Article 134), but the detailed processes etc. are defined in the Civil Procedure Code (2004 Code, Article 282 onwards).

Problems with cassation instance under the old law were that the Chief Justice of the Supreme People's Court or the Prosecutor-General of the Supreme People's Prosecutors could raise an objection even if the parties were satisfied with the judgment, there was a long 3-year objection period after the final judgment, the preliminary examination process was not open to the public, and the parties did not have the right to plead.

Therefore, the Japanese side submitted comments on the cassation instance process. Proposals were made regarding matters such as, for example, limiting the ability of the Chief Justice of the Supreme People's Court to raise an objection to only when requested by a party to the judgment, involving the parties in the cassation instance process and providing them with the right to submit arguments, and making the cassation instance process public. Although these proposals were adopted at one stage during the drafting process, ultimately they were not included in the 2004 Civil Procedure Code.[29] (Regarding these points, see the 2004 Code, Articles 288, 292 and 285; also see Chap. 3, Section 4). The government sees the cassation instance system as a way to forbid the incorrect application of the law, and although it is a system peculiar to socialist law, similar systems can be seen in the criminal procedural law of capitalist countries such as Japan.

The role of the judiciary in not allowing but correcting incorrect judgments by way of the retrial system on the ground of newly found fact (The process is defined in the 2004 Code, Article 304 onwards) is similarly appropriate.

The right of the public prosecutor to inspect the court's activities has a basis in Article 137 of the Constitution, but with the enactment of the 2004 Civil Procedure Code, the system where a public prosecutor could commence a lawsuit on behalf of a rights holder has been removed (see 2004 Code, Article 162), and the right to

---

[28] Iseki, supra note 7 at 89.

[29] Id.

attend oral pleadings is limited to the case in which there is an objection from a party concerning the examination of evidence (2004 Code, Article 21). This point guarantees and respects the parties' right to self-determination mentioned above. However, the public prosecutor's right to appeal (2004 Code, Article 250) and the right to raise an objection for cassation instance (2004 Code, Article 285) have been retained from the old law.

During the process of supporting the drafting of the 2004 Civil Procedure Code, the Japanese side also introduced a summary court process without peoples' jurors which judge is only in charge of.[30] In Vietnam, all civil cases are tried and judged by a three-person trial panel (one judge and two citizen lay judges) (Article 129 of the Constitution, Article 11 of the 2004 Code). As this does not allow for a summary civil procedural trial, the Japanese system of a summary process conducted by a lone judge was presented in order to allow the effective processing of cases. With reference to this, systems similar to Japan's demand procedure and small claims procedure appeared in the draft at one stage of the drafting process of the 2004 Civil Procedure Code, but ultimately they were not adopted into the Code. However, the results of this will take shape later (see Chap. 3, Section 3).

6.2.2.4 The New Civil Procedure Code as the General Law of Civil Proceedings

At the theoretical level, in a socialist country a dualistic relationship between production and consumption is maintained, and corresponding to this, the structure of substantive law is divided into economic contracts and civil contracts and the format of procedural law also agrees, with separate procedural regulations established.[31] Economic contracts draw from the area of the state-owned sector and collectively-owned sector, while the civil contract area relates to the private sector, which can used to be thought to have a limited existence in a socialist economy. This is reflected in the procedural law, where the aforementioned procedure under the old law was defined separately in the Order of Economic Case Resolution Procedure and the Order of Civil Case Resolution Procedure Regulation.

In these legal conditions, even when a market economy was introduced under the socialist economy, from the aspect of the legal format, there was large significance in the 2004 Civil Procedure Code which established a trans-substantive civil procedure. As identified by Professor Kaneko, "the act of systematically placing the civil procedure law, which was a dispute resolution system related to minor private consumption, as the general dispute resolution system for civil and commercial matters including advanced commercial disputes regardless of whether they were in the state-owned, collective or private sector, has a significant meaning."[32] Moreover, the establishment of this trans-substantive, or in other words, uniform civil procedure

[30] Regarding the following see Iseki, supra note 7 at 90.

[31] The following is according to Kaneko, supra note 11 at 82.

[32] Kaneko, supra note 11 at 82.

eventually led to the establishment of a "Civil Code" as a general judicial law.[33] Such a legislation approaches or concords with capitalist law from a structural aspect and means that a common economic foundation has been obtained through the law. The shape of the nation, even if it is classified as a socialist country, from a legal form and systemic aspect is fundamentally not different from the legal system of capitalist liberal economies. However a problem is the operation of the law; depending on the degree of the custodial role of the court within the civil procedure with adversary system, the socialist government's orientation towards forming a social welfare state through the civil procedure process may remain. In fact, it seems the 2004 Civil Procedure Code has kept sufficient room for that possibility.

Finally, I would like to take a look at the biggest topic from the enactment of the 2004 Civil Procedure Code, namely the adversary system.

6.2.2.5 Civil Procedure Trials and the Reality of "Conciliatory Judgments"

After the 2004 Civil Procedure Code came into force, one of the Japanese people who provided support during the drafting sat in on a trial. He was satisfied that it was appropriately conducted in accordance with the Code and published his impressions.[34]

However, generally the reality of Vietnamese civil procedure process is not always clear.

In Vietnam, the meaning of conciliation i.e. settlement by parties' consent within the procedure is important. A principle of putting conciliation in which settlement by both parties is conducted by the court first has been adopted within the 2004 Civil Procedure Code (2004 Code, Article 180(1)) and settlement is promoted strongly,[35] but in Japan also procedural settlement is currently extremely flourishing. The significance and value peculiar to settlement, which might exceed the function of a judgment, are loudly publicized.[36] Also for Vietnamese judges, the success rate of conciliation is linked to favorable evaluation and increased respect as a socially capable judge, and a report found that "it is easy to understand the motive for young judges who are strongly oriented towards gaining promotion to be particular about conciliation".[37]

---

[33] Id.

[34] Iseki, supra note 7 at 92.

[35] A dispute resolution system called "grassroots conciliation" also exists within conciliation groups of residents' cooperative bodies. See the 1998 regulation regarding grassroots conciliation organizations and activities (published in Tatara (2013) *Betnamu Roppou* (*Vietnam Law Code*)).

[36] For example, see Kusano (2003) *Wakai Gijutsuron, Dai 2 Han* (*Conciliation Techniques Theory, 2nd ed.*), 1.

[37] Kaneko, supra note 11 at 116. On this point I had the similar impression in Vietnam. At the seminar I attended, questions regarding the resolution rates of conciliation cases in Japan were asked several times. At the seminar concerning family law, the procedural conciliation rate in divorce procedures was discussed and the judges attending appeared satisfied that the rate is considerably higher in

Although there are various backgrounds, it has been found as a result of conducting field work that in actual civil trials, even in the instance where conciliation was not successful, "conciliatory judgments" are sometimes delivered. When I sat in on a few civil cases, I gained the impression that the judge was enthusiastically recommending conciliation. "Conciliatory judgments" in this context means that when procedural conciliation could not be reached even though the judge and citizen lay judges urged compromise between the parties and recommended conciliation during preliminary examinations and trial, a judgment with conciliatory contents is delivered, as if it were a substitute for conciliation[38] (judgments that are partially approved are also seen). This sort of trial that fosters conciliation is reminiscent of the argument/conciliation (conciliation/argument. Benron ken Wakai in Japanese) previously seen in Japan. Although the trial in Vietnam is conducted in open court, it seems as if it were the non-contentious disposition (Hisho teki Shori in Japanese) of a contended action rather than being a trial of a contended action. Because the inclination for the parties themselves to make applications of claim and assertions of fact and to produce evidence is relatively weak, and because it is difficult to make factual findings and identify the focal point of applicable law due to delays in establishing substantive laws, it has been identified that the trend for judges to be favorable towards conciliation is growing even stronger.[39]

As the Japanese concept of "separation of contended actions and non-contentious cases",[40] is not present as for proceedings in Vietnam,[41] the format of a trial with oral pleadings is also used in cases that would be classified as non-contentious in Japan, such as those related to inheritance. Therefore, in cases that would be non-contentious in Japan, particularly in these cases a judgment that is conciliatory to a certain degree would also be useful (in Japan, before contended actions and non-contentious cases were separated, cases such as the division of deceased estates were

---

Vietnam than in Japan. However, in Vietnam all divorce cases must pass through the legal judicial procedure, but in Japan divorce is also recognized by the joint submission of divorce papers through the consent between husband and wife. Further, mediation is a prerequisite, therefore negotiated divorces are achieved at the divorce mediation level too (there are also arbitrated divorces in special cases), so most cases do not reach the stage of filing a lawsuit and those which do reach that stage were unable to reach agreement until that point, therefore a simple comparison of conciliation rates at the procedural level is not much use as a reference.

[38] In Japan the procedural process in summary courts is limited and the conditions are clearly defined, but there is also an "order in lieu of settlement" system (Japan Code of Civil Procedure, Article 275-2).

[39] Kaneko, supra note 11 at 119. As an opinion from field work, it was found that "there is a trend for a series of conciliation opportunities led by the judge within a civil trial, from the preliminary examination processes until the trial as the oral pleadings and evidence examination". Further, because of the delaying in developing substantive law, it is difficult to define the findings of fact and the focus of application of law, and it is predicted that the judges' inclination towards settlement and compromise will get stronger still.

[40] For the debate in Japan, see Kawashima, supra note 23 at 22.

[41] In Vietnam cases are divided into contended and non-contentious based on whether there is contention. Accordingly, for example, cases in Appendix List 2 of the Family Cases Procedural Law (e.g. distribution of deceased estates) are contended cases.

also contended actions.). The non-contentious disposition of cases is the embodiment of the judiciary's custodial, discretionary, purposeful and future-oriented disposition and may be appropriate to non-contentious cases, but seems to be purely out of touch with the adversary system in a contended case.

The mechanism to make civil trials possible within these conditions in Vietnam in fact may have already been included in the legislation at the time of enacting the 2004 Civil Procedure Code. To make this sort of conciliatory trial and conciliatory judgment possible, there may have been an intention to keep the previous actual practice of authoritative procedure after the enactment of the new law, or an intention to accept the smooth operation of the new law,[42] for example, by the adoption of a system of giving preference to conciliation, a lack of detail regulations concerning preliminary examinations, the preparation of processes for related parties to participate, the absence of requirements for a "same basis of claim" and "written documentation" in order to change a claim (see 2004 Code, Articles 217–218), which is different from Japan, the avoidance of establishing clear provisions regarding factual assertions (provisions regarding the principle of assertions), and provisions that specifically define the contents of judgments yet seem undeniably abstract.

Under Vietnam's civil procedure, where it can be presumed that the law will not always be correctly applied and civil trials that force conciliation are often conducted, the easy importation of Japan's conciliation methods must be a negative point. First, it is desirable to construct a procedural environment where well-organized civil trials are performed, the law is accurately applied under the correct finding of facts, and judgments are prepared and delivered in accordance with the law. For this reason, a project to prepare a judgment manual and the development of a system of precedents is desirable.[43] Needless to say the bribe to the judge and peoples' jurors should be forbidden naturally.

---

[42]In Japan the term "conciliatory judgment" has a considerably different meaning to that in Vietnam. In Japan "conciliatory judgment" is understood as meaning a good judgment that reflects the pretrial and trial process as a result of "the similarities and differences in the interests of the parties becoming clear from the background circumstances of the case and negotiations inside and outside the court and broad communication that incorporates future circumstances and conditions being conducted." See Inoue (1993) Benron no Jouken (Advocacy Conditions), in *Minji Tetsuzukiron* (*Civil Process Theory*), 87, 116 (originally published in 1991).

[43]The background to Japan's flourishing conciliation is that there is a well-organized judgment process in the civil procedure system, judges that obey the law and are capable of correctly using legal syllogisms (judgment syllogisms) exist, and further, many rules of precedent have been developed under the civil procedure law, which can be thought of as becoming a guideline for the format of details of conciliation within the procedural process. Generally, for example, if judges with a high conciliation rate are favorably treated at performance reviews, there is some apprehension of falling into forced conciliation to avoid giving judgment. Moreover, in the world where it can be said that bribes are being passed in court, attempting conciliation by way of non-public alternating meetings with parties seems a danger to maintaining the integrity of the judiciary.

6.2.2.6 The Position of Cassation Instance

Japan's legal system development support gave a negative evaluation of the cassation instance system itself.[44] That is because of its position as a system peculiar to socialist civil procedure law. Furthermore, it appears to be an inappropriate system for an adversary system centered upon the parties' self-determination.

However, (even though the purpose of the system differs) if it is positioned as an extraordinary method of relief, a similar system can be seen in Japanese law, although it is in criminal procedure as mentioned above.

That system is the proceeding of "extraordinary appeal", a process of extraordinary relief to rectify breaches of the law. Although the word "appeal" is used here, it is a process of relief after a judgment has been finalized, as in the case of a retrial process. However, it differs from a retrial in that it applies to errors of law, not errors of fact. Parties do not have a right of appeal, but only the Prosecutor-General may commence an extraordinary appeal (Japan Code of Criminal Procedure, Article 454). Historically, this system came from French law of "cassation application in the interest of the law" (France Code of Criminal Procedure, Article 620), but differs from the French law in that when an error of legal interpretation disadvantages the defendant, that portion of the judgment is reversed, which fulfils a function of relief for the defendant (Japan Code of Criminal Procedure, Article 458(1) proviso).

The future procedural development of cassation instance as a system of extraordinary relief is thought to be desirable in Vietnam.

6.3 Activity Related to Civil Procedure After the Enactment of the 2004 Code

6.3.1 Human Resource Development

The reform of civil proceeding law has continued in Vietnam following the enactment of the 2004 Civil Procedure Code and has covered various aspects of civil procedural law including, for example, the establishment and development of a judgment enforcement law (corresponding to compulsory execution in Japan) and a bankruptcy law (an insolvency law that includes a reorganization type insolvency process), as well as policies for handling domestic cases. Below I will take a glance at the subsequent developments concerning the Civil Procedure Code (judgment enforcement law).

First, regarding the development of judicial officers, the establishment of a unified training system for judges, public prosecutors and lawyers modeled upon Japan's Legal Research and Training Institute was considered. It is possible that such a system could have the objective of sharing information about procedural processes

[44] Iseki, supra note 7 (*ICD News,* (26)) at 15 etc.

and develop human resources that can realize smooth procedural operation under the adversary system of the 2004 Code.

Joint seminars for Vietnamese drafters were conducted by the short-term Japanese experts, which had a main theme of the specifics of the "adversary system", and participants at that time were particularly interested in the "cross-examination in the trial" education provided in Japanese legal training. This presented the topic of the "adversarial principle" (2013 Vietnam Constitution, Article 103(5)) which is a continuing issue (i.e. the realization of an adversary system). As Vietnam has become a country having explicit law of the civil procedure code which is a formally "civil procedure with adversary system", this means that the genuine effort to make the system substantially adversarial has commenced. Particularly in civil trial under the adversary system, matters such as the specifics on how the judge's authority to ask for explanations should be utilized and the relationship with specific cases (e.g. cases related to a statute of limitations) have become a matter of great interest in Vietnam. However it would be the most important thing for all of lawyers to understand and realize adversary system on the base of self-determination and private autonomy.

At that time in order to make new civil procedure feasible, the "Unified Legal Training Institute" was debated and planned. This institute aimed to be the organ in which people wishing to become judges, public prosecutors and lawyers all undergo legal training in the same training period, like in Japan's Legal Research and Training Institute. However it did not see the light of day afterwards. Such a conclusion might have resulted from differences in the interests and expectations of the three types of legal officers, but it also seems that the opportunity to communize the image of the adversarial civil procedure was lost.

6.3.2 Activities Towards Developing Precedents

Afterwards, cassation instance precedents were disclosed for the first time as a "Cassation instance Judgment Law Report" which is covering the period of 2002–2006. Following the enactment of the new Civil Procedure Code in 2004, support of drafting judgments was given as Japan's legal system development support. As part of the results of this, a report[45] was published in 2007. This report was published in Vietnamese, English and Japanese.

As described in the Japanese title "Vietnamese-Japanese Joint Research on the Development of Precedents in Vietnam", this was a result of joint Vietnamese-Japanese research and had the purpose of providing information to the executive of the Supreme People's Court regarding the importance of introducing a system of precedents during judicial reform centered around a precedents system and the courts.

[45] JICA (2007) *Betonamu ni okeru Hanrei no Hatten ni kansuru Etsunichi Kyoudou Kenkyuu (Vietnam-Japan Joint Research Regarding the Development of Precedents in Vietnam)*.

This is linked to Japan's legal system development support currently being provided for the establishment of a "precedent system" which is a system for judgment of subordinate court not to conflict with the legal opinions expressed by the country's highest court in a similar case.[46]

6.3.3 2011 Partial Revision of the Civil Procedure Code

After the enactment of the 2004 Civil Procedure Code, Vietnam passed a revision in 2011 in order to establish a more convenient civil procedure code. I'd like to leave the details for another day, but the subjects of the revision were as follows.[47]

(1) Jurisdiction: addition of contended and non-contentious cases, expansion of the jurisdiction of the provincial-level people's courts, etc.
(2) The court's authority to reverse individual decisions of other agencies
(3) Expansion of the public prosecutor's role in the process
(4) Parties' rights: clarification of the parties' right to self-determination, guarantee of the parties' right to advocate
(5) Party's legal guardian of rights and interests
(6) Amendment of provisions regarding time limit for commencing a contended action, time limit for requirements of a non-contentious cases
(7) Amendment of provisions regarding return of a complaint
(8) Collection of evidence: collection of evidence by the court, and asset appraisal, etc.
(9) Provisions of conciliation process in order to promote conciliation
(10) Decision to stay a process
(11) Absence from the trial
(12) Appeal process
(13) Cassation instance process: grant of right for the party to submit a proposal to the objector while limiting the period for submitting proposals, etc.
(14) Special process for reconsidering a decision made by the Judges' Council of the Supreme People's Court
(15) Civil non-contentious cases process.

These revisions also referred to the opinions of the Japanese experts, but the revision provisions were independently drafted and passed by the Vietnamese side. This provided a glimpse of the shape of voluntary, autonomous civil procedure reform. It is thought that, on the one hand, there were aspects which strengthened the adversary system, but on the other hand, there were also aspects that strengthened and restored the authoritative system of the Vietnamese court.

---

[46] Id., at 112.

[47] Tatara (2013) Kaisei Betonamu Minji Soshouhou no Gaiyou (Outline of Vietnam's Revised Civil Procedure Code) in *Betnamu Roppou (Vietnam Law Code).*

6.3.4 2015 Partial Revision of the Civil Procedure Code

In 2013 a new Constitution was enacted and as a result Vietnam's National Assembly revised many laws towards realizing a legal structure that complied with the new Constitution.[48]

The overall structure of the 2015 Civil Procedure Code did not make changes to the previous system of civil procedure and non-contentious cases at its roots, and the fundamental frame of the 2004 Civil Procedure Code was maintained. The subjects of the revision were as follows.

(1) Enhancement of the adversarial principle: As the 2013 Constitution defines the "adversarial principle" as one of the principles that must be guaranteed in trial in People's Courts (Vietnam Constitution, Article 103(5)), while the provision regarding the right to advocate in the old Vietnamese Civil Procedure Code, Article 23a was assumed (Vietnam Civil Procedure Code, Article 24(1)), the rights of the parties to collect evidence etc., duty to notify the other parties, the duty to state opinions on evidence etc., were prescribed (Vietnam Civil Procedure Code, Article 24(2), (3)). There is a right to submit arguments focused upon evidence. Further, regarding the period for the trial in a contended action, the rights are clarified to include not only assertions based on facts and the submission of evidence at the trial, but also to give opinions on the evidence and the applicability of laws to the evidence (Vietnam Civil Procedure Code, Article 247(1)).

(2) Criteria that the court should apply to the handling of a case and clarification of authority aimed at the uniform application of the law: This included standards regarding articles of laws and regulations that should be applied, the introduction of the precedent system (see Sect. 5), and handling when a legal normative document that requires correction is discovered.

(3) Case handling by way of a summary process: In this, a civil procedure process conducted by a single judge, which is a single-judge procedure that excludes the two people's jurors (Vietnam Civil Procedure Code, Articles 103(1), (3) and 317) and a process for court approval of out-of-court conciliation (Vietnam Civil Procedure Code, Article 416 onwards) was introduced. This was an issue from the time that the 2004 Civil Procedure Code was enacted.

(4) Arrangement of jurisdictional provisions: The organization of the courts was reformed with the revision of the Law on the Organization of People's Courts in 2014. The appellate benches which until then had existed as a division of the Supreme People's Court became independent Superior People's Courts based in three locations. Those are located in Hanoi, Danang and Ho Chi Minh City. In addition the family-juvenile bench of court was established as the 6th specialized

---

[48]The following is according to Sakai (2016) 2015 Nen Betonamu Minji Soshouhou no Gaiyou (Outline of Vietnam's 2105 Civil Procedure Code), *ICD News*, (68), 43. According to this, following the 2011 revisions, the 2013 revision has approximately 100 extra articles compared to the 2004 Civil Procedure Code.

bench. The Civil Procedure Code was partially revised in accordance with these revisions.

Procedural reform for cases related to family law is progressing and it seemed that at one time establishment of a court corresponding to system of the Family Court in Japan was considered; however, eventually it stopped at being just established as a specialist bench of the court i.e. family and juvenile bench. The proceedings for family and personal status cases still currently use the provisions of the standard civil procedure because of no existence of the special family court procedure.

(5) Arrangement of laws regarding cassation instance: There was no change to the three categories of conditions for commencing a cassation instance procedure, namely (1) the conclusion of a decision conflicts with the substantive facts; (2) significant procedural error; or (3) error in the application of a law (see 2015 Civil Procedure Code, Article 326(1)), but regarding each category, an extra condition requiring infringement upon a party's right or a lawful right, or infringement upon the interests of the government or the public was added (Vietnam Civil Procedure Code, Article 326(1)). Further, a provision allowing the cassation instance to enter its own decision was also promulgated (Vietnam Civil Procedure Code, Article 343(5)).

The revisions to date have retained the court's leading position while making the trend towards enhancing the rights of the parties within the process consistent; it says for judges to respect the rights and intentions of parties, but at the same time it has been identified that the sense that the court must take the initiative itself rather than the parties is strongly-rooted.[49] For this reason follow-up research is desirable.

6.3.5 *Activity Towards Establishing a System of Precedents*

As already mentioned, the integration of the training system for human resources development to carry the system was planned immediately following the enactment of the 2004 Civil Procedure Code (see Sect. 1 above). Along with this, the development of precedents within Vietnamese judiciary was also searched for (see Sect. 2 above).

When the Act on the Organization of People's Courts took effect in 2015, the development of a "precedents system" was clearly defined as a duty of the Supreme People's Court. In short, it was provided that the Supreme People's Court is to select, summarize, and develop and publish as precedents the cassation instance decisions of the Judges' Council of the Supreme People's Court, judgments that have legal effect on each court and decisions that are standard so that each court can research and apply the precedents to a case in charge (Law on the Organization of People's Courts, Article 22(2)(c)). In accordance with this, the Supreme People's Court established the "Resolution on the Process for Selection, Publication and Application of Precedents" (effective December 2015).

[49] Id., at 48.

In Vietnam the National Assembly (Standing Committee of the National Assembly) has the authority to "interpret laws" according to the Constitution (Vietnam Constitution, Article 74(2)), and a fundamental thinking exists that the court does not have the authority to "interpret"; it seems that until now the court has not developed any approaches that illustrate rules for legal interpretation. This seems to be a problem related to the idea of the separation of powers of government and the definition, significance and legal source of precedents, and also an issue related to the significance and role of legal interpretation.

Even so, even for a country of codified law that does not adopt a system of case law, as it is impossible to prescribe within the law all of societal phenomena in advance, defining in detail the scope within which the interpretation of legal terminology will be accepted, in other words, identifying "interpretation rules", should be accepted as the duty of a judge. Further, in the resolution of specific individual cases, the identification of "law application rules" for applying specific provisions to specific found facts can be thought of as a regular method for judges to deliver decisions. Because each of these includes certain generic rules, they may become beneficial policies for decisions by other courts, so it is desirable that they will be published as "precedents". In addition, regarding "precedent decisions" (relief precedents) that identify special determinations in specific individual cases also, even though they have no versatility per se, it is possible that they may become reference materials for a notion, so it is desirable that they too be published.

Anyway precedents are a kind of public good.

Currently, legal system development support is being provided under special conditions imposed by the court regarding selection by the Vietnamese side of decisions that should become precedents and the fundamental thinking of a precedents system, in order to materialize the rule of law, secure equality under the law (Vietnam Constitution, Article 52), increase the predictability of decisions and make the standardization of judges' decisions possible. During this support, in the area of civil law it is desirable that the results of research regarding precedents within civil jurisprudence[50] and the results of research regarding "precedents" that were stipulated in Japanese legislation for the first time with the 1996 enactment of Japan's Code of Civil Procedure[51] be utilized.

6.4 Conclusion; Realization of an Adversary System?

The support of drafting Vietnam's civil procedure law is an interesting example of competition between the supporting countries which is called the donors. Vietnam received legal system development support from both the United States and Japan

[50]For example, see Hirai (2010) Minpou ni okeru 'Hanrei' Ron no Shindankai (New Stage in 'Precedent' Theory in Civil Law), in *Houritsugaku Kisoron no Kenkyuu* (*Research of Fundamental Legal Theory*) (p. 325). (originally published in 2010).

[51]For example, Takada et al. (2016) *Chuushaku Minji Soshouhou, Dai 5 Kan (Annotated Code of Civil Procedure, Vol. 5)*, p. 315 (written by Kazuhiko Teshigawara).

and reached the enactment of the 2004 Civil Procedure Code. When conducting support from multiple countries in this manner, it is presumed impossible to avoid problems like confusion on the recipient country's side and confrontation between the supporting countries.[52]

- However, regarding this point, the internal circumstances are unclear but it seems the Vietnamese side adopted a flexible position to skillfully avoid the confrontation between the supporting countries. Of course, in Vietnam's case a style where the supporting countries meet in one place to provide support did not occur, and moreover, because the support was limited to the supporting countries considering drafts prepared by the Vietnamese side and providing comments, it can be said that the adopted system inherently avoided any direct confrontation between the supporting countries.
  Furthermore, the interesting thing is that, according to the research of Professor Kaneko,[53] it is thought that Soviet Russian civil procedure laws i.e. the 1961 law "Soviet Union Basic Principles of Civil Procedure" and the 1964 law "Code of Civil Procedure of Russian Soviet Federal Socialist Republic" had a large influence upon the drafting of the civil procedure code by the Vietnamese side. These laws were civil procedure laws with an adversary system. For Vietnam these laws were a good prior example from a socialist country, as they were able to meet the demands of the United States regarding an adversary system. In doing so, because the degree of connectedness particularly between the civil procedure system that embodies the government's political system and the basic principles of civil procedure is not always strong, it seems it was not so difficult for Vietnam to clear the conditions set by the United States by the aspect of the form of civil procedure.
- Finally, I would like to look at what seems to have been the largest pending issue, namely the adversary system.
  During the enactment of the 2004 Code, within the conditions required of Vietnam by the United States was, as mentioned previously, "the transition from an inquisitorial system to an adversary system". However, this requirement was considerably abstract and the idea of an adversary system itself is ambiguous, and moreover, because so called inquisitorial systems which might be replaced as an authoritative system are not completely avoided in capitalist countries in the modern world, even though the elements of the adversary system are placed at the center of their civil procedure laws, it seems that there is a sense of a complimentary existence of adversarial and authoritative systems while contributing to the correct and prompt pre-trial, trial and judgment under civil procedure.[54]

---

[52]As a general finding, for example, Kagawa and Kaneko, supra note 1 at 2–3 (written by Yuka Kaneko).

[53]Kaneko, supra note 11 at 89.

[54]In Japan this is called a blend of the adversarial system and authoritative system, which is found to have a complementary relationship. That is, on the one hand, from the aspect of the substantive form of the case, the adversarial system (procedural jus dispondi, principles of advocacy) is suitable, while from a procedural aspect the authoritative system (progression by authority) is used. See Kawashima, supra note 23 at 297.

The central basic principle of American civil procedure is the "adversary system". This can be interpreted in Japanese as a "system that consists of structure of opposing parties", "system of confrontation structure between parties" and "system of competing arguments", but it is used as the fundamental way of thinking to express the adversarial system in American civil procedure. The same expression is similarly used in criminal procedure in the United States. Procedurally, the basic thinking is that the opposing parties each submit legal and factual assertions and evidence that benefit their own interests, and based upon this, a judge positioned as a neutral third party enters a judgment. Under this system in the United States, it seems that the civil procedure can be justified as a process of discovering the truth, and is evaluated as being not just a simple dispute resolution process, but also has the notion of an enlightened system for the realization of rights.[55]

Compared to Japanese law and continental law such as German law, the interesting part of American law, although it is an aspect that is unavoidable under the common law, is that fundamental rules regarding procedural jus dispondi and advocacy, which are discrete contents of the adversarial system, do not seem to exist.

For example, it is clear that, when looked at from a formal aspect, the principle of restriction to the subject of the suit (Japan Code of Civil Procedure, Article 246) within procedural jus dispondi does not exist in the United States. Rule 54 (c) of the United States Federal Rules of Civil Procedure provides that, as long as it is not a default judgment (namely, as long as the parties' right to attend court and submit arguments is guaranteed so as to realize the their right to day in court is realized), the court can provide relief which is not restricted to the subject of the suit.[56] However, regarding this legislation, within the common law a prerequisite to the grant of such relief is that there is no element of surprise in the process of argument between the parties, in other words, the opportunity for the opposing party to argue against such a grant of relief is substantially guaranteed and is clearly identified as a prerequisite condition of granting the relief.[57]

The interesting thing about American procedural law, which is deficient from a formal aspect but is functionally compensated for by the substantive aspects of the process of civil procedure, is that it differs from the relative resolution of disputes intended in countries such as Japan and in a sense creates an opportunity for leading towards an all-inclusive resolution of social disputes.[58] This has an aspect

---

[55]Asaka (2016) *Amerika Minji Tezuzukihou, Dai 3 Han (American Civil Procedural Law, 3rd ed.)*, p. 6.

[56]The same clause reads as follows. "A default judgment must not differ in kind from, or exceed in amount, what is demanded in the pleadings. Every other final judgment should grant the relief to which each party is entitled, even if the party has not demanded that relief in its pleadings".

[57]Taniguchi (2013) Amerika minso ni okeru atarashii kenri no seisei (Creation of new rights in American civil procedure). in *Minji tezuzukihou no kiso riron I: Minji tezuzukihou ronshuu – Dai 1 kan* Basic theory of civil procedure 1 (Essays on civil procedure – vol. 1), p. 125 (Originally published in 1970).

[58]Taniguchi, id., at 152 finds that modern American civil procedure intends to provide an all-inclusive resolution to social disputes (real disputes, not a dispute where the plaintiff has artificially cut out and removed aspects), and furthermore suggests this is not a legal fiction of simple resolution

that approaches the form of procedural resolution under the old law in Vietnam mentioned earlier. However, in order to realize the substantive guarantees of the self-determination and autonomy of the parties and the substantive, all-inclusive dispute resolution seen in the United States, there seems to be a large amount of reliance not only upon the capability of judges, but also the ability of the parties and in particular lawyers. In that way, the issues of human resource development and the practical permeation of the results of legislative amendments become apparent.

Also, Vietnam's 2004 Civil Procedure Code does not address the first principle of the principles of advocacy relating to the fact that should be base of judgment i.e. the "burden of pleading principle".[59] If the provisions regarding the parties' right to submit evidence and burden of proof (2004 Code, Article 6(1) and 79) are presupposed, it seems that the principle of separating facts and evidence, in other words, the principle of separating factual materials and evidentiary materials, has not been put into effect. But in reality, if facts are not asserted then the issue of dispute does not become clear, nor does what needs to be proven. Evidence establishes the facts that are the issue of dispute, and considering the burden of proof, the facts to be proven must be accepted; also, looking at the contents to be included in a written judgment (2004 Code, Article 238(5)), it is possible to recognize the substantive weight of the assertion of facts. Under Japanese law too, there is in fact no provisions on this point, but the fundamental principle is recognized in precedents and in grand and general theory there is theoretical argument regarding the identification of the facts in issue (criteria for separating the relevant facts in issue and indirect/tangential facts).[60] This fundamental idea can be substantively achieved if the function for preventing surprise regarding the fact is realized in the trial process. Accordingly, it is hard to imagine that the principles of advocacy regarding the fact are instantly contradicted by the absence of provisions regarding the first principle of the principles of advocacy regarding the fact. However, at the same time, securing the fundamental principle relied upon in actual trials in individual cases also conceives a large problem.

Moreover, in American law also, this point is not always clearly defined within the United States Federal Rules of Civil Procedure either.[61]

---

through the expansion of res judicata, but is attempting to realize a substantive resolution through the completeness of the trial facts. Civil procedure for Indian law within the United States is, as it were, a "public trial with all people gathered".

[59] Yoshimura, supra note 18 (*ICD News,* (26)) at 6; Kaneko, Note 11 at 88 etc.

[60] See Kawashima, supra note 23 at 436.

[61] For example, Rule 15 (b) of the United States Federal Rules of Civil Procedure provides as follows regarding pleadings and facts. "(1) If, at trial, a party objects that evidence is not within the issues raised in the pleadings, the court may permit the pleadings to be amended. The court should freely permit an amendment when doing so will aid in presenting the merits and the objecting party fails to satisfy the court that the evidence would prejudice that party's action or defense on the merits. The court may grant a continuance to enable the objecting party to meet the evidence. (2) When an issue not raised by the pleadings is tried by the parties' express or implied consent, it must be treated in all respects as if raised in the pleadings. A party may move—at any time, even after judgment—to amend the pleadings to conform them to the evidence and to raise an unpleaded issue. But failure to amend does not affect the result of the trial of that issue." Also, this seems to suggest that similar to when a party submits a motion, the importance of substantive factual assertions within the trial

Incidentally, it seems that the adversarial system in the United States is backed by the classical argument about the foundation of civil procedure. Classical research in the United States, particularly regarding the distinguished "form of adjudication", includes the classic work by Fuller.[62] According to this, the essential "form of adjudication" is "evidence and participation through rational argument" and this form can be best achieved by a certain set of procedural attributes, for example, the adversary system, a neutral adjudicator who has excellent understanding, justification of a decision and a retrospective decision. If so, the adversary system in the United States consists of "evidence and participation through rational argument", and if a fundamental structure of civil procedure to guarantee such participation is provided, it seems that judicial jurisdiction, judicial independence and an assurance of delivered judgments endorsed by retrospective reasoning will be fulfilled along with the requirements of the adversary system to eliminate the inquisitorial system. If this Fuller's theory does not include the principle of adjudicative restriction to the subject of the suit or the principle of assertions but has evidence and participation as the central elements, it seems that Vietnam's 2004 Civil Procedure Code, which appears to provide a "deliberation forum" where related parties get entangled in a wide civil procedure process, can be evaluated as having cleared the fundamental conditions instructed by the United States.[63]

Moreover, in the United States, it seems there is also a background where the prominence of public law litigation/structural reform litigation/institutional reform litigation together with a kind of an authoritative system was not evaluated that negatively. This is transformation in the adversary system in the United States, as well as the removal of poly-centric disputes from the subject of civil procedure as lacking the essential attributes of Fuller's "form of adjudication" theory, and provided the highly-respected opportunity to incorporate contended cases.[64]

Having come to view it in this way, the frustration between the supporting countries and Vietnam of living together but in different worlds or the flexibility of the recipient country in order to realize the results can be felt.[65]

The persevering effort to practically realize the civil procedure law can be felt from the subsequent reform of Vietnam's civil procedure law including strengthening

---

is greater than the formal contents of the pleadings. This seems to suggest the importance of the parties' right to submit evidence that is mentioned below.

[62] Fuller (1978) The Forms and Limits of Adjudication, *Harvard Law Review*, *92*, 353.

[63] Findings of fact in American civil procedure is conducted on a "preponderance of the evidence", which is understood as being lower than the "high probability" level of proof under Japanese law. Kawashima, supra note 23 at 467. In the United States also, comparing the mildness of legislation regarding factual assertions, emphasis is placed on the value of the evidence. This is also the value of Discovery.

[64] Chayes (1976) The Role of the Judge in Public Law Litigation, *Harvard Law Review*, *89*, 1281; Damaška (1986) *The Faces of Justice and State Authority: A Comparative Approach to the Legal Process*. Also see Kawashima (2016) *Koukyou Soshou no Kyuusai Houri (Jurisprudence of Relief in Institutional reform Litigation)*, p. 43.

[65] It has been identified that there is a "trend for the adversarial system to be nothing more than additional formal conditions". See Kaneko, supra note 11 at 119.

of parties' rights and reinforcement of the authoritative system. Also, the activity towards publishing precedents is useful for judicial system and it would be able to trace the reality of civil process from the results. Such an activity also can be thought of as being inspection and supervision work.

I want to keep watch over the future developments.

References

Asaka, K. (2016). *Amerika minji tezuzukihou, dai 3 han (American civil procedural law* (3rd ed.). Tokyo: Koubundou.

Chayes, A. (1976). The role of the judge in public law litigation. *Harvard Law Review, 89,* 1281.

Damaška, M. R. (1986). *The faces of justice and state authority: A comparative approach to the legal process*. New Haven: Yale University Press.

Dang, Q. P. (2005). lecture: Betonamu minji soshouhou no seitei to shikou ni okeru Betonamu saikou jinmin saibansho no yakuwari (Role of the supreme people's court in the enactment and operation of Vietnam's civil procedure code). *ICD News, 20,* 32–38.

Fuller, Lon L. (1978). The forms and limits of adjudication. *Harvard Law Review, 92,* 353.

Hirai, Y. (2010). *Houritsugaku kisoron no kenkyuu (Research of fundamental legal theory)*. Tokyo: Yuhikaku.

Inaba, K. (2008). Houseibi shien jigyou no ima (Current legal system development support projects). *Jurist* (1358).

Inoue, H. (1993). *Minji tezuzukiron (Civil process theory)*. Tokyo: Yuhikaku.

International Cooperation Department, Ministry of Justice. (2005). Houseibi shien katsudou nenhyou (Annual table of legal system development support). *ICD News, 20,* 196–197.

Iseki, M. (2005). Nihonhou to Hikakushite no Tokuchou; Saibankan, Kantokushin, Kinkyuu Hozen Shobun (Features compared to Japanese law; Judges, cassation and emergency preservation disposition). *ICD News, 21,* 58–90.

Iseki, M. (2006). Betonamu minji soshouhou no shourai no mondai (Future issues for Vietnam's civil procedure code). *ICD News, 26,* 13–26.

Kagawa, K., & Kaneko, Y. (Eds.). (2007). *Houseibi shien ron; Seido kouchiku no kokusai kyouryoku nyuumon (Legal system development support theory; Introduction to international support of system development)*. Tokyo: Minerva Shobo.

Kaino, M. (2001). "Houseibi shien" to hikakuhougaku no kadai (Legal system development support and comparative law issues). *Asia Keizai, 42*(1), 52–62. https://ci.nii.ac.jp/naid/40000088038.

Kaneko, Y. (2010). *Ajia no houseibi to houhatten* (Asian legal system development and legal development). University Education Press.

Kawashima, S. (2001). Houseibi shien to sono purosesu wo tsuujita naisei-teki shiza no kakutoku; Minji soshou hou kenkyuusha no shiten kara (Acquisition of introspective viewpoints from legal system development support and its process; Viewpoint from a civil procedure law researcher). *ICD News, 48,* 1–4.

Kawashima, S. (2007). Nihon ni okeru houseibi shien no kadai to tenbou ni tsuite (Issues and views regarding Japanese legal system development support). *Housei Kenkyuu, 73*(4), 685–714.

Kawashima, S. (2013). *Minji soshouhou (Civil procedure law)*. Tokyo: Nihon Hyoron Sha.

Kawashima, S. (2016). *Koukyou soshou no kyuusai houri (Jurisprudence of relief in institutional reform litigation)*. Tokyo: Yuhikaku.

Kusano, Y. (2003). *Wakai gijutsuron, dai 2 han (Conciliation techniques theory* (2nd ed.). Tokyo: Shinzansha.

Maruyama, T. (2005). Betonamu minji soshouhou seitei; Waga kuni no kisou shien (Vietnam's civil procedure law enactment; Japan's drafting support). *ICD News, 21,* 5–9.

Ozaki, M. (2002). Houmusho Sougou Kenkyuusho Kokusai Kyouryoku-bu ni okeru min-shouji hou wo chuushinn ni shita houseibi shien katsudou ni tsuite (Legal system development support centered upon civil and commercial law by the International Cooperation Department of the Ministry of Justice's Research and Training Institute). *Hou no Shihai, 126,* 5–16.

Sakai, H. (2005). Betonamu minji soshouhou seitei; Hishou/kokusai minji soshouhou oyobi hanketsu shikou tezuzuki no gaisetsu (Establishment of Vietnam's civil procedure code; Outline of non-contentious cases, international civil procedure law and judgment execution processes). *ICD News, 21,* 85.

Sakai, H. (2006). Betonamu minji soshouhou no shourai no kaisei mondai (Future revision issues for Vietnam's civil procedure code). *ICD News, 26,* 27.

Sakai, N. (2016). 2015 nen Betonamu minji soshouhou no gaiyou (Outline of Vietnam's 2105 civil procedure code). 68 *ICD News*, (68), 43.

Takada, H., Miki, K., Yamamoto, K., & Yamamoto, K. (2016). *Chuushaku minji soshouhou, dai 5 kan* (Annotated code of civil procedure, Vol. 5). Tokyo: Yuhikaku.

Taniguchi, Y. (2013). *Minji Tezuzukihou no Kiso Riron I (Minji Tezuzukihou Ronshuu – Dai 1 Kan) (Basic theory of civil procedure 1 (Essays on civil procedure – Vol. 1)*. Tokyo: Shinzansha (Originally published in 1970).

Tatara, S. (2013). Kaisei Betonamu minji soshouhou no gaiyou (Outline of Vietnam's revised civil procedure code). In JICA, Technical Assistance for the Legal and Judicial System Reform (Ed) *Betnamu roppou* (Vietnam law code).

Yoshimura, T. (2005). Betonamu minji soshouhou seitei; Seiritsu no haikei to tokuchou—Dai-Ichi Shin ni okeru shinri tezuzuki wo chuushinn toshite (Establishment of Vietnam's civil procedure code; Background to realization and its features, focused upon the trial process at first instance). *ICD News, 21,* 10–57.

Yoshimura, T. (2006). Betonamu minji soshouhou no kongo no kadai; Nihon minji soshouhou tono hikakuhouteki shiten kara (Future issues for Vietnam's civil procedure code; From a comparative law viewpoint of comparison with Japan's code of civil procedure). *ICD News, 26,* 2–12.

Yoshimura, T. (2011). *Hikaku minji tetsuzukihou (Comparative civil process law)*. Tokyo: Shinzansha.

Chapter 7
Issues of Compulsory Execution in Myanmar: A Comparative Approach from Practical Viewpoints

Yoshifumi Akanishi

7.1 Introduction

Each nation has its' own civil execution system which reflects its history and socio-economic system. On the other hand, in a certain degree, there are similarities in devices directed to the same purposes, including attachment and sales. Especially for developing countries, civil execution system is expected to change with the progress of internationalization of economy. As the economic relationship between Japan and Myanmar is deepened through increasing investments, now is the time to try compare the civil execution systems both countries to consider the needs for legal reform movement which is already being sought between both governments.

Compulsory execution in Japan deals primarily with execution of monetary claims and the compulsory execution law prescribes primarily about execution against real property. Further, the structure of attachment and sale of subject real property is thought of as being to some extent a versatile process even in compulsory execution systems outside of Japan. On this occasion, limited to the above situation, this paper will attempt to compare points noticed in the processes under Japanese and Myanmar law, primarily focusing on the efficiency of execution. However, due to limitations in the available materials and lack of examination, there may be several misunderstandings, and I await everyone's findings and will accept them as future areas of examination.

This paper is an only attempt of comparative view from practical viewpoints, and does not enter into a comprehensive structural comparison of the details.

Yoshifumi Akanishi—Professor of Law, Kinki University, Japan; Former Presiding Justice at Osaka High Court; LL.B. Kyoto University; LL.M., Kyoto University.

Y. Akanishi (✉)
Kinki University Law School, Higashi Osaka, Japan
e-mail: marzo_1@kindai.ac.jp

Y. Kaneko (ed.), *Civil Law Reforms in Post-Colonial Asia*,
Kobe University Monograph Series in Social Science Research,
https://doi.org/10.1007/978-981-13-6203-3_7

7.2 Myanmar's Compulsory Execution System

7.2.1 Overview

Myanmar's compulsory execution system[1] is defined in the *Code of Civil Procedure* (India Act V of 1908) as contained in Volume XII of the *Burma Code* (hereinafter referred to as "the CPC", as is customary); besides the main clauses of the CPC, compulsory execution is primarily prescribed in the Rules contained in Order 21 (In this paper, the main clauses of the CPC are referred to as "Sections" and Rules within an Order will be referred to by the Order and Rule number; however regarding compulsory execution the Rules in Order 21 will be referred to by omitting "Order 21"). The materials examined include the "Status Paper" and "Report" mentioned in Footnote 1, a document received from the Yangon Western District Court (a pamphlet titled "The Procedure of the Court in Execution" written by Judge Daw Swe Swe of the same Court, hereinafter referred to as the "District Court Pamphlet") during our visit to Myanmar in February 2017,[2] and knowledge obtained from a discussion with judges of the same Court at a roundtable meeting that was arranged during the same visit.[3] Discussion of the compulsory execution system within Japan will be limited in this paper to providing a brief explanation where necessary. In Japan, the number of cases concerning compulsory execution against real property is decreasing (according to the judicial statistics for Fiscal Year 2015 there were 2,278 outstanding cases that year), and although there were more cases of exercising security interests via auction of real property (21,222 outstanding cases according to the same statistics), the execution of security is subject to the compulsory execution provisions. Regarding the execution of security in Japan, even if there is no document that evidences the right to claim (Title of Obligation), a creditor can apply for an auction sale if there is a document that evidences the security interest (e.g. a certificate of registered matters). On this point, in Myanmar execution based on a mortgage is prescribed in Order 34, but there does not appear to be any provisions that allow execution based on a security interest itself without a Decree, therefore it is necessary to sue for a Decree that orders an auction and the amount to be repaid.[4] This scenario will be excluded from this examination.

---

[1]Regarding Myanmar's execution system, refer to page 45 onwards of *Status Paper on the Civil and Commercial Dispute Resolution System in Myanmar* by Yukawa et al. in Nishimura & Asahi law firm (2015) http://www.moj.go.jp/content/001179166.pdf (hereafter referred to as the "Status Paper"); and page 204 onwards of Chapter 5 "Civil Procedure and Arbitration Law in Myanmar" of *2012 Report on the Legal System in the Republic of the Union of Myanmar* by Mori Hamada & Matsumoto law firm (2013) http://www.moj.go.jp/content/000110250.pdf (hereinafter referred to as the "Report").

[2]The author studied the Myanmar legal system in a group of three with Professor Yuka Kaneko, Graduate School of International Cooperation Studies, Kobe University, and Professor Shiro Kawashima, Faculty of Law, Doshisha University.

[3]If there are errors in this paper concerning the results of the discussion, such errors are the responsibility of the author.

[4]See page 62 onwards of the "Status Paper".

7.2.2 *Purpose and Scope of Compulsory Execution for Monetary Claims*

While in Japan a compulsory execution is a process to compulsorily realize a claim (monetary claim) and the debtor's property is subject to execution of a monetary claim, in Myanmar also, the purpose of execution is to realize a monetary claim that was determined by way of a court judgment, but in the CPC it is described as the execution of a Decree (Section 38).[5] Decrees for the payment of money can be executed by detention in a civil prison or attachment and sale of the judgment-debtor's property (Rule 30) ("judgment-debtor" is hereinafter referred to as the "debtor"). Accordingly, both the debtor's property and the debtor's physical self are within the scope of execution.[6]

"Decree" is defined in Section 2(2)(9) as a formal expression of an adjudication which determines the rights of the parties that are contesting a suit in the Court, and is issued by a judge based on a judgment. Further, Order 20 Rule 6(1) defines that a decree must contain the name of the suit, the names of the parties, particulars of the claim, and clear specification of the relief granted or other determination of the suit. A decree is not the judgment itself, but is understood as an order for execution based on the judgment.[7]

In Japan, a Title of Obligation, such as that issued pursuant to a final judgment, is a requirement for execution and is a document that notarizes a right of claim for the purpose of execution; because a decree itself is expressed as being for the purpose of execution, it can be thought of as being a little different in concept to a Title of Obligation. However, as a decree is a public document that describes the details of the relief that should be realized via execution and is executed on this basis, it may be appropriate to say that it corresponds in function to a Title of Execution (a Title of Obligation with a certificate of execution attached).[8]

7.2.3 *Jurisdiction*

In Japan there is exclusive jurisdiction (Article 19 of the Civil Execution Act). Therefore, for execution against real property for a monetary claim, the District Court that has jurisdiction over the location in which the real property is located has juris-

---

[5] In the CPC, general provisions concerning compulsory execution are defined in Section 36 onwards, and detailed provisions are defined in the Rules of Order 21.

[6] Nakano and Shimomura (2016) *Minji Shikouhou* (Civil Execution Act) Supplementary Edition 6, Seirin Shoin, on p. 6 says "Execution that makes a person (their life, body or labour) the subject of execution (i.e. execution against the person) is not only inconsistent with our cultural notions, but because of its ineffectiveness it is generally concealed in the shadows.".

[7] Kenta (2016) Adversary System in Myanmar Civil Trials (1). *ICD News,* (68), p. 72.
For a specific example of a decree, see Attachment IV-2-15 of the "Status Paper".

[8] Of course this is a figurative expression and there is no process for granting a certificate of execution.

diction, but when several pieces of land and or buildings are subject to execution, discretionary transfer is permitted (Article 44 of the same act). In Myanmar the court that issues a decree has jurisdiction, but when executing against real property outside of the court's geographical jurisdiction, the decree may be sent to another court upon the application of the decree-holder (Sections 38, 39) (The "decree-holder" here refers to a judgment-creditor, but will hereinafter be referred to as the "creditor".). Also, where the real property is located across the jurisdiction of two or more courts, it is provided that any court may order the attachment and sale of the entire real property (Rule 3). Therefore, jurisdiction lies with both the judgment court and the court where the real property is located, but it is thought that in principle the court with jurisdiction is the one that delivers the judgment. In Myanmar, there is a time limit for applying for execution, which in principle is 3 years from the day that the decree is issued but may be extended to 12 years in some circumstances, after which time an order for execution cannot be issued (it will be dismissed pursuant to Section 48 and Articles 182, 183 of the First Schedule of the Limitation Act). In Japan, execution is possible as long as the right of claim has not been extinguished by a time limitation. But, an effect of extinguishment of the right of claim can't be arise until the debtor alleges against the creditor that the right of creditor is extinguished due to the lapse of time period (Civil Code Article 145). And whether the effect of extinguishment of the right of claim due to the lapse of period is determined not by the execution court, but by the institution that issued the Certificate of Execution (e.g. the clerk of the judgment court) (Articles 25, 26 of the Civil Execution Act).[9]

7.2.4 *Executive Agency*

In Japan the executive agency is the execution court and court execution officer (Article 2 of the Civil Execution Act). The execution court differs from the court that formulated the final judgment or other Title of Obligation (judgment court). The execution court performs execution with the aim of effectively realizing the relevant right of claim based on the Title of Obligation formed from the judgment.

As described above, in Myanmar the execution court is in principle the court that issued the decree (and a court which receives transfer of a decree) (Section 38), and the court which issues a decree is the same court that delivers judgment. Therefore, during the execution process the execution court must also determine substantive objections and the court has accumulated large discretion to order a stay of the execution, which can be thought of as a background factor for causing delays. In Myanmar, the division of the roles of the execution court and court execution officer are not clearly defined in the legislation.

[9]On the other hand, I think, the fact of lapse of time period and debtor's allegation is an easy to judge, so, if execution court find out the aforesaid facts, the court also can dismiss the application (in my opinion).

7.2.5 *Appeals/Objections and Stay (Suspension) of Proceedings*

In Japan, objections to the disposition of an execution and appeals against disposition of an execution are the avenues of appeal against procedural issues. Such objections and appeals do not have the effect of staying execution as a matter of course (the court has the authority to stay execution pursuant to Articles 10(6) and 11(1) of the Civil Execution Act). In an appeal against disposition of an execution, there is provision for the court to dismiss the appeal if it has been filed for the purpose of delaying the execution procedure (Article 10(5) of the same act).

Avenues for appeal based on substantive reasons (e.g. absence or extinguishment of a right of claim, or a third party possesses a right that obstructs the delivery of the property subject to execution) include actions to oppose execution (Article 35 of the Civil Execution Act), third-party actions against execution (Article 38 of the same act) and actions to oppose a grant of a certificate of execution (Article 34 of the same act). Actions to oppose execution and third-party actions against execution are law suits where the creditor is the opposing party (An action to oppose execution disputes, for example, whether there is a right to claim, and is filed in the court that delivered judgment. A third-party action against execution is a claim that the third party has ownership or some other right over the subject property which obstructs assignment of the property and seeks rejection of the compulsory execution; it is filed in the execution court.). These actions do not stay the execution as a matter of course, but the person who raises the objection may apply to the court hearing the objection for a provisional stay of execution (Article 36(1) of the same act), or must submit an authenticated copy of a successful judgment to the executive agency and request a stay or revocation of the execution (Articles 39(1) and 40(1) of the same act).

In Myanmar, it appears that procedural objections and substantive objections are not clearly separated in the legislation in the way that they are in the Japanese law. This may be because the execution court and judgment court are not separated. Also, it appears that the provisions for staying execution when an objection is filed are not as organized as they are under Japanese law. In Myanmar, there are provisions for third-party objections to an attachment (Rules 58–62) and Rule 63 specifies that a person dissatisfied with the determination of an objection may commence a law suit.[10] According to Rule 58(1), when investigating a third-party objection, the court can examine the parties and other relevant persons in the same manner as a law suit, and as a result has the authority to postpone the sale of property (Rule 58(2)), which in practice does not differ greatly from the Japanese law. However, the creditor is not named as a party to the objection like in Japan, but instead it is a process of objecting to execution; further, there are no provisions regarding stay or revocation of the process that are individually defined for each of the methods of objection. There

[10]See pp. 208–209 of the “Report”.

is a provision for dismissing an objection that is filed for the purpose of delaying execution (Rule 58(1)).

In Myanmar law, stays of the execution process are defined in Rules 26–29. According to these rules, the court that receives a decree for the purpose of execution shall, upon sufficient cause being shown, stay the execution for a reasonable time to enable the debtor to apply to the court that issued the decree or a court of appellate jurisdiction for a stay of execution (Rule 26). Further, if a suit is pending between the creditor and debtor, the court may accept a security and stay execution until the pending suit is decided (Rule 29). The court therefore has a very large scope of authority to stay execution (according to Section 151, in Myanmar the court generally has a wide discretion to make orders necessary for the ends of justice or to prevent abuse of the process of the court.). However, the relationship a stay of execution has with substantive objections and suits is not clear, and it seems that the substantive provisions regarding when a stay should be ordered and for how long are insufficient (but there are individual provisions such as Rule 58(2) mentioned above).

In Japan, excluding stays under the authority of the court (for example, in appeals against a disposition of execution under Article 10(6) and actions to oppose a grant of a certificate of execution under Article 32(2) of the Civil Execution Act), execution may be stayed based on an application for a provisional stay of execution (Article 36(1) of the same act) and when a document staying execution is submitted to the execution court (Article 39 of the same act). Other than the authority to stay an execution that derives from an objection to a disposition of execution, the execution court does not make a substantial decision regarding a stay of execution; rather the substantial decision is left to the judgment of the appeal court or the court that receives the action to oppose execution, etc. In other words, even if an appeal against the execution process is submitted, the execution is not stayed as a matter of course on the basis of the appeal submission itself. This is due to consideration for the efficient progression of the execution process.

In Myanmar, unlike under Japanese law, regardless of whether it is a procedural objection or substantive objection, the submission of an order staying execution is not required to stay the execution, and if an objection is submitted or there is another pending suit between the creditor and debtor, the execution court is either obliged to stay execution or has the discretion to do so (however, the wording of Rule 29 can be read as the court mentioned in the Rule refers to the court that received the objection). Then, if waiting for the result of the objection or appeal takes a considerable amount of time, this too can be said to be a factor in causing delay. That the execution court and judgment court are not separated may be thought of as a background factor, but establishing requirements for a stay of execution based on the filing of an appeal or submission of an objection are desirable.

In Myanmar, when an objection is submitted concerning a procedural issue and the decision is appealed, the entire record of the case is sent to the responsible court, meaning the execution process cannot practically proceed (information received during the discussion with the Yangon Western District Court judges). On this point, in Japan, Article 7 of the Rules of Civil Execution provides that "If an appeal against a disposition of execution is filed and the execution court finds no need to send the record of the civil execution case, it is sufficient for the court clerk of the execution court to send only the record of the appeal case to the court clerk of the court of appeal." in order to prevent suspension of the process.

In Japan, appeals against a decision on an objection to a disposition of execution are in principle not allowed (as an exception, Article 12(1) of the Civil Execution Act allows an appeal against an order to rescind a civil execution procedure) and re-appealing an appeal against a disposition of execution is also in principle not allowed (as an exception, Article 10(8) of the same act allows an appeal against a dismissal). It seems that no such limits apply in Myanmar.

7.2.6 Classification of Subject and Mode of Compulsory Execution

In Japan, monetary execution and non-monetary execution (delivery, surrender, manifestation of intention, action/inaction) are separated by the type of Title of obligation (type of right of claim); monetary execution is further classified into execution against real property, execution against movables and execution against a claim based on the type of property that is subject to the execution. Modes of execution against real property are compulsory auction (attachment and sale) and compulsory administration.

In Myanmar, under the heading of "Procedure of Execution" in the CPC, the authority of the court is to, upon application of a creditor to execute a decree, order the (1) delivery of property, (2) attachment and sale or sale without attachment of property[11] (3) civil detention, (4) appointment of a receiver, or (5) other action appropriate to the nature of the relief granted (Section 51). Within these, in (1) and (5) the details of the right of claim can be considered consistent with the mode of execution, but (2), (3) and (4) are not details of a right of claim but a mode of execution. Further, within Order 21 under the heading of "Mode of Execution", Rule 30 onwards defines execution methods corresponding to the classification of the contents of the decree. That is, decrees are classified into decrees for the payment of money (Rule 30), decrees for specific movable property (Rule 31), decrees for specific performance of a contract, restitution of conjugal rights, or an injunction (Rules 32, 33), decrees concerning a document or negotiable instrument (Rule 34), decrees for delivery of real property (Rule 35) and decrees for delivery of real property in the occupancy of a tenant (Rule 36), with execution methods defined for each type of decree. Amongst those, concerning a decree for the payment of money (monetary claim), it is prescribed that attachment and sale of the debtor's property, civil detention, or both can be applied.[12] According to the "District Court Pamphlet", beyond that an order for payment in installments (over a period of 6 months) is also a stand-alone execution method for a monetary claim. Decrees for payment in installments are defined in

[11]According to the judges of Yangon Western District Court, "sale without attachment" means the mode of execution for security right.

[12]See pages 205–207 of the "Report" for a translation of this part of the CPC.

Order 20, Rule 11, and according to this provision, when issuing a decree for the payment of money the court may order payment in installments; also, after issuance of a decree for the payment of money, upon application of the debtor and after notice to the creditor, the court may order payment in installments after adding such conditions as the attachment of the debtor's property or taking of a security. According to the discussion with the Yangon Western District Court judges, in most cases the debtor will apply for payment in installments and the court often allows this. There are also often objections from both the creditor and debtor regarding the order for payment in installments (the debtor objecting to the conditions of the installments), and awaiting the result of the investigation, decision and appeal of the decision requires time, which becomes a cause of delay. Further, as the creditor must wait (for 6 months) to see whether the debtor defaults on the payment of the installments before being able to execute, this is also a cause of delay.

Concerning modes of execution, Section 51 contains general provisions and Order 21 Rule 30 onwards contains separate provisions applicable to specific decrees, but the relationship between the right of claim and mode/subject of execution is not always clear; apart from the legislation there are execution methods that are used in practice (e.g. payment in installments), which gives the feeling that, different from the law in Japan, there is a deficiency regarding classification based on the right of claim and subject of execution. However, in Myanmar, such classification is, from a practical standpoint, prescribed in detailed execution methods that correspond to the specific contents of the decree.

Regarding payment in installments, in the case of a Title of obligation for payment in installments in Japan, the creditor can seek execution on a certificate of execution alone, without having to allege or prove that the debtor has failed to make installment payments (Supreme Court decision delivered 15 December 1966 reported in *Minshu* Vol. 20, No. 10, p. 20 "debtor must prove the fulfillment for installment payment"). Further, regarding a Title of Obligation for simple repayment, the execution court cannot permit a change to payment by installments ex officio. The parties may reach an agreement between themselves, but in such case, the creditor must withdraw the execution, or the debtor must prepare and submit to the court a record of proceedings of settle the case (Article 39(1)(iv) of the Civil Execution Act), or a document granting a grace of performance (Clause (1)(viii) of the same article) in order to obtain a stay of execution.

7.2.7 *Flow of the Compulsory Execution Process for Execution Against Real Property for Monetary Claims*

A. In Japan, the sale of real property is generally performed in the following pattern: (Article numbers refer to the Civil Execution Act except where specified)

(1) The creditor sends the Title of Obligation (e.g. final judgment) and Certificate of Execution to the debtor, identifies the real property that is subject to execution, and applies for compulsory execution to the court that has jurisdiction over the location of the real property (Articles 22, 26, 29, 43 and 44)
(2) The court issues a commencement order for compulsory execution and attachment declaration (Article 45)
(3) Court investigation of claim: The court determines and gives public notice of a time limit for demands for liquidating distribution, and a notice requiring the notification of claims (Article 49)
(4) Court preparation for sale: Investigation of the current conditions (court execution officer), order for appraisal (appraiser), description of the property (court clerk) (Articles 57, 58 and 62)
(5) The court determines a standard sales price (Article 60)
(6) The sale is performed (court clerk, court execution officer) (Article 64, etc.)
(7) Bidding and bid opening (Article 66, Rules of Civil Execution Articles 44–48, etc.)
(8) Permission for sale is determined (Articles 69–71, etc.)
(9) Payment of the purchase price (Article 78)
(10) Delivery order (Article 83)
(11) Distribution of the proceeds (Article 84).

B. Comparison with Myanmar System (Identification of points from a comparative law stance, following the pattern of execution in Japan described above.)

(1) Concerning decrees for payment of money, the creditor applies for compulsory execution to the court that issued the decree, with a copy of the decree attached (Section 38 and Rules 10, 11),[13] and the court issues a process to commence execution; the process must bear the date on which it was issued, be signed by the judge, sealed with the seal of the court, and delivered to the "proper officer" (it is unclear whether this means an execution officer) (Rule 24).

The order for an execution commencement process can be thought of as corresponding to the commencement order for compulsory execution under Japanese law, but according to the above Rule, unlike in Japan, it appears that an order for attachment of the real property subject to execution is not described in the execution commencement process. This may instead be according to the order for attachment issued in relation to the separately conducted application for attachment (Rule 54).

An application for compulsory execution is in principle made in writing (Rule 11(2)). Within the application, the creditor selects from the execution modes defined in Section 51 (in the case of execution against real property pursuant to Rule 11(2)(j), the options are attachment and sale or sale without attachment, civil detention, or

[13] See Attachment IV-10-(5)-(b) of the "Status Paper" for an actual example.

both). If the creditor selects attachment and sale of the real property, they apply for attachment and specify the applicable real property by identifying the lot number or attaching a map (Rule 13(1)).[14]

(2) A court which receives an application (in principle the court of first instance that issued the decree) shall summons the parties.[15]

Concerning the summons, Rule 22 defines that where an application is made more than 3 years have passed since the date the decree was issued, the court shall give notice to the person against whom the application is made and require them to provide a reason why the decree should not be executed. However, rather than being limited to these circumstances, summons are widely used as a preliminary process before commencing execution (page 49 of the "Status Paper", and information obtained from the discussion with the Yangon Western District Court judges); the debtor rarely appears at this time, but often appears after the execution commencement process has been issued (page 49 of the "Status Paper"). Regarding summonses, where a decree is for the payment of money and the creditor selects civil detention, the debtor must be summonsed as a preliminary process in order to be given notice and the opportunity to be heard (Section 51, Rule 40); it is further prescribed that when attachment is selected, the creditor can apply for the debtor or other person to be summonsed to attend court for oral examination regarding whether the debtor has any property or other means of satisfying the decree (Rule 41). These provisions can be read as being performed after execution has commenced and civil detention or attachment is used as the individual execution method, and are separate from the general summons issued at the time of commencing the execution procedure.

Japan's system does not have a summons as a process to commence execution, but this is because the subject of execution is the debtor's property, which the creditor specifies when applying to commence execution, so summonsing the debtor is unnecessary. In Myanmar, it is inferred that a summons is a prerequisite to the decision to commence execution, but when looking at the practice described above, it is actually more often performed after execution has commenced, so it seems that the difference from the abovementioned summons issued when detention or attachment is selected is unclear. If the operation of the abovementioned payment in installments is also considered, in Myanmar the court's discretion in the operation of the execution process is large and the circumstances of the debtor are given as much consideration as possible, but the role of the summons system and a detailed description of its operation in the provisions seem insufficient. In its operation, the time required for a summons seems a factor causing delay in the process.

Summons for an attachment can also be read as being used as a property disclosure method; on this point Japan has a similar property disclosure procedure (Civil Execution Act Article 196 onwards). However, the system is not used often, and there are strong opinions that the conditions for non-fulfillment and sanctions (a non-penal fine of 300,000 yen or less) should be revised. Further, currently in executions against

[14] See Attachment IV-10-(6) of the "Status Paper" for an actual example.

[15] See pages 48–49 of the "Status Paper".

a claim, a system is being considered where the court can make enquires with banks etc. regarding the savings account information of a debtor who breaches an obligation to pay money. The status of the use of Rule 41 in Myanmar is a point of interest.

(3) Attachment

In Japan, when commencement is ordered the attachment of the subject real property is declared and registration of the attachment is commissioned (Articles 45(1) and 48 of the Civil Execution Act). During this it is proclaimed that the auction process has been commenced. The attachment becomes effective when the debtor is served with the commencement order, or when the attachment is registered, whichever is earlier (Article 46(1) of the same act).

Registration as a public notice is important as any further transfer, offering as security or grant of usufructory rights between the debtor and a third party essentially cannot countervail the execution process.

In Myanmar, there appears to be no provisions defined regarding the registration of attachment based on the authority of the court (Section 17(1) of the Registration Act includes "order of a court that contains a limit on a right related to immoveable property" as a document subject to mandatory registration, which seems to apply to attachment[16] but is not interpreted that way in Myanmar[17]). Therefore, in Myanmar, even if an attachment order is issued as a compulsory execution method, it seems the public notice of such cannot be said to be sufficient. In Myanmar, the provisions on attachment prohibit actions such as the debtor transferring rights in the subject property to a third party or setting the property as security, have the effect of prohibiting a third party from gaining a benefit from any such actions by the debtor, and specify that the attachment is to be proclaimed by traditional methods such as beating a drum and by affixing a copy of the attachment order to the subject property (Rule 54(2)); however this system of public notification cannot be thought of as sufficient. The attachment becomes effective against transferees of the property without consideration from the date of the attachment order, and against all other persons from the time they reasonably should have had knowledge of the attachment order or the time that the order was proclaimed by the beating of a drum or other method defined in Rule 54(2), whichever is the earlier (Rule 54(3)). However, according to the above provisions, it seems that in many cases persons who receive a transfer of rights or a security via a transaction with the debtor (who conceals the existence of the attachment) are actually unaware of the existence of the attachment order at the time of the transaction.[18] Further, because the attachment is not registered, it

[16]See Mori Hamada & Matsumoto law firm's Yangon office "Front Line of Myanmar Law", p. 225.

[17]But, according to Yuka (2017) "Issues of the Civil Execution System in Myanmar" published in *Kokusai Kyouryoku Ronsyuu*, Kobe University Graduate School of International Cooperation, A registration office (under the office of Agricultural Land Management and Statistics of Myeik District in Tanintharyi Region) transcribes the attachment order to the Record 1A by the court's request. So, we need to confirm the status of practice of the registration office at that point.

[18]According to p. 60 of the "Status Paper", in the case of land the execution officer erects upon the land a notice with the attachment order affixed, so if the site is inspected then the existence of the attachment should be clear.

seems that persons who acquire ownership of the subject property from the debtor after the attachment order is made, for example via a contract of sale, can register the contract of sale, and subsequent acquirers can inspect the register and conduct subsequent good faith transactions of rights in the property. In that case, because the acquisition of rights after the attachment order become invalid or cannot countervail against the buyer of the property at auction, regardless of the good or bad faith of the acquirer, and because there is insufficient public notice of the attachment, doesn't it have severe results for a good faith acquirer of rights? In particular, following future economic development, whether problems will occur if transactions are conducted without always inspecting the property subject to the transaction is a point of interest. In Japan, the acquisition of rights after attachment is effective between the parties to the transaction but is ignored by the execution process; that is, it will not prevail against the purchaser of the subject property.

(4) Preparation for Sale

In Myanmar, there does not appear to be any provisions in a form similar to Japan's for a survey and appraisal of the property's value initiated by the court, or the preparation of documents by the court regarding the relationship of rights. However, according to Rule 66(2) and (3), the court must prepare a notice that details the revenue assessed against the property, any encumbrances, the amount for the recovery, and any other thing that is important for the purchaser to know. Also, as the court has the authority to summons any person to court for examination and require the submission of necessary documents pursuant to Rule 66(4), the court does proactively investigate the property subject to sale. Further, according to pages 60–61 of the "Status Paper", the debtor submits the Grant, map, price information, etc. concerning the subject real property and an expert conducts an appraisal, upon which the court determines the minimum bid price. In this way, it can be thought that in practice the court takes the lead in having the debtor submit documentation and preparing for sale, but instructions regarding specific tasks such as an execution officer inspecting the site and reporting are unclear, and the establishment of provisions is desirable.

(5) Sale process

In Japan, the sale process is conducted by an execution officer, and currently most cases are by way of period bidding (Article 34 of the Rules of Civil Execution). In Myanmar, the sale (auction) is conducted by an execution officer or deputy execution officer (Bailiff or Deputy Bailiff), and all sales appear to be via auction. Other provisions regarding the sale process are defined in Rule 64 to 68 (a Japanese translation is in pages 55–56 and 60–61 of the "Status Paper").

In Myanmar, if the amount of the decree may be raised (via mortgage, lease or private sale of the property) the debtor can apply to the court for postponement of the sale and the court may consider the reason and postpone the sale for an appropriate period (Rule 83). This point also gives consideration to the debtor's circumstances, but the discretion of the court is large and can be thought of as being linked to delay of the process. In my opinion, the court should not allow postponement unless the debtor's application has concrete reason and based on the clear evidence.

(6) Payment of the purchase price and acquisition of ownership by the purchaser

In Japan the purchaser acquires ownership upon payment of the purchase price (Article 79 of the Civil Execution Act). In Myanmar ownership is transferred at the time of sale (Section 65), which doesn't seem to differ from Japan (however, the relationship with the system for later cancellation of the sale is unclear). However, regarding payment of the purchase price in Myanmar, the purchaser must pay a 25% deposit at the time of declaration of purchase and pay the balance within 15 days; if such payment is not made the property will be re-sold (Rules 84–87). In effect, this means that payment in installments is accepted, which seems to give instability to the sale process and invite delay in the process. On this point, in Japan payment in installments of the purchase price is not accepted (In Japan, a person who makes a purchase offer for real property shall provide money of 20% of standard sales price as a guarantee beforehand. Article 66 of the Civil Execution Act and Article 39 of the Rules of Civil Execution). However, in the case of a creditor who is to receive a distribution, they may pay the difference in price after deducting the amount they are to be distributed or receive (Article 78(4) of the Civil Execution Act); in Myanmar the same provision exists (Rule 72).

In Japan, the effect of the purchaser acquiring ownership via payment of the purchase price is not affected even if the right of claim in the Title of Obligation is non-existent or extinguished. Justifiably, if A and B conspire to defraud a Title of Obligation (an order for payment declared provisionally executory) against C, the effect will be that it is invalid against C, and if A applies for compulsory execution against the property of C on the basis of the Title of Obligation and D is the successful bidder, D will not acquire title to the relevant real property (Supreme Court decision 27 February 1968, reported in Minshu Vol. 22, No. 2, p. 316). Also, in the case that the debtor did not have ownership of the real property subject to execution in the first place, the successful bidder will not acquire ownership as there is no basis for acquiring such ownership. In Myanmar, the thinking in such cases is unclear, but it appears the same considerations are given in the procedure for subsequent cancellation of a sale.

(7) Cancellation (setting aside) of sale

In Myanmar, persons with certain interests may apply for the sale to be set aside if a certain amount is paid as a deposit, or for the reason of there being a fraud or major irregularity in the process (see Rules 89–90 and pages 57–58 of the "Status Paper"). In the case where the debtor did not own a saleable interest in the property, the purchaser can apply to the court for the sale to be set aside (Rule 91). An application under the above Rules 89 or 90 seems to be possible even after the purchase price has been paid and it is unclear whether there is a time limit (According to pages 61–62 of the "Status Paper", objections related to the auction may be submitted within 30 days after payment of the purchase price, therefore it seems the same time limit would apply to setting aside, but it is unclear in the provisions). Regarding fraud and procedural irregularity, it depends on the specific reasons, but the acceptance of circumstances outside of the execution process as a reason to set aside the sale may make the process unstable and become a factor in causing delay. The provisions for allowing objections within the abovementioned 30-day period can be thought of in the same way. Defining specific conditions for setting aside the sale and submitting objections may be beneficial for avoiding complications. In Japan, as described in (6) above, acquisition by the purchaser via payment of the purchase price (Article 79 of the Civil Execution Act) is not affected by the absence of an executable claim, but ownership will not be acquired if (1) the debtor was defrauded of a Title of Obligation, or (2) the debtor did not have ownership of the subject real property. On this point, the provisions of Myanmar's Rule 91 can be said to be based on the same reasoning as (2). If Myanmar's provisions in Rule 90 concerning setting aside the sale due to procedural irregularity or fraud are said to have the same reasoning as (1), then it is in common with the effect of the Japanese case precedents. However, the specific conditions are not clear within the provisions.

(8) Confirmation of sale

In Myanmar, when the sale is confirmed the court grants a certificate to the purchaser identifying the purchased property and the purchaser, a copy is sent to the Sub-Registrar within the district in which the relevant land is located, and the purchaser's information is certified by the superintendent of land records (Rules 94, 94A, 94B). If this carries the meaning that a purchase via auction is described in the land registrar or is registered under the authority of the Registration Act,[19] then it has the same meaning as the commissioning of registration in Japan (Article 82 of the Civil Execution Act). Provisionally, if the result of public sale is the mandatory registration under the court's authority, then registration of the attachment under the court's authority at the commencement of the execution process would be more consistent and avoid confusion in transactions concerning the real property subject to the attachment. However, according to page 62 of the "Status Paper", if the debtor does not respond to the change of title, the purchaser can apply to the court for a change of title, and the execution officer (Bailiff) can sign and issue documents instead of the debtor (obligee) and take them to the government office for registration; it appears as if there is not a system of registration under the authority of the court.

(9) Distribution

When there are multiple creditors in Japan, the creditors other than the person who applied for compulsory execution can request and receive a distribution (Article 87(1) of the Civil Execution Act).

[19]Regarding registration in Myanmar, according to p. 218 onwards of "Front Line of Myanmar Law", when transferring or leasing real estate the two processes of registration under the Registration Act and changing the contents of the Land Record are necessary. Concerning the history of land rights and registration systems in Myanmar, see Okamoto (1997) Land Tax Systems and Land Ownership in Colonial-Period Burma, in *Southeast Asian Economic Development and Land Systems* (Institute of Developing Economies).

In Myanmar, when there are several persons holding a decree for the payment of money, they may receive a proportional distribution by applying to the court for compulsory auction (Section 73(1)). That means multiple applications for auction are required in order to receive a distribution.

But, the order of distribution is that, first, the cost of the sale, second, the amount due under the decree of decree-holder (who applied the execution first), third, the interest and principle money due on subsequent incombrances, forth, the amount of money of claims of the other decree-holders is distributed rateably (Section 73 1(C)).

If a separate execution process is performed for each application this may hinder the efficiency of the process, but in essence an application for auction may achieve the same function as a request for distribution. In Japan, if there are multiple applications to commence an auction the applications will be received, but processing of the first application will proceed first, and the subsequent application will be processed in the case that the first is ended due to withdrawal etc. (Article 47 of the Civil Execution Act).

(10) Order for delivery (Rule 95)

In Myanmar, the court may order delivery to the purchaser even when a tenant or other person is entitled to occupy the property (Rule 96). On this point, in Japan, an order for delivery cannot be made against a tenant who occupied the property prior to attachment if there is no mortgage, and occupancy by a tenant who has occupied the property after a mortgage was provided but prior to attachment will be recognized for a period limited to 6 months (Article 83 of the Civil Execution Act, Article 395(1)1 of the Civil Code). Myanmar's provisions can be read as allowing an order of delivery against an occupant who is entitled to occupy the property, but in practice the occupancy is recognized until the end of the tenancy period (according to the discussion with the Yangon Western District Court judges). Consistency between the practice and provisions is desirable.

(11) Obstruction of Transfer of Possession

Rules 97–99 provide for the civil detention of the debtor or others who obstruct the purchaser from obtaining possession (see page 59 of the "Status Paper"). Described in practical terms, the same provisions may be inferred as having the effect of providing indirect compulsion (impression gained from the roundtable meeting with the Yangon Western District Court judges). In Japan, police assistance can be received in the case of malicious interference (Article 6(1) of the Civil Execution Act), but in Myanmar there is not an impression of smooth cooperation with the police. If this is the case, improvement on this point is desirable.

7.3 Conclusion

Under Myanmar law, there is a system of civil detention, which is touched upon in pages 207–208 of the "Report" and pages 51–52 of the "Status Paper" (the "Status Paper" says that civil detention is used but not frequently, as the creditor must bear the debtor's living expenses). The author heard from the Yangon Western District Court judges that they had not experienced receiving an application for civil detention, so it seems civil detention is rarely used, at least in Yangon city. From the point of view of Japanese law, as described in Footnote 5, there is no room for the adoption of a similar system, but it can be thought that its practical function in Myanmar is not large (although the impression from the roundtable meeting with the Yangon Western District Court judges was that it has a practical function of indirect compulsion). This point is a question for future examination within Myanmar.

In Myanmar, the fundamental law is the CPC based on the India Act V of 1908, and other provisions have been subsequently established based on practical requirements. In practice, the circumstances of the parties are given consideration, which is an aspect that should be regarded highly. However, following social and economic development, there are some areas where the contents of the legislation and the actual practice are not always consistent. On this point, it appears necessary to make the operations and regulations consistent. Further, the legislation itself has a complex structure, divided into general provisions and Rules under Orders, and they are not always well organized.

Also, because the room for judicial discretion is large and detailed requirements for practical processes are not clear, the consequences of the various applications or objections of both parties are difficult to see, which places a heavy burden on the court and may be a factor in bringing out delays in the process.

A few other points that were noticed are summarized as follows.

(1) Establishment of a system for submitting appeals and objections that is appropriate to each stage of the process is desirable.
(2) Further, clarification of the relationship between the submission of appeals and objections and a stay of execution seems to be necessary. Also, practical measures concerning sending the record of the case to other court seem to be required. Limiting the circumstances where the decision on an objection can be appealed should also be examined for the purpose of efficient execution.
(3) The position of the procedure for summonsing people within the execution process needs to be clarified.
(4) The practice of payment in installments and its role seems to require clarification, including whether it is an order of the court (and should be granted in a decree) or by agreement between the parties.

(5) In relation to the current status of the registration system in Myanmar, if the registration of land transactions under the Registration Act has become common (according to the discussion with the Yangon Western District Court judges), then it may be good to consider the registration of attachments under the authority of the court also.[20]
(6) It seems provisions regarding the acquisition of rights after attachment and coordination with security holders and tenants are insufficient. Even if it is not much of a problem at present, instances of acquiring ownership, security or tenancy without knowledge of the existence of an attachment will increase as real estate transactions become more dynamic, which means coordination with the execution process will become necessary. On this point, the Japanese system for addressing rights that compete against the attachment may be a helpful reference. In any case, examination of the public proclamation of attachment may be necessary.
(7) Establishment of a process for investigating the current conditions of the real property subject to execution and the relationship of rights is desirable.
(8) Regarding the sales process, an examination of the following matters is desirable, including whether the provisions for postponing the sale upon the debtor's request, the practice of paying the purchase price in installments and the system for setting aside a sale should be retained, and the establishment of conditions if they are retained, as well as the establishment of conditions for distribution when there are multiple creditors.[21]

This paper has examined Myanmar's compulsory execution law from the procedural aspect of efficient operation, using comparison with Japanese law as a benchmark. However, it has been limited to superficial observations without knowledge of the actual practices within Myanmar and there may be many points based upon misunderstandings that do not conform with the actual circumstances. About these points I would like to receive all of your findings and advice, and conduct further examination in the future.

---

[20] At this point further investigation is needed to confirm the actual practice.

[21] Refer to Yuka (2017) Issues of the Civil Execution System in Myanmar 2(4).

Table Outline of the comparison of Japanese and Myanmar law: on the compulsory execution against real property for a claim of payment of money

	Japan	Myanmar
	Civil Execution Act (CEA) Rules of Civil Execution (RCE)	Code of Civil Procedure (CPC) Sections and Order (esp. 21)-Rules
1. Classification of compulsory execution	1. Monetary claim (CEA-Article 34 onwards) "CEA" hereinafter omitted (Subject of execution) Assets of debtor i.e. Immovable property • Movable property • Claim etc. (Mode of execution) • Attachment and sale • Compulsory administration • Collection of monetary claim etc.	1. Monetary claim—Decree for payment of money (Order 21, Rule 30) "Order 21" hereinafter omitted (Subject of execution) • Assets of debtor • Body of debtor (Mode of execution) • Attachment and sale • Detention in civil prison • Other manner as the nature of the relief granted may require (section 51(e)) Installment?
	2. Non-monetary claim (Article 168 onwards) (Categories) • Delivery/vacation • Manifestation of intention (registration process) • Performance/Non-performance of an action (Mods of execution) • Direct execution (delivery etc.) • Execution by substitute (removal of a house etc.) • Indirect compulsory execution	2. Non-Monetary claim (Section 51, Rule 31 onwards) (Categories) • Delivery/vacation • Performance/Non-performance • Execution of document of endorsement of negotiable instrument etc. (Mods of execution) • Direct execution • Appointing a receiver • Detention in civil prison (effect of indirect compulsory execution?) • Attachment and sale (as substitution measures?) etc.
2. Base of execution	Title of obligation + Grant of a certificate of execution (Articles 22, 26)	Decree (Sections 36–38)
3. Executive agency	Execution court (including clerk)—different court to the judgment court Enforcement officer (Article 2)	Execution court—same court as the judgment court (Enforcement officer?) (Sections 2(2), 38)

(continued)

(continued)

	Japan	Myanmar
	Civil Execution Act (CEA) Rules of Civil Execution (RCE)	Code of Civil Procedure (CPC) Sections and Order (esp. 21)-Rules
4. Jurisdiction	Principal: • The district court having jurisdiction over the location (where the real property is situated) • Transfer to another court is possible (Articles 19, 44)	Principal: • The district court which issued the Decree (same as the judgment court) • Transfer of decree to another court is possible (Sections 37–39) • Where immovable property is situated within the jurisdictions of two or more courts, any court may attach and sell the property (Rule 3)
5. Objections and appeals	1. Substantive objection • Action to oppose execution (Article 35) • Third party action against execution (Article 38) 2. Procedural objection • Appeal against a disposition of execution (Article 10) (When specially provided) Within one week • Objection to a disposition of execution (Article 11)	1. Substantive objection • Action to oppose execution (Separate suit between creditor and debtor)? • Third party objection against execution (Rules 58–63) 2. Procedural objection There are not concrete provisions?
6. Stay of procedure (suspension)	1. Due to substantive objection: A. The court upon a petition may order a stay until the final judgment (Article 36(1)) B. Mandatory Stay or Revocation due to submission of the certain documents (Articles 39(1), 40) 2. Due to procedural objection A court of appeal or an execution court may order stay (Articles 10(6), 11(2))	The court has the general authority to stay the execution (Rule 26(1)) 1. Due to substantive objection: a. Where a suit is pending against the decree holder—the court may stay execution until the pending suit has been decided (Rule 29) b. Third party objection against execution The court has authority to postpone the sale (Rule 58(2)) 2. In case of appeal Order of stay by appellate court or the court which passed the decree (Order 41 Rule 5 (1) and (2))

(continued)

(continued)

	Japan	Myanmar
	Civil Execution Act (CEA) Rules of Civil Execution (RCE)	Code of Civil Procedure (CPC) Sections and Order (esp. 21)-Rules
7. Restriction of appeal against judgment of objection	1. Appeal is possible against a judgment about a substantive objection 2. Judgment about a procedural objection • Against the decision of appeal against a disposition of execution → As a rule re-appeal is impossible (Exception Article 10(8)) • Against the decision of objection against a disposition of execution → As a rule appeal is impossible (Exception Article 12)	There are no restrictions on appeal? The court may restrict an appeal if the court thinks it is an abuse or delays the procedure? (Section 151)
8. Application for execution	By written application (RCE. Article 1) Submission of a copy of title of Obligation with a certificate of execution Identification of subject of attachment by creditor (RCE. Article 21)	As a rule by written application Submission of a copy of Decree (Rule 11) Selection of mode of execution (when attachment is selected, identification of subject of attachment by creditor is necessary) (Rule 13 (1))
9. Commencement order	When the required preliminary measures have been taken, execution court issues a commencement order and declares an attachment of the real property (Article 45(1))	The court executing the decree issues a notice to the debtor for requiring him to show cause why the decree should not be executed (Rule 22) When the required preliminary measures have been taken, the court issues its process for the execution of the decree (Rule 24)

(continued)

(continued)

	Japan	Myanmar
	Civil Execution Act (CEA) Rules of Civil Execution (RCE)	Code of Civil Procedure (CPC) Sections and Order (esp. 21)-Rules
10. Attachment	Creditor identifies subject of attachment beforehand, and applies for execution (RCE. Article 21) An execution court declares an attachment pertaining a commencement order (Article 45(1)) A court clerk commissions registration of the attachment (Article 48) Any transaction between the debtor and a third party after an attachment is valid, but the outcome of that transaction cannot prevail over the creditor and the purchaser thorough the execution process (Article 46 etc.)	When the creditor chooses attachment as a mode of execution, the creditor must identify the subject of attachment beforehand (Rule 13(1)) Summon and examination of the debtor upon an application of the creditor (Rule 41) Notification by beat of drum or other customary mode and affixment of a copy of the order on a conspicuous part of the property etc. (Rule 54(2)) Whether the attachment is effective between the parties is unclear (Rule 54(1))
11. Preparation for sale	Court–lead procedure (Articles 57–62) • Investigation of the current conditions (enforcement officer) (Article 57) • Appraisal (appraiser) (Article 58) • Making the description of the property (court clerk) (Article 62)	Court–lead procedure? The Court may summon any person and examine him in respect to any matters (material things for a purchaser to know) and require him to produce any document in his possession (Rule 66(2)-(4)) (The role of the enforcement officer is unclear, and as a whole, the investigation procedure is not as clear)

(continued)

(continued)

	Japan	Myanmar
	Civil Execution Act (CEA) Rules of Civil Execution (RCE)	Code of Civil Procedure (CPC) Sections and Order (esp. 21)-Rules
12. Sale procedure	A court clerk specifies the method of sale, and an enforcement officer implements the sale (Article 64(1) (3)) In practice, period bidding is adopted in almost all cases (CER. Articles 46–48) Next-highest purchaser offer system is adopted (Article 67) Appeal against an order of permission or non-permission of sale (Article 74)	Bailiff or Deputy Bailiff implements the sale (Rule 65(1)) (Rules 64–68) Public auction at the site (provisions for period bidding etc. do not exist) Re-sale on default (Rule 84(1), 86, 87) Postponement of sale to enable debtor to raise amount of decree (Rule 83) Application to set aside sale (Rule 89, 90) Objection against auction (30 days)?
13. Payment of the price	Acquisition of ownership of the property by purchaser (Article 79) Acquisition of ownership is not affected by non-existence of an obligation (Exceptions) 1. When the debtor did not have ownership (due to lack of grounds for acquiring ownership) 2. When the title of obligation was obtained by deception (because the debtor as the owner of the subject property has been excluded from the execution procedure) (Supreme court precedent) Commission of registration (Article 82)	Acquisition of ownership of the property by purchaser (Section 65) Whether acquisition of ownership is affected by non-existence of the obligation is unclear 1. When the debtor did not have ownership, the purchaser may apply to the court to set aside the sale (Rule 91) 2. Any person whose interests are affected by the sale may apply to the court to set aside the sale on the ground of a material irregularity or fraud (what constitutes a material irregularity or fraud is not clear) Registration by official authority is not performed Deposit by purchaser (payment by installment) is adopted (Rule 84–87)

(continued)

(continued)

	Japan	Myanmar
	Civil Execution Act (CEA) Rules of Civil Execution (RCE)	Code of Civil Procedure (CPC) Sections and Order (esp. 21)-Rules
14. Delivery order	Arrangement between the possession (occupancy) by the tenant and the attachment or the setting of a mortgage (based on the timing of the contract and the order of the attachment and setting of the mortgage) (Article 83, Civil Code 395(1) (-1)) Delivery order is a title of obligation (Article 22(-3)). Purchaser can apply the court to execute the delivery upon a delivery order	Arrangement between the possession (occupancy) by the tenant and the attachment is not clear In practice, the possession (occupancy) of the tenant before the attachment has priority over the purchaser? (Rule 95, 96) Purchaser must file a suit to remove the person?

References

Kenta, K. (2016). Adversary system in Myanmar civil trials (1). *ICD News, 68,* 72–74.

Mori Hamada & Matsumoto. (2013). *2012 nendo Myanmar Renpo Kyowakoku houseido chosa hohkokusyo* (2012 Report on the legal system in the Republic of the Union of Myanmar). Ministry of Justice. http://www.moj.go.jp/content/000110245.pdf; http://www.moj.go.jp/content/000109989.pdf; http://www.moj.go.jp/content/000110246.pdf; http://www.moj.go.jp/content/000110247.pdf; http://www.moj.go.jp/content/000110248.pdf; http://www.moj.go.jp/content/000110249.pdf; http://www.moj.go.jp/content/000110250.pdf; http://www.moj.go.jp/content/000110252.pdf; http://www.moj.go.jp/content/000112674.pdf; http://www.moj.go.jp/content/000112675.pdf.

Mukawa, T., Manabe, K., & Inoue, A. (2017). *Front line of Myanmar law*. Shoji Houmu: Tokyo.

Nakano, T., Shimomura, M. (2016). *Minji shikouhou* (Civil execution act), supplementary edn 6. Tokyo: Seirin Shoin.

Okamoto, I.(1997). Land tax systems and land ownership in Colonial-Period Burma. In Mizuno, Shigetomi (Eds.), *Southeast Asian economic development and land systems* (pp. 81–114). Institute of Developing Economies.

Yuka, K. (2017). Issues of the civil execution system in Myanmar. *Kokusai Kyouryoku Ronsyuu, 25*(1), 1–22.

Yukawa, Y., Harada, M. et al. (2015). *Myanmar ni okeru min-syoji kankeitou no hunsou kaiketuseido no jittai* (Status paper on the civil and commercial dispute resolution system in Myanmar). Ministry of Justice. http://www.moj.go.jp/content/001179166.pdf.

Chapter 8
Japan's Civil Code Drafting Support for Socialist Reform Countries: Diversity of Normative Choice

Yuka Kaneko

Abstract This article will review the context of civil code drafting in the the"transition" countries in Asia after the collapse of the Soviet Union in 1991, with a focus on the changing relation between the economic law and the civil law in the historical path of socialist legal reforms. Japanese ODA which has taken a unique position in the process. While most of the capitalist code systems still maintain the binary structure of civil code (as modernist ideal) and commercial code (as merchandize practice), the Russia 1995 Civil Code was an avant-garde attempt to integrate the code norms. Asian civil codes seem to be deviated from Russian influence, probably as a result of the pressure of international donor agencies calling for investor-friendly legal reforms. The normative confrontation in the boundary of civil, commercial and consumer laws will be investigated on selected issues of debate in civil code drafting.

8.1 Introduction

The Japanese ODA took a unique position in legal technical assistance, began in the mid-1990s, maintained its attitude centering on the drafting and implementation of civil basic laws. Vietnam 1995 Civil Code, Vietnam 2005 Civil Code, Vietnam 2004 Civil Procedure Code, Vietnam 2015 Civil Code, Vietnam 2015 Civil Procedure Code, Cambodia 2006 Civil Code, Cambodia 2004 Civil Affairs Lawsuit Code, Laos 2017 Civil Code, among others. Also, since 2011, legal assistance for Myanmar began, initially specializing in support of commercial laws but gradually reaching to such basic areas as civil procedure law. There are pros and cons in the policy of Japanese ODA that has continued to provide support to the fundamental codes that constitute the core of one country's normative order. There are criticisms that it is

Yuka Kaneko—Professor, Law & Development Program; Graduate School of International Cooperation Studies, Kobe University, Japan; LL.B. Tokyo University, LL.M., Georgetown University, LL.D. Kyushu University.

Y. Kaneko (✉)
Kobe University, Kobe, Japan
e-mail: ykaneko@kobe-u.ac.jp

Y. Kaneko (ed.), *Civil Law Reforms in Post-Colonial Asia*,
Kobe University Monograph Series in Social Science Research,
https://doi.org/10.1007/978-981-13-6203-3_8

an export of Japanese legal system from an economic intention (Taylor 2005), as apposed to another extreme of criticism that civil-oriented legal asssitance does not directly benefit investors (e.g. 24 Aug. 2017 edition of the nihon Keizai Shimbun).

Motivated by the purpose of reconsidering the outcomes of Japan's legal assistance, this article will review the context of civil code reform in the "transition" countries after the collapse of the Soviet Union in 1991, with a focus on the changing relation between the economic law and the civil law in the historical path of socialist legal reforms. An inquiry will first be made into the 1995 Russian Civil Code, which has influenced the legal reforms in Asian market reform countries since the 1990s.

Second, the normative confrontation in the boundary of civil, commercial and consumer laws will be investigated on selected issues of debate in civil code drafting. In Asian market reform countries, as discussed in the Preamble of this volume, establishment of an integrated normative regime to get rid of the "legal pluralism" has been a goal of law-making since independence from colonial rule. By establishing a Civil Code as an integrated source of norms, these countries will be able to achieve true independence from the remaining influence of colonial law. The Civil Code will also extend an integrated regime to coordinate individual laws in commercial spheres brought by the contemporary "legal transplants" of various international donors.

Whether Japan, as one of the donors of legal assistance, has attempted to direct the code drafting toward a certain policy orientation, or instead has provided mere technical support based on the policy choices already made by the recipient countries, the author has no intention of answering this question due to a lack of access to the inside information. This chapter only intends to investigate the provisions of the codes which are the direct products of Japan's assistance projects in Vietnam, Cambodia and Laos, as well as the result of interviews with those who took part in the drafting committees in these recipient countries, in order to identify the policy direction to address the normative issues in debate. Target issues will be selected by a review of socialist law reforms (Sect. 8.2); and focus will be made on the standardization of general principles as the hierarchical bases of normative interpretation (Sect. 8.3); the norm conflict between the protection of true intention and the promotion of transactions (Sect. 8.4); and another norm conflict between consumer protection and the commercial customs in the sphere of breach of contract (Sect. 8.5).

8.2 Legal Reforms in Transition Economies

8.2.1 Implications of Russian Civil Code

The trend of legal development in the countries in transition from socialism after the collapse of the Soviet Union provides one viewpoint for analysis of the Asian market reform countries, which are known for following the trends in post-cold war Russian legal reforms as well as that of Chinese.

Influential donor agencies such as the World Bank, the European Bank for Reconstruction and Development (EBRD), and the United States Agency for International Development (USAID) developed legal technical assistance for the transitioning countries immediately after the collapse of the Soviet Union in 1991. It is remarkable that formation of the theories that promoted such "legal transplants " also occurred at this time, centered around American institutional economists. "Legal transplant" is originally a term in comparative law that suggests the inheritance of Roman law by Western countries (Watson 1974/1993) , but the contemporary "legal transplant" is primarily an argument promoting the American law to the transition countries, with the neo-liberal legal orientation that features the contract freedom and ownership maximization (Posner 1998; Trubek 2006). This inclination is prominent in the "Legal Origin" theory by the so-called LLSV group (La Porta et al. 1997, 2007), which is, however, arbitrary in its grouping of legal systems, and inductive of its conclusions. In particular, that it includes Russia and the other former socialist countries as well as the debt-burdened countries of Central and South America and Asia as being incorporated in the "French legal origin" is a surprising distortion. Using economic data as of 1993, when Russia had just gone through a change of political system and the cumulative debt-burdened countries from the 1980s were at the lowest point of the economic crisis, induces the categorical conclusion that countries that inherited French law have lower economic performance than the countries that inherited Anglo-American law. Regardless of this academic flaw, the LLSV group's theory boasts remarkable influence and has become an obstacle to countries trying to advance the development of a continental law system centered around a civil code.

In the same mid-1990s, international organizations such as the World Bank and the EBRD launched so-called "model laws" in key economic law areas such as secured transaction law, insolvency law, corporate governance and competition law, as well as "legal indicators" that evaluated the degree that these model laws had been introduced in the countries subject to reform (World Bank 2001/2003). The "Legal Indicators Survey" by the EBRD and "Report on the Standards and Codes" (ROSC) promoted by the World Bank and IMF are typical examples of such legal indicators. The contents of the model laws often overlapped with the above-mentioned LLSV group's tone, representing the neo-liberal route among the American laws (Kaneko 2009a, b, 2011, 2012). The law reforms have also been linked with trade negotiations such as WTO accession negotiations, FTAs (free trade agreements) and BITs (bilateral investment treaties).

In Russia, the 1990s was a turbulent period of legal development that was tossed about by pressure mechanisms such as these model laws and legal indicators and WTO accession negotiations. The incoming pressure of the American model and the independent route of Russian law centered on a parliament conflicted, indicating a situation that could be described as a battlefield of legal reforms. The rapid introduction of the American model did occur with the enactment of a competition law and securities exchange law immediately after the collapse of the Soviet Union in 1991, a bankruptcy law and securities law in 1992, and a revision of the civil procedure law in 1995; however, a subsequent reversal has continued with the 1995 revision of the competition law, 1998 revision of the securities law, 1999 revision of the bankruptcy law and enactment of a new civil procedure law in 2002.

In 1995, Part One of Russia's Civil Code was introduced into this whirlpool of rebounding revisions. This has been followed by Part Two of the Civil Code (details of debtor law) in 1996, Part Three (inheritance) in 2001, Part Four (intellectual property rights) in 2006 and revisions in 2013.

A characteristic of the current Russian Civil Code is its comprehensiveness, which integrates and does not distinguish boundaries between civil, commercial and consumer laws. It is clear that its position as the fundamental rules of private law extends over every aspect of the social space that has shaken by the transition. This comprehensiveness in the Civil Code may be understood as an intention to build a breakwater to protect the autonomous legal system from the incoming tide of the American model. At that time, the United States' corporate law support team was passionate about transplanting into Russia a comprehensive company law model with a strong flavor of charter autonomy and deregulation (Black and Kraakman 1996; Hansmann and Kraakman 2000), but this attempt was prevented by Part One of the 1995 Civil Code which introduced its own corporate law provisions. As a result of the establishment of the 1998 Limited Liability Company Law via support from the United States, Russia's corporate law system took on a binary structure: the system for joint stock companies prescribed by the Civil Code, on one hand, incorporated a corporate governance system that included strengthening the power of general shareholders meetings and emphasizing stakeholders such as employees and creditors, while the 1998 Limited Liability Company Law which received US support prescribed a deregulated form of corporate governance; speculative foreign investors utilized only the latter. It would seem as if the legislative sovereignty of the country had been split and the social phenomenon of legal pluralism was caused by the intervention of external pressure.

In the midst of external pressure, the choice that Russian legislators connected to the hopes of overcoming the confusion of normality order through the re-establishment of the "Civil Code" which has been the forerunner of socialist legal reforms since the 1960s. The first Civil Code in 1922 of the New Economic Policy was substituted by the 1961 Civil Fundamental Principles as well as each republican civil code such as the Russian Republican Civil Code in 1964 during the reform of the socialist law in the 1960s, where the dogmatic dualism of "economic contract" as a means of implementing the specialist production plan in state or collective sectors, on one hand, and "civil contract" as a means of consumer relation, on the other, was being overcome through a gradual increase of contractual autonomy. It was a remarkable leadership taken by the Russian reformist "civil law" school to rescue the normative confusion after the collapse of the Soviet Union by way of the drafting works of the 1995 Russian Civil Code.

8.2.2 *Donor as a Side Runner: Support by the Netherlands*

A shadow-minded person who supported this wish was the team of legal assistance provided by the Leiden University of the Netherlands (Feldbrugge 2008; Snijders 2008).

At this time, the LLSV group mentioned above supported vigilance against the establishment of the Civil Code in Russia, behind the backdrop of developing an allegation that the French law system has lower economic performance than common law system. It is possible to read the hostility to this assistance by Leiden University to Russia by the common law circle, given the tendency that the Dutch law had been regarded to belong to French legal family, at the time the LLSV group wrote "Legal Origin" theory, despite the fact that the Netherlands had already abolished the 1938 Civil Code, which was a copy of the Napoleonic Civil Code, and introduced the new Civil Code of 1992 that adopted a deductive Pandecten form with the general rule as the apex, and adopted the concept of "legal acts (Rechtsgeschäft)" in Germany.

Rather, a hybrid character that makes us feel the influence of British law is pointed out in the 1992 Civil Code of Netherland, leaving numbers of comparative issues to the judicial interpretation to be developed into the case law based on the newly added general principles (Hartkamp 1994; Honduce 1994). The reason why the Leiden University group supported the Russian Civil Code seemed to be other than an intention of entering into a battle for law bearing each national flag, but a purely academic intention to contribute in the legislative process (Snijders, ibid.).

One characteristic of the Civil Code of 1995 of Russia is a comprehensive range that does not establish the normative boundary of the civil, commercial and consumer laws.[1] Netherlands 1992 Civil Code was as well attracting attention as an attempt to unify the private law, integrating all spheres of civil, commercial, consumer protection and labor law. In the French law, which was regarded as the mother law of the Dutch law in the past, the Civil Code and the Commercial Code are arranged side by side, while the consumer law is externally attached. Although the German law took in the consumer law into the Civil Code by the obligation law reform in 2002, it maintains the binary composition of the Civil Code and the Commercial Code. The trend of such normative pluralism of the binary structure of civil code (as modernist ideal) and commercial code (as merchandize practice) implies that the code system is yet self-sufficient as a basic law of capitalist market regime, needed to be adjusted by the governmental intervention through the competition law and law on unfair trade practices that applied in the intersection of civil, commercial and consumer transactions.

Among them, the Russian law was an avant-garde attempt to reestablish the civil code as a self-sufficient source of basic norms.

[1]Consumer Protection Law in 1992 explicitly mentions to its subordinate relation to the Civil Code (Article 1), mainly providing for compulsory provisions for consumer sales contracts.

8.2.3 *Policy Implications of a Comprehensive Civil Code*

But then, did Russia centralize the choice of norms to either civil, commercial or consumer law? The Russian Civil Code has no general principles such as the principle of good faith, while the Dutch law relies on a number of provisions, leaving room for flexible interpretation by the court. Perhaps Russia inherits the socialist legitimacy, purporting to rule by the legislature that is the people's representatives, instead of the judicial branch to create the law.

As previously mentioned, the socialist civil code has evolved in the interaction of "economic law" and "civil law," while these two axes have come closer to each other towards the realization of policy goals of the socialist plan within the framework of contractual autonomy. Points of debate include the contract according to the plan (e.g. 1964 Russian Civil Code Article 159), the principle of actual performance to implement the socialist plan (Article 168), prohibition of unilateral termination (Article 169), specific performance as the rule in contract infringement (Article 218), the principle of full compensation having a function as indirect compulsion on contract performance according to the socialist plan (Article 218), and the obligation of actual performance maintained regardless of payment of compensation (Articles 191, 221, also 1961 Civil Fundamental Principle Article 36). The question is how these principles changed their implications after the collapse of the planned economy.

The 1995 Russian Civil Code maintains the basic structure of strict performance, by differentiating the concepts of imperfect tender and the impossibility in the general provisions on obligations, making it a rule for the former that the obligation of actual performance is not substituted by the payment of contractual damage unless specifically provided by the law or contract (Article 396, Section 1), detailing the standards for contractual damage in imperfect tenders (Articles 393–406). Further, the specific provisions on sales contracts explicitly provides for remedies for imperfect tender based on the perfect tender rule (Article 478), while providing separately for risk sharing rules in cases of force majeure (Article 459–476). Particularly, the principle of actual performance is made a strict rule for the consumer contracts (Article 505), which is confirmed by the Consumer Protection Law (Article 13, Section 3). In other words, the Russian 1995 Civil Code maintained the basic legal designs which have been developed for the reform of "economic contracts," which could be explained as either an overly contractual intervention by compulsory legal provisions or a contemporary policy consideration as a remedy to contractual asymmetry such as for consumer protection.

On the other hand, the Russian 1995 Civil Code maintains a stance of prioritizing the true intention of contractual parties rather than the interests of bona fide third parties to the transaction, which had been a firm principle in the socialist civil code. It simply invalidates an expression of intention in legal acts that is the result of a fraud or compulsion, without considering the interests of bona fide third parties (Article 179). It lacks the system of apparent representatives on unauthorized acts of agency to protect the interests of a bona fide third party (Article 183). It recognizes the original ownership in loss of possession against his intention (Article 302), despite the principle of protection of a bona fide third party who trusted registration as evidence of ownership (Article 223, Section 2). Even though such a stance seems a remnant of the specialist dogma, we cannot deny its contemporary reformist implication for policy-oriented intervention by compulsory provisions to correct contractual asymmetry for the interests of weaker parties such as consumers and small and medium enterprises.

Thus, the Russian Civil Code has interventionist provisions that were carried over from the tradition of socialist law, against full-scale contractual autonomy, but such an interventionist tendency implies a chance of advanced policy balancing in the intersection of normative conflicts.

A related question is, then, how and by whom such a policy balancing can be implemented. In contrast to the Dutch Civil Code which contains varieties of general principles as the basis of flexibility of judicial interpretation for normative integration, the Russian 1995 Civil Code has limited mention to the general principles, as if denying the judicial discretion.[2] The number of provisions under the code is remarkably many, as if guiding the literal application of law by the judiciary.[3] A question is the dualism of civil and economic legal spheres maintained in the Russian procedural law from the socialist era, in contrast to the integrity of the Civil Code as a substantive law, where the economic arbitration court deals with disputes between economic entities under the Arbitration Procedural Code. Though the Civil Procedure Code applied in the ordinary court only assumes a civil case in a narrow sense, its unique procedural tradition is known as a social dispute resolution where the court summons all stakeholders in a face-to-face relationship, and through advisory functions lead the overall solution of the dispute, giving effect of the judgment to all parties concerned. While the 1995 amendment of the Russian Civil Procedure Code accepted American-style adversarial system, the 2002 Civil Procedure Code restored the original tradition of social dispute resolution by reinstating the judge's obligation to explain and obligation of ex officio collection of evidence.

The implication of setting the Civil Code as the highest legislation of private law was not only as the symbol of the unification of substantive norms, but might also include the extension of the ideal of social dispute resolution to the wider spheres of socio-economic phenomena, including consumer relations and SME disputes. Nevertheless, the question remains what adjustments will be possible in the intersection of norms, while avoiding dualization of the dispute resolution rules, especially when the judge's discretion of interpretation is narrow?

---

[2]The general principles of the Russian 1995 Civil Code refers to the equity, contractual freedom, non-intervention to civil relation, civil remedies, and compliance to the laws (Articles 1–3) while lacking mention to such principles as the good faith, prohibition of abuse of rights, and the social order and good morals. There is mere reference to the good faith and justice as the basis of interpretation on the ambiguity of contractual terms (Article 6, Section 2).

[3]For example, the number of provisions on contract under the Russian code amounts to 650, in contrast to 180 in Japanese civil code.

8.2.4 *Civil Codes of Asian Market-Reform Countries and Japanese Support*

Challenges of Russian Civil Code are likewise handed down to transition countries that follow the Russian law. As in the transition countries in East Europe and Central Asia, codification works in socialist market reform countries in Asia, as seen in China's 1997 Contract Act, Vietnam 1995, 2005 and 2015 Civil Code, Cambodia 2008 Civil Code, Laos 2016 Civil Code Draft, have shared the same question of structural choice (Kaneko 2010a, b, 2011).

In particular, in Vietnam, the Civil Code (1995, 2005 and 2015) coexists with the Comercial Law (1997 and 2005), the 2010 Consumer Protection Law, the 2011 Labor Code, and the 2013 Land Code. Initially it was thought that the "economic contract" dominated by the directive plan of the Soviet era was extracted from the Civil Code as independent provisions in the Commercial Law. It seemed to be a Vietnamese attention to the Russian conservative "economic law school" confronting Russian "civil law school" attempting norm reunion by the Civil Code. However, in the process of the code revision of 2015, a policy was turned to clearly establish the Civil Code as an abstract normative source, by dropping concrete specific provisions to lower legislations. In the 2015 Civil Code, the general provision of Article 1 of the 2005 Civil Code that set the range of application of the Civil Code was deleted, and even the term of "civil" was deleted from the previous usage of terms of "civil contract" and "civil obligations". While such policy highlights the Civil Code as the highest norm for all private laws, it also seems to contain a risk to invite a diversification of norms, and to make mutual coordination with fragmented subordinated laws difficult.

For example, with regard to the contract law, the 2015 Civil Code has established a Pandect deductive structure by introducing an abstract concept of "civil transactions" (equivalent to "juridical acts" referred to in Japanese law) in the general principles in Part I, and also places the rules on defects of intention (mistakes, frauds, obsessions, etc.) as the general principles applicable to such "civil transactions" (Articles 127–138), and then deductively applies these rules on defects of intentions to Part III on the general rules of obligations and contracts (Article 410). Defective rules of the Vietnamese Civil Code clearly follows the tradition of the socialist civil code emphasizing the integrity to the intention, and finds contracts with a defect of intention simply invalid: in case of mistake, contract is invalid unless there is an explicit agreement to amend in accordance with the intention of the parties, without differentiating the mistakes on fundamental factors of contract and the mistakes on motivations; similarly, fraud and compulsion make a contract simply invalid. The relief is a restoration of the original situation (Article 131). However, in the 2010 Consumer Protection Law (Articles 10–11) that was placed in the outer frame of the Civil Code, remedies for the defects of intention such as fraud and compulsion are regarded as civil damage compensation incidental to administrative and criminal penalties: which is a remedy led by an administrative intervention, a deviation from the traditional civil approach of finding defective contract "invalid" and restoring the original state. As another example, while the provisions on the sales contract in the Civil Code prescribe three choices of remedies in an incomplete performance of a contract, namely, the repairmen and exchange, the acceptance with claims for damages, and the cancellation (Articles 437–445), but the 2005 Commercial Law (Articles 39–41) put in the outer frame of the Civil Code maintains the actual performance as the rule, while allowing damage compensation only incidentally on the basis of buyer's good faith. In other words, even though the Civil Code assumes the autonomous rule of private contract order, the Consumer Protection Law and the Commercial Law are based on administrative oversight which makes it reminiscent of the "economic contract" field of the socialist planning era. Whatever the Civil Code provides for the abstract principles as the highest legislation of private law order, there is a limit to the spatial range of its application.

The limit of the highest normality of civil law in Vietnam is more prominent in the area of procedural law. Following the Russian way of dual court system separately maintaining the civil and the economic courts, Vietnam also separately had the civil procedure law and the ordinance on economic disputes resolution originally two-way parallel. Although they were unified according to the 2004 Civil Procedure Law, the "civil department" and the "economic department" are still divided within the court.

Further noteworthy is the impact of Japan's legal technical assistance. In parallel with Russia supported by the Leiden University team, Vietnam, Cambodia and Laos implemented the drafting of the Civil Code under the assistance by Japanese scholars' team sponsored by the Japan International Cooperation Agency (JICA) and the Ministry of Justice of Japan. A notable difference between these two outcomes of drafting work is the incorporation of the general principles (such as the good faith and the public order and morals) that reminiscent of the Pandecten style in the Civil Codes drafted by Japanese assistance, with an implication to rely on in the judicial interpretation to elaborate these principles by accumulating case law. The politburo of Vietnamese communist party issued the resolutions No. 48 and No. 49 in 2005 explicitly referring to the bounding effect of judicial precedents, which has been materialized by the 2015 Civil Procedure Code (Article 45, Section 2) and further elaborated by a series of resolutions by the Supreme People's Court.[4] However, in reality, the principle of socialist legitimacy that do not permit the creation of law by justice has been maintained in Vietnam and Laos. In Vietnam, the 2014 revised Civil Procedure Code clearly states the effect of *stare decisis* of the cassation judgements selected by the resolutions at the juducial council of the Supreme People's Court, but visible changes have not yet occurred to the formation of judicial interpretation except a limited number of cases dealing with procedural issues, without addressing the interpretation of substantive law.

[4]Resolution of Justice Committee of the Supreme People's Court No. 3 in 2015, etc. However, most of the cases selected as the precedents by the Supreme People's Court are technical detailing of court procedures (e.g. Decision No. 4/2012/NQ-HDTP) without touching on debated substantive issues.

8.3 General Provisions as the Basis of Interpretation

In considering the question of whether the normative conflicts under the civil code is solved through the detailed standardization of legislations or though the judicial interpretation, a focus will be made on the general provisions under the code, which guides the integrated application of norms. General principles are often given at the beginning of the civil code as the fundamental norms to bind the entire provisions of the code, particularly in a Pandectae-style code featuring a hierarchical structure of norms to be interpreted in a deductive way. The initial stance of civil code drafting in the Asian market reform countries was to entrust the legislature to elaborate the details of subordinating legislations, which seemed to be a stance of following the Russian 1995 Civil Code which repeatedly emphasized the obligation of civil actors to be bound by state laws and regulations (Articles 1–3). But gradually, perhaps in response to the Japanese involvement in the drafting process, the drafting stance has shifted to streamline the general principles under the civil codes in an expectation to entrust the judiciary to incrementally develop case law to identify the normative contents of such general principles through the accumulation of individual dispute resolution. At the same time, the drafters seem to aim at a standardization of such general principles within the code itself.

8.3.1 Vietnam

While Book One (General Provisions) of the 2005 Civil Code of Vietnam used to include a long list of general principles consisting of ten clauses (Articles 4–13), the present 2015 Civil Code (Article 3) has reduced this list to only five items. The deleted items included the obligation of civil actors to follow the laws and regulations, as well as the obligation to follow public order and good morals, while the reason of deletion was explained as to remove the possible basis of public intervention in contract freedom,[5] which is a deviation from the aforementioned stance of the Russian Civil Code. The deletion also included the encouragement of flexible dispute resolution through the traditional culture of conciliation.

The remaining items in the list are the principles of equality, freedom of contract, good faith, national and public interests, and civil liabilities based on fault. A certain effort of the drafters to standardize such inherently abstract principles are recognized in some provisions, such as the explicit reference to governmental organizations as a civil actor (Articles 97–100) which was meant to materialize the principle of "equality" in the bargaining position between both public and private participants in market

[5]The result of the author's interview as of October 25th, 2017 with Prof. Nguyen Hong Hai, the drafter of Vietnam 2015 Civil Code.

transactions.[6] The principle of "good faith" was also the target of such standardization in individual provisions in various parts of the Code.[7]

As for the basis of interpretation of any vagueness of provisions of contract law, the 2015 Civil Code of Vietnam (Articles 5–6) provides for analogy based on customs and the sense of justice, following the stance of the Russian Civil Code (Article 6). However, the Vietnam 2015 Civil Code (Article 121) further details the basis of such interpretation in the general provisions for "civil transactions" which is the equivalent of "juridical acts (Rechtsgeschäft)," setting the priority of the true intention of the parties, the purpose of the civil transaction, and the local custom in the place of conclusion of the civil transaction. A remarkable change to the original clause in the 2005 Civil Code (Article 126) is the deletion of the reference to the "literal wording," and the inclusion of the "purpose" instead. Further, in the general provisions for contracts, the basis of contractual interpretation is detailed such that the true intention should be prioritized to the wording, as well as the benefits of parties, nature of the contract, local customs, and the interests of the party in the weaker bargaining position (Article 404).

Thus, an obvious tendency of the Vietnam 2015 Civil Code is to reduce the legislative guidance on private relations so as to place more importance upon contractual freedom, while shifting the mode of guidance on such contractual freedom from the legislative/administrative mode to the judicial mode, by standardizing the general principles as the basis of judicial interpretation of contracts. Such a shift in contractual intervention is in other words a shift from the public mode of supervision implemented by the government to the autonomous mode of contractual realization initiated individually by the parties at the court, which might be a result of Japan's involvement.

However, the outcome of this shift cannot be tested until the capacity of the judiciary is improved, to enable a logical interpretation of general principles to accumulate in the integrated regime of case law. Also, there remains the trend of subsidiary legislation such as commercial and consumer protection laws to keep functioning as the basis of administrative intervention in contractual freedom, even if the Civil Code makes much of the autonomous mode guided by the role of the judiciary.

8.3.2 Cambodia

Cambodias constitution is a product of Japanese assistance in the drafting work over four years (1999–2003), which was adopted in the yearend of 2007, and entered into force at the end of 2011. It consists of eight chapters (general provisions, persons,

[6]See Footnote 13 of Nguyen Hong Hai (2018) in this volume Chap. 5.

[7]See Footnote 25 of Nguyen Hong Hai (2018) in this volume Chap. 5, which refers to some examples of such standardization, including the prior notice requirement in foreclosure of mortgages (Article 300), obligation of the creditor to mitigate the damage in the causal link (Articles 362, 585, Section 5, etc.), *clausula rebus sic stantibus* or changes of circumstances in the general provisions on contract (Article 400).

property rights, obligations, contract and tort, secured credits, relatives, inheritance), with general provisions in the chapeau of each of the eight chapters. Though such a hierarchical structure of general provisions, as well as the separation of real property rights and obligations, reminds us of a Pandectae system, its general provisions only contain five provisions, and it lacks the concept of "juridical acts" (Rechtsgeschäft). Detailed explanation of technical terms which could have been defined as elements of a "juridical act" (such as the expression of intentions, terms, defects in intention, invalid expression of intention, voidable expression of intention, agency) are all given in the general provisions on the obligations.

The general provisions in Part One include the principles of human dignity and equality (Article 2), private autonomy (Article 3), prohibition of abuse of rights (Article 4), and good faith. These general provisions are in principle applied to all spheres of the Civil Code, except property law and family law where special legislation can be excluded from the application of these general provisions (Article 1).

Given the scarcity of normative provisions as well as the loosened hierarchical order, the hurdle seems to be lowered by the Civil Code drafters for the convenience of local judges making their first attempt at judicial interpretation of the Code. However, the judicial activism is yet to be seen (Kamiki 2011).

8.3.3 Laos

As of the end of 2018, the Civil Code was adopted by the people's national assembly in Laos after more than two year long deliberatons, but the official translation is still unknown to the author. Instead, reference will be made to the commentaries given by the Japanese team that assisted drafting of the Code, based on the 2012 version of the draft Civil Code (Matsuo 2015). A simplified method of codification was chosen to consolidate the existing laws in the private spheres (such as the 2003 Land Law, 2005 Secured Credit Law, 2005 Inheritance Law, 2008 Law on Contract and Out-of-Contract Obligations) with general provisions put at the top of the entire draft code and consisting of a total of nine chapters (general provisions, persons, family, property and ownership, contractual obligations, secured credits, tort, inheritance, final provisions). Among the total of 615 articles, 112 are simply transplanted from the existing provisions, 251 contain some modification from the original provisions, and 252 are newly introduced provisions. While the structure of the draft code reminds us of the Institutiones style, it also incorporates some characteristics of the Pandectae system by placing general provisions in the chapeau of each chapter, as separately provided for property (Book 4 and Book 6) and obligations (Book 5). The Japanese assisting team describes the draft as a hybrid model (Matsuo, ibid., p. 109).

Accordingly, the bases of judicial interpretation are given in a hierarchical order of norms such that Book 1 provides for the general principles for "legal acts", which are transformed from the original 2008 Law on Contract and Out-of-Contract Obligations (Article 5) with certain modifications. Such general principles include the principles of voluntary agreements, equality, good faith, observance of law and customs. Further, the draft code (Article 16) provides for legality of purpose, voluntariness, capacity to act, and legality of forms as the requirements of a "judicial act" borrowed from the original 2008 Law on Contract and Out-of-Contract Obligations (Article 10), and further detailing the elements of each requirement (draft Articles 17, 18). The draft (Article 390) is expected to further detail the basis of contractual interpretation in the general provision on the Book on obligations.

Although the Japanese assistance team holds a view that these general provisions are not the normative basis for judicial interpretation in a strict sense (Okawa 2015), the attempt at a hierarchical order of norms as well as the efforts of standardization of their elements appearing in the draft Code are good enough evidence of the intention of Lao drafters to entrust the integrated implementation of the Civil Code to the initiative of the parties and the judiciary.

8.4 Protection of True Intention Versus Promotion of Transactions

As the socialist civil code was started as a rule to regulate civil relations in a narrow sense, in contrast to the economic law to regulate production relations, it pays full respect to the true intention of the parties, invalidating a legal act due to defects in intentions, without incorporating devices for the protection of bona fide third parties. The 1995 Russian Civil Code, as aforementioned, that integrated the civil and commercial spheres maintains the tradition of protection of true intention, by lacking the system of apparent representatives for unauthorized acts of agency; prioritizing the original owner who lost the property against his intention over a bona fide third party. Interestingly, the civil codes of the Asian market reform countries show a shift from the Russian style protection of true intentions to the promotion of transactions, which implies the influence of Japanese involvement.

8.4.1 Vietnam

According to a drafter of the 2015 Civil Code of Vietnam, the drafters held an explicit policy stance to modify the previous 2005 Civil Code toward the promotion of transactions.[8] In this context, the system of apparent representatives was newly incorporated in Book One on the clauses of "civil transactions" to bind the agent's act against the principal in cases of express authorization (Article 142, Section 1 c) and unauthorized acts of agency (Article 142, Secion 2) which is equivalent to the concept of legal acts. This is a remarkable shift from the original stance maintained

[8]The result of the author's interview as of October 25th, 2017 with Prof. Nguyen Hong Hai, the drafter of Vietnam 2015 Civil Code.

since the first Vietnamese 1995 Civil Code, whose drafters were highly skeptical of the idea of validating an agreement against the true intention of the parties.

Another remarkable change under the Vietnam 2015 Civil Code was the introduction of an independent Book Two titled "ownership and other property rights," which was meant to clearly separate the concepts of real rights and personal rights.[9] While the Russian 1995 Civil Code chosen this separated structure of property and obligations, the 1995 and 2005 versions of Vietnam's Civil Code did not follow it, and instead had a chapter titled "property and ownership" which listed the dogmatic types of ownership according to the categories of actors, while the issues of the secured interests and the transfer of land use rights, a major category of property right, were dealt with in separate chapters despite their major roles in the real economy (Kaneko 2012). The drafter of the 2015 Civil Code explains that this change is due to the policy stance of promoting transactions to accelerate further economic growth.[10] Not only was there a change in the chapter's title, but also its substance included major changes to the property rules to reflect the promotion of transactions, such as abstracting rule for the transaction of real properties for the benefit of bona fide third parties (Article 133, Section 2) as well as the immediate acquisition of movables by a bona fide third party in transactions (Article 133, Section 1). A real property transaction takes three steps: first, an initial contract between the parties, second, the transfer of the posession of property, and third, the perfection against third parties by registration, where the trust of the once-established perfection by a third party cannot be denied by asserting the invalidity of the original contract. This effect of protecting third parties is explained as the result of the abstraction rule by the Vietnamese drafters. Such substantive rules in the Civil Code on real rights are automatically applied to the land use rights regulated under the Land Law, since the land use right is treated as superficies defined as one of the real rights restricting an ownership (Article 159, Section 2; Article 106, Section 1).

On the other hand, the 2015 Civil Code of Vietnam has a strict basis for public intervention in contractual freedom when the true intention of the parties has been violated. The general provisions on "civil transactions" provides for strict rules on defects in intentions such as mistake, fraud, compulsion, and failure to meet with formalities, where such defects in intentions simply result in the invalidity of a civil transaction (Article 127-8), and whose remedy is simply a restoration of the status quo. Such upper-level rules are duplicated in a deductive way in the general provisions on contracts (Article 410). The 2010 Consumer Protection Law of Vietnam (Articles 10–11) further provides for administrative and criminal penalties, as well as the civil damage claimed attached thereto, in fraud and compulsion cases causing defects in consumer contracts.

The Code seems to carry two policy orientations that are in mutual conflict, namely the promotion of market transactions for the pursuit of economic development and the

---

[9]See Nguyen, ibid.

[10]The result of the author's interview as of October 25th, 2017 with Prof. Nguyen Hong Hai, the drafter of Vietnam 2015 Civil Code.

protection of weaker parties in transactions, and is incapable of defining a theoretical integration of the two.

8.4.2 *Cambodia*

The promotion of transactions seems to be a basic policy stance consistently established in the Cambodian Civil Code, which received Japanese assistance. Book Four on obligations contains the system of apparent representatives to validate an agent's act beyond the scope of authorization and the agent's acts after the termination of representation (Article 372).

Book Three on property rights provides for the immediate acquisition of movables by a bona fide third party in transactions (Articles 134, Section 2; Article 192). As for real property transactions, the drafting process of the Civil Code experienced controversy, where the initial draft code that the Japanese assisting team handed over to the Cambodian minister in 2003 did not provide for an abstraction rule, envisaging a registration system that only had the effect of public notice. However, the 2001 Land Law drafting assistance provided by the World Bank and the Asian Development Bank introduced the Torrens style land title registration system which aimed at the perfection of title or the absolute proof of freehold ownership once registration is finalized through the cadastral dispute resolution. In order to fill the gap between the draft Civil Code and the Land Law, the former was amended to recognize the perfection effect of land registration as a requisite of the transaction of real estate (Article 135).[11] As this Torrens-style title registration perfects ownership without differentiating between a third party with or without knowledge of the defects in the original contract, the policy effect is more for the promotion of transactions than in the case of protection of bona fide third parties.

8.4.3 *Laos*

The draft Civil Code being debated in the people's national assembly of Laos included the system of apparent representatives that did not exist in the 2008 Law on Contract and Out of the Contract Obligations (Okawa 2015, p. 118).

On the other hand, the draft code doesn't have a provision on the immediate acquisition of movables nor the abstracting rules for the transaction of real estate for the benefit of bona fide third parties (Matsuo 2015, p. 130). Even though title registration is a requisite of the transfer of real estate, the effect of registration is not considered as absolute proof of ownership, as in the case of Torrens style registration, since contrary evidence is admissible even after the finalization of registration, according to Rule No. 500/2008 of the Prime Minister's Office Land Management Agency,

[11] See Kaneko 2010a, b.

etc. (Matsuo, ibid., p. 131). The majority opinion in the code drafting committee is against the prioritization of a second purchaser with registration in the case of double sales of real estate (Matsuo 2012, p. 170). In sum, the policy orientation of the drafters in Laos does not amount to the prioritization of the promotion of transactions at the expense of the protection of true intention, whose nuance is different from the aforementioned Vietnamese drafters.

8.5 Remedies for Contracts Violation

The Russian 1995 Civil Code (Article 393 and thereafter) maintains, as aforementioned, a series of detailed compulsory provisions on the compensation for damage caused by imperfect performance of a contract. This is a remnant from the socialist civil code that saw a gradual integration of the concepts of "economic contract" and "civil contract" through the development of strict damage compensation rules as a compulsion of actual performance as a means of implementation of socialist plans. Such intervention by the compulsory provisions of law might be considered as an impediment to freedom of contract in the trend of international commercial sales contracts which mitigate the perfect tender rule, but could have an advanced implication friendly to the interests of vulnerable parties.

A comparative review tells that the majority of civil law tradition has placed an importance on the specific performance while narrowing the unilateral termination, in contrast to the common law tradition based on the monetary compensation upon a termination. While the former is inclined for consumer's interest, the latter seems to facilitate the sellers in the commercial transactions.

Inquires will be made in the following section as to the trend in the Asian market reform countries, which have been influenced from not only Russian law but also from different legal traditions since the colonial period as well as the contemporary external pressures of legal reforms.

8.5.1 Vietnam

The drafters of the 2015 Vietnam Civil Code paid special attention to the standardization of contractual liabilities so as to guide transparent judicial rulings, in response to the criticism that the Vietnamese judiciary is still inflexibly bound by the notion of perfect performance of contract that follows the tradition of socialist economic plans.[12] Book Four on Obligations first differentiates the general rules on delayed performance and imperfect performance where the party's negligence is involved (Article 351, Section 1), on one hand, and the force majeure which is a matter of

[12]The result of the author's interview as of October 25th, 2017 with Prof. Nguyen Hong Hai, the drafter of Vietnam 2015 Civil Code.

distribution of risk (Article 351, Section 2; Article 441), on the other. As for the former, the principle of perfect performance is maintained as the principle (Article 352), and damage compensation is elaborated in details (Articles 360–364), without identifying whether such compensation is a substitute or a supplement to the perfect performance. The general provisions on contracts basically deductively accept such standardized compensation rules given in the upper provisions on obligations (Article 419), but newly referred to the principle of *clausula rebus sic stantibus* (Article 420) where the parties (or the court) are obliged to modify the contract so as to let the contractual relation continues, instead of termination. On the other hand, the chapter on sales details the remedies for contract violations as an alternative choice between a claim for completion (reform or exchange), damage compensation while accepting the imperfect tender, and cancellation of the contract (Articles 437–445).

Thus, the Civil Code drafting policy is to maintain the socialist contract tradition of actual performance in the principle of civil obligations, but modify it for the sales contract, making a strange use of the pandect system.

However, the subsidiary legislation such as the 2005 Commercial Law provides for stricter rules of contract liability outside of the Civil Code, making perfect tender a principle while admitting compensation for damage only as a supplementary means of remedy for a bona fide purchaser (Articles 39–41). Even if the Civil Code chooses to follow autonomous rules for sales contracts, the subsidiary legislations may maintain the administrative intervention into the commercial and consumers' sales contracts.

8.5.2 Cambodia

Book Four, Chapter 4 of the Cambodian Civil Code provides for the remedies in case of contract infringement, referring to three categories: delay of performance, impossibility of performance, and imperfect performance (Article 389), and the remedies of completion of performance based on the defect, compensation for damage, and cancellation (Articles 390, 398), to which the claimant has a freedom of choice (Article 395). Further, the provisions on sales refer to the remedies in the case of latent defects, including substitution and repair, cancellation, reduction of price, and compensation for damage (Articles 543–546). Thus, the basic stance is the promotion of party autonomy by providing a variety of remedies and the free choice of the parties to the contract, in accordance with the Japanese assistance. The question is how this stance of the Code has been interpreted by the judiciary in response to the needs of the actual socio-economy after several years' of implementation since the adoption of the Code.[13]

8.5.3 *Laos*

The 2008 Law on Contract and Out of Contract Obligations, which is the origin of the contract provisions of the Civil Code of Laos which was adopted in the yearend 2018, had only a few provisions on remedies for contract infringement. While non-performance of an obligation results in compensation for damage except in the case of force majeure (Article 33), additional penalties can be imposed according to the legal standards and by mutual agreement (Article 36). The party whose interest is adversely affected by the contract infringement can unilaterally alter or cancel the contract (Article 37). As for the individual provisions for sales contract, compensation for damage can be claimed for a defect in quality in addition to other remedies such as substitution, reduction of price, and cancellation (Article 40). It is explicitly stated that a buyer can both cancel and claim compensation for imperfect performance by the seller (Article 43).

A member of the Japanese team that assisted the drafting of the Laos Civil Code criticizes the Lao drafters' choice on contract provisions, which are a deviation from the original 2008 Law on Contract and Out of Contract Obligations that basically follows the lines set by the United Nations Convention on the International Sales of Goods (CISG).[14] For example, the Lao Civil Code draft (Article 408) exempts not only compensation but also all other types of claims of the buyer in case of force majeure, which is criticized as being a result of misunderstanding the stance of the CISG. The CISG only exempts compensation in the case of force majeure, without affecting other claims of the buyer such as reduction of price and cancellation (Article 79, Sections 1–5), which is considered to be the result of a theoretical differentiation of the contractual liabilities involving the seller's fault and the principles of risk allocation while incorporating the principles of remedies for latent defects, which are based on risk allocation without requiring the element of seller's default.

It may be true that the Japanese assisting team found difficulties in transferring highly theoretical concepts needed for code drafting to the Lao drafters.[15] The question is how code drafting assistance can be pursued in a country whose technical capacity does not always meet the expectations of the donor. Perhaps, the stance of assistance could have been modified to meet with the local socio-economic needs, as

[13]A review of the implementation of Civil Code has been attempted through the supplementary projects for training addressed to local lawyers. The result of the author's interview as of March 25th, 2015 with JICA legal assistance office in Pennon Penh, as well as the participants of such training.

[14]See Nozawa 2015, p. 143.

[15]The author's interview as of August 18th, 2016 with a person who used to be a member of civil code drafting team but intended anonymous interview confessed the technical difficulties and mental stress that he had experienced throughout the involvement to the project.

Laos has a special need to protect the interests of consumers as the final market in the ASEAN region as the region's least developed economy in terms of industrialization.

8.6 Conclusion

This article paid attention to the evolution of the socialist civil codes in considering the results of civil code drafting assistance for the Asian market reform countries. Particularly when the context of overcoming the dualistic socialist tradition of public regulation in economic legal spheres and private autonomy in a narrow sphere of consumer relations is viewed from the contemporary reformist stance to mitigate the disparity of bargaining position between commercial actors and consumers, some of the tendencies of these Asian codes are understood more clearly. Although there are criticisms on the Japanese involvement in the code drafting in these market reform countries being the exportation of the Japanese model in order to serve the interests of Japanese investors in these countries, perhaps such criticisms fail to recognize the implication of socialist civil code development in these countries. Japanese involvement has basically been mere technical assistance to meet the needs of local code drafters, which is equivalent to the role taken by the Netherlands-Leiden University team in its support of drafting the Russian 1995 Civil Code. However, a fundamental difference between the two assistance projects was in the fact that the counterparts of Japanese assistance have often lacked the knowledge and experience of code-drafting at all, which couldn't help but have resulted in more substantive involvement of the Japanese team in the Asian codifications, which might have caused a misunderstanding on its overly intense involvement with national interests. Also, as a natural effect of such intense involvement, the substantive contents of the codes sometimes reflect the trends of debates in Japanese academia or in industrial sectors on the reform of Japan's own Civil Code, which do not always directly meet with the local needs of the counterpart countries.

As for the points of debate in the contemporary context, this chapter reviewed such issues as the conflict of policy choices protecting true intention and promoting capitalist transactions, and the controversies in contract law reforms between the stances of following the trend of international commercial customs and consumer protection. As the Asian market reform countries pursue their individual paths for economic growth, through their participation in international economic frameworks such as the World Trade Organization (WTO) and free trade agreements (FTA), as well as the reception of international assistance from various foreign donors, they are increasingly exposed to conditionalities and other forms of foreign pressures to perform legal reforms that meet with the needs of investment promotion. The introduction of the Russian 1995 Civil Code seemed to be an attempt to establish higher norms that integrate all spheres of civil, commercial, and consumer transactions by extending the reach of a single highest code that has a reformist tendency to protect the party in the weaker bargaining position. Such a policy stance is not, however, always taken by the Asian market reform countries, whose codification often reveals a positive tendency to follow the international commercial customs which promote transactions at the expense of true intention and limit contract liabilities for the benefit of sellers.

As for the impact of Japanese involvement in such a process of policy choices in the Asian civil codes, a hypothetical view might find that the deviation of the Asian civil codes from the Russian reformist stance might be a direct result of Japanese involvement. But another possible hypothesis would be that Japan's role has been mere technical assistance and the tendency of these Asian countries had already selected policies toward the prioritization of economic growth. Although this chapter could not clearly conclude which was the case, due to limited access to insider information on the Japanese assistance projects, so far the author is inclined to favour the second hypothesis based on the fact that each civil code in the target countries (Vietnam, Cambodia and Laos) more or less reveals mutual differences in the policy choices on the debated aspects, even though they received similar assistance from Japanese teams led by similar members.

Perhaps, a more crucial issue will be the common law vs. civil law conflict in the law reforms in these Asian market reform countries, who will increasingly be affected by commercial law models imposed by international donor agencies which bases on Anglo-American law traditions, in a deviation from continental law models applied in Japanese legal assistance as well as in the Russian influence. The continental contract law is evolving toward the flexible intervention by the judiciary for the modification of asymmetrical bargaining position of parties, with numbers of bases for judicial intervention incorporated in the civil code such as the interpretive principle of good faith, judicial practice to consider pre-contract negotiations, judicial consideration of change to the circumstances (*clausula rebus sic stantibusation*), admission of the defense of lacking of fault in the breach of contract, etc. When the judiciary of these socialist reform countries intends to follow such policy-guided judicial activism in the contractual intervention, more conflicts will inevitably occur between such judicial intervention and the commercial norms guided by international commercial practice.

Further, when the position of the Civil Code is considered within a holistic system of civil, commercial and consumer laws as a whole, an obvious tendency in these Asian market reform countries has been the substantial role played by pubic supervision over the private spheres, as observed in Vietnam, where the Civil Code is considered as the supreme law which is supplemented by subsidiary legislation such as the Commercial Law and the Consumer Protection Law, which are increasingly providing the basis for administrative intervention in market transactions. In this trend of increasing public methods of regulation, the role of the Civil Code is expected to go beyond a general law for the private sphere only, but should be the supreme law that provides the basic norms to regulate the entire market mechanisms, through both public and private means of supervision. The role of donor assistance in drafting civil codes should also reach into the administrative system of implementation as well as the judicial system. Otherwise, the Civil Code will lose its importance, without having an effect on the increasing administrative regulations placed on the market. In that sense, for example, the fact that the 2015 Civil Code of Vietnam deleted the list of human rights which the 2005 Code advocated could be seen as a retreat in the role of the Civil Code as the ultimate source of norms to regulate the limit of public intervention in private relations.

Perhaps, the goal of legal assistance of code drafting is not reaching the point in time when the code is adopted, but rather such adoption is the starting point for a second stage of involvement in the further evolution of the code. All of the countries that received Japanese code drafting assistance are still in the initial stage of adoption, and remain interested in receiving continuous involvement of the Japanese technical support. For example, the Vietnamese Civil Code has been amended every ten years, and the preparation for the next amendment was started soon after the adoption of the 2015 Civil Code, in which the code drafters had a keen interest on the joint empirical research with Japanese counterparts on the impact of code implementation in the socio-economic reality in Vietnam.[16] For the least industrialized countries Laos and Cambodia, there must be further needs to identify country-specific issues for code development to meet with local socio-economic conditions. As the initiator of code drafting assistance in the Asian region, Japanese technical assistance is expected to continue to take the role of a side runner in the long journey of Asian civil code development, which will be a difficult process of seeking out an integrated, normative regime through numerous conflicts between the different interests of civil, commercial, consumers, laborers and SMEs as actors in the market, and which will also go together with the continuous historical process of the post-colonial efforts of re-establishing an integrated legal system.

References

Black, B., & Kraakman, R. (1996). A self-enforcing model of corporate law. *Harvard Law Review, 109,* 1911.

Feldbrugge, F. J. M. (2008). The codification process of Russian civil law. In J. Arnscheidt, B. Van Rooij & J. M. Otto (Eds.), *Law making for development: Exploration into the theory and practice of international legislative projects.* Leiden University Press.

Hansmann, H., & Kraakman, R. (2000). The end of history for corporate law, Yale Law School working paper no. 235; Harvard Law School Discussion Paper No. 280.

Hai, N.H. (2018). *Some fundamental studies of the 2015 civil code of Vietnam.* In Y. Kaneko, (Ed.), Civil law reforms in post-colonial Asia: Beyond western capitalism, Springer.

Hartkamp, A.S. (1994). Development of Dutch Private Law—viewed from European Law. *Civil and Commercial Law Journal, 109*(4-5), 623–660.

Honduce, E. (1994). Protection of weak parties in contract law. *Civil and Commercial Law Journal, 109*(4-5), 661–691.

Kamiki, A. (2011). *Report on the review of judgement writing in Cambodia.* International Cooperation Department, Ministry of Justice of Japan (in Japanese).

Kaneko, Y. (2009a). A review of model law in the context of financial crisis: Implications for procedural legitimacy and substantial fairness of soft laws. *Journal of International Cooperation Studies, Kobe University, 17*(3), 1–16.

[16]The result of the author's interview as of October 25th, 2017 with Prof. Nguyen Hong Hai, the drafter of Vietnam 2015 Civil Code.

Kaneko, Y. (2009b). An Asian perspective on law and development. In *Symposium: The Future of Law and Development, Part III. Northwestern University Law Review Colloquy* (Vol. 104, pp. 195–200).

Kaneko, Y. (2010a). A procedural approach to judicial reform in Asia: implications from Japanese involvement in Vietnam. *Columbia Journal of Asian Law, 23*(2), 315–358.

Kaneko, Y. (2010b). An alternative way of harmonizing ownership with customary rights: Japanese approach to Cambodian land reform. *Journal of International Cooperation Studies, Kobe University, 18*(2), 1–21.

Kaneko, Y. (2011). Accompanying legal transformation: Japanese involvement in legal and judicial reform. In J. A. Sanchez Cordero (Ed.), *Legal culture and legal transplants* (Vol. I & II). International Academy of Comparative Law.

Kaneko, Y. (2012). Reevaluating model laws: Transplant and change of financial law in Vietnam. *Journal of International Cooperation Studies, Kobe University, 19*(2–3), 1–37.

La Porta, R., Lopez-De-Silanes, F., Shleifer, A., & Vishny, R. W. (1997). *Law and finance*, NBER working paper no. 5661.

La Porta, R., Lopez-De-Silanes, F., & Shleifer, A. (2007). *The economic consequences of legal origins*, NBER working paper no. 13608.

Matsuo, H. (2015). Civil code drafting in Laos and legal assistance-Property, ownership, and security interests. *Comparative Law Journal, 77,* 128–136. (in Japanese).

Nozawa, M. (2015). Civil code drafting in Laos and legal assistance—Contract and out-of-contract obligations. *Comparative Law Journal, 77,* 137–144. (in Japanese).

Okawa, K. (2015). Civil code drafting in Laos and legal assistance—General provisions and persons/legal persons. *Comparative Law Journal, 77,* 111–119. (in Japanese).

Posner, R. (1998). Creating a legal framework for economic development. *World Bank Research Observer, 13*(1), 1–11.

Snijders, W. (2008). Russian experience: A Dutch perspective on legislative collaboration. In J. Arnscheidt, B. Van Rooij & J. M. Otto (Eds.), *Law making for development: Exploration into the theory and practice of international legislative projects.* Leiden University Press.

Taylor, V. (2005). New markets, new commodity: Japanese legal technical assistance. *Wisconsin International Law Journal, 23*(2), 251–281.

Trubek, D.M. (2006). The rule of law in development assistance: Past, present, and future. In D. M. Trubek & A. Santos (Eds.), *The new law and development: a critical appraisal*. Cambridge University Press.

Watson, A. (1974/1993). *Legal transplants: An approach to comparative law*. GA: University of Georgia Press.

World Bank (2001/2003). *Initiatives in legal and judicial reform.* World Bank.

Index

Y. Kaneko (ed.), *Civil Law Reforms in Post-Colonial Asia*,
Kobe University Monograph Series in Social Science Research,
https://doi.org/10.1007/978-981-13-6203-3

The manufacturer's authorised representative in the EU is Springer
Nature Customer Service Centre GmbH, Europaplatz 3, 69115 Heidelberg,
Germany. If you have any concerns regarding our products, please
contact ProductSafety@springernature.com

Printed and bound by CPI Group (UK) Ltd, Croydon, CR0 4YY
25/09/2026
02222900-0001